Spiritual Wayfarers, Leaders in Piety

HARVARD MIDDLE EASTERN MONOGRAPHS
XL

Spiritual Wayfarers, Leaders in Piety

Sufis and the Dissemination of Islam in Medieval Palestine

Daphna Ephrat

DISTRIBUTED FOR THE
CENTER FOR MIDDLE EASTERN STUDIES
OF HARVARD UNIVERSITY BY
HARVARD UNIVERSITY PRESS
CAMBRIDGE, MASSACHUSETTS
LONDON, ENGLAND

ISBN-13: 978-0-674-03201-9
ISBN-10: 0-674-03201-2
Printed in the United States of America

Library of Congress Cataloging-in-Publication Data

Ephrat, Daphna.
Spiritual wayfarers, leaders in piety : Sufis and the dissemination of Islam in medieval Palestine / Daphna Ephrat. — 1st ed.
p. cm. — (Harvard Middle East monographs)
Includes bibliographical references and index.
ISBN-13: 978-0-674-03201-9
ISBN-10: 0-674-03201-2
1. Sufism—Palestine—History. I. Title.
BP188.8.P34E64 2008
297.4095694—dc22

2008018319

Dedicated to the memory of Nehemia Levtzion

Contents

List of Figures and Table

Note on Transliteration, Names, and Dates

In general, I have adopted the system of transliteration of Arabic words and names used by the new edition of the *Encyclopedia of Islam (EI3)*. For certain Arabic words and names that are commonly found in English texts or dictionaries and atlases, I have preferred the less technical form: for example Koran, not Qur'ān; 'Abbasids, not 'Abbāsids; Acre, not Akkā. I have also frequently indicated the plural Arabic nouns simply by adding an "s" rather than giving the correct Arabic form (e.g. *ṭarīqa*s rather than *ṭuruq; zāwiya*s rather than *zāwāyā*).

For the sake of convenience, dates are generally given according to the Western calendar, except for dates of birth and death and dates in figures for which I have used both the Islamic (AH) and Western (AD) systems of dating.

Spiritual Wayfarers, Leaders in Piety

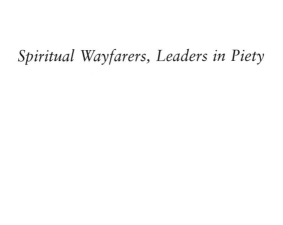

Introduction

This book draws a comprehensive picture of the history of Sufism that is rooted in a particular time and place. My central aim is to show how prominent representatives of Islam's ascetic and mystical currents in medieval Palestine (mid-seventh to late fifteenth centuries) disseminated their traditions, formed communities, and helped shape an Islamic society. Their role, I propose, must have acquired a special significance in a land that was demographically and culturally dominated by Christians, at least during the first four centuries of Islamic rule (seventh to eleventh centuries). Scholarship on the establishment of Islamic rule and the official sphere is vast, but historians of the field have generally neglected the dissemination of Islam's religious traditions and the crystallization of local communities of believers in medieval Palestine under the Arab caliphate and the successive Seljuk, Ayyubid, and Mamluk regimes. Similarly, the development of a public space around pious and charismatic leaders warrants further study.

During the long period under consideration, the geographical area of Palestine (or southern Bilād al-Shām)[1] underwent significant political, administrative, and economic shifts (see figure I.1). The changeover from Umayyad to 'Abbasid and later Fatimid rule and the resultant shifts of governmental centers from Damascus to Baghdad and Cairo were major milestones in the

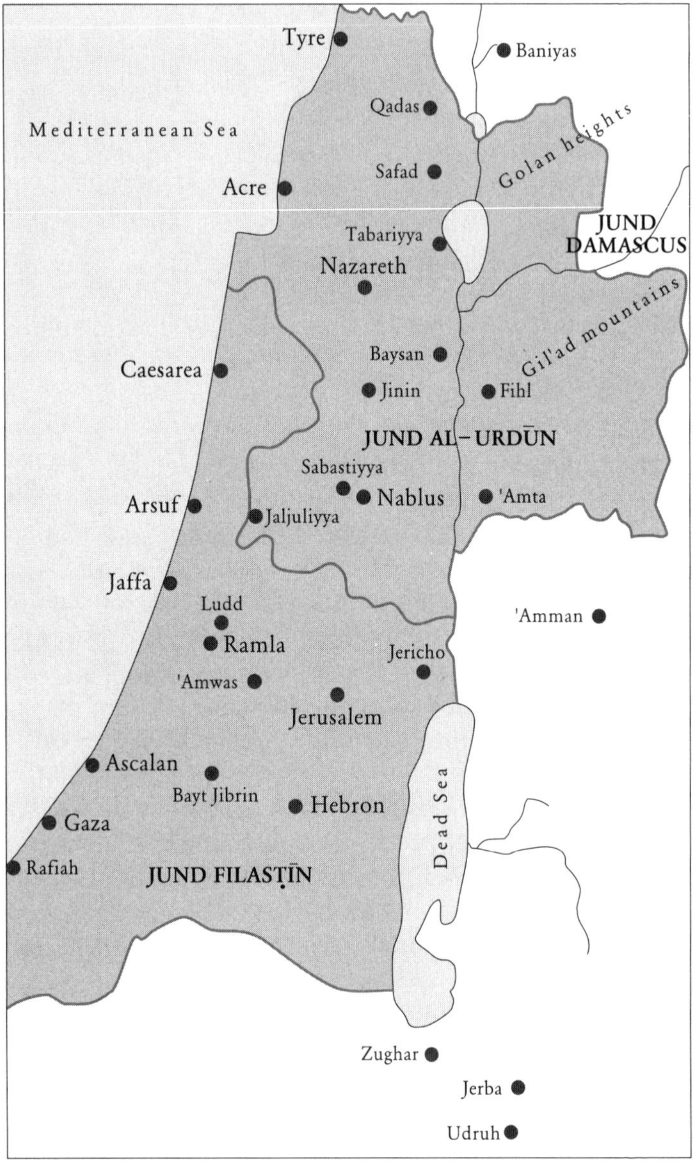

Figure I.1. Palestine (Southern Bilād al-Shām) in the early Islamic period (634 to 1099)

early Islamic period (634–1099). The establishment of the first Crusader kingdom and the subsequent Ayyubid and Mamluk conquests inaugurated new phases in the history of Palestine and of Bilād al-Shām as a whole. At times, the Holy Land stood on the sideline, far from the central areas of the Muslim state. In other periods, it became a major stage of struggles against external and internal enemies and a focus of attempts to restore the rule and glory of Islam. All the while, Palestinian cities, towns, and villages were becoming an integral part of the world of Islam. People and ideas made their way to rural and urban areas. Immigrants of diverse ethnic and geographical origins augmented the local Muslim population, and religious traditions that had their origins in other parts of the Muslim world met with thriving locally embedded cultural legacies, struck roots, and matured. Of them, the tradition that came to be known as Sufism played a prominent role in imprinting Islam on the human and physical environment and in consolidating an Islamic society and space.

Islamicists have long noted the gradual evolution of Sufism from a marginal steam of spiritual wayfarers into the most prominent religiously based and led association in the public sphere of Islamic societies in the course of the Islamic middle periods (1000 to 1500).[2] Sufi shaykhs disseminated the tradition that provided the Muslim believer with the unique combination of spiritual-emotional religious experience, intellectual teaching, and moral guidance; established their position as charismatic figures (channels to God); and expanded their following far beyond the small circles of ascetics and mystics. By the end of the middle periods, the Sufi friend of God (the *walī Allāh*) had become the focus of veneration, and his lodge-tomb complex had been transformed into a public space—a center of devotional life shared by all segments of society.[3] The concrete manifestations of the forces at work have hardly been studied. Little is known about the social and institutional dimensions of Sufism before the golden age of the Sufi brotherhoods under the Ottomans. Spencer J. Trimingham's *The Sufi Orders in Islam* is still the only comprehensive historical account of the birth and early development of the major Sufi brotherhoods (orders). This work merits attention especially for providing a general schema of different modes of Sufi organizations as they developed throughout Islamic history, tracing the origins of the main Sufi orders, and locating them in time and place. Despite its contributions, however, *The Sufi Orders in Islam* has been criticized for the monolithic historical pattern that it applies and the historical inaccuracies that it generates and perpetuates.[4]

Although it is commonly perceived to be a universal Islamic phenomenon, the diffusion of Sufism and the gradual extension of its social horizons were a product of a concrete historical setting. In medieval Palestine, Sufism was influenced primarily by the sanctity of its cities, their long-established position as centers of pilgrimage, and a cultural environment that was imbued with the living legacy of Eastern monasticism and direct encounters with Christian monks and holy men. Added to the impact of the cultural milieu was the proliferation of Sufi lodges and saintly tombs under the Mamluk regime (1250 to 1517). This proliferation led in turn to the intensification of social and religious life surrounding local Sufi shaykhs of recognized virtue and deepened the notions of affinity to local society and landscape. Even though distinctive spiritual centers such as Baghdad or Nishapur did not emerge, with the passage of time the Sufism that was spreading in medieval Palestine acquired its own particular features.

Drawing largely on Sufi and non-Sufi biographical and hagiographic material written in Arabic and incorporated in the pages of general dictionaries and in obituaries, this study revolves around the universal and peculiar features of the body of ascetics, mystics, and holy figures who were living in medieval Palestine and collectively labeled *Sufis.* It examines the origins and diffusion of their traditions, the content and methods of their guidance, the nature of their circles of followers, and their operation in the public sphere.

At the same time, the study branches out to major themes that relate to the universal evolution of medieval Sufism. The social significance of the consolidation of the Sufi main tradition lies at the center of my investigation. I address, among other issues, the interrelationships between the doctrinal institutionalization of Sufism and its institutionalization in the form of fraternities (or between *ṭarīqa* as a spiritual path and *ṭarīqa* as a religious and social association), between the Sufi guide's teaching and the emergence of an association around him, and between Sufism and sanctity. Through this investigation, I seek to contribute to the study of classical and medieval Sufism, where research has often focused either on the lives and legacies of the great mystics of the East or on the spiritual dimensions of Islamic mysticism while tending to overlook the practice of Sufism and the dynamic of religious and social evolution.[5]

Preceded by a solid overview of the theoretical themes in their historical context, each of the three chapters of this book corresponds to a major phase in the evolution of Sufism in medieval Palestine and the medieval Islamic Near East as a whole. Chapter 1 is devoted to representatives of nascent asceticism and mysticism who lived in Palestine from the time of the Arab-Muslim conquest to the late tenth century, their incorporation into the universal world of ascetic and Sufi piety, and their mode of life, teachings, lines, and networks. It traces the origins of the Sufi main tradition to the ascetic piety and community-oriented outlook of the early ascetics and shows how as early as the end of classical Sufism the seeds were planted for the birth of a coherent congregation around Sufi shaykhs who settled in Palestinian cities and their environs.

Chapter 2 covers the Islamic earlier middle period (late tenth to mid-thirteenth centuries). By drawing the profiles of renowned Sufi traditionalists and legalists living in Palestine of the time, it focuses on the assimilation of Sufis into the scholarly world of the religiously learned (the *ʿulamāʾ*) and the social order. It outlines how they perceived their role and place in society and disseminated the truth of Islam and how, parallel with their integration into the world of the *ʿulamāʾ*, they developed their own inner life and organizational forms and devised their own ways of integrating into the fabric of social and communal life. The early development of a coherent local Sufi congregation out of the loosely knit and dispersed circle of disciples around the Sufi guide is closely tied to the change in the concept of guidance for advancement along the path and the change in the relationship between master and disciple.

The final chapter explores the expansion in Palestine in the Islamic later middle period (mid-thirteenth to late fifteenth centuries) of the locally embedded Sufi-inspired community—the people of the path *(ahl al-ṭarīqa)*—around the venerated Sufi *walī Allāh* and his tomb. Since affiliation with the local *ahl al-ṭarīqa* was often through the so-called cult of saints, this examination touches on the linkage between Sufism and sanctity *(walāya)*. Historians of religious thought who study this linkage offer extensive discussions on the role that Sufism played in providing the theoretical basis for the rise of the Muslim holy man that here can be only briefly summarized. The attachment of Sufi shaykhs to the prophetic model through a recognized spiritual genealogy and their scrupulous observance of the Shariʿa and the Sunna enabled them to embody the Prophet's personal charisma. At the same time, Sufi shaykhs drew their inspiration and legitimacy from the idea of a path *(ṭarīqa)* by which to approach God, which implied that man not only was the creature and servant of God but also could become his friend. Gradually, a complete, albeit varied, mystical worldview of sanctity developed concerning miracles, sanctity, saintly intermediaries, and pious role models. This tradition had its origins in the philosophical and gnostic theories of such major figures in the development of classical mystical thought as Ḥakīm al-Tirmidhī and was elaborated on dramatically by Ibn Arabī. At its heart lay the idea of intercession: due to his nearness to God, the *walī* could intercede with him on behalf of others, calling down divine grace *(baraka)* into the world during his lifetime or at his tomb.[6] This status and role of the *walī* were not attained through the formal mechanism of saintly recognition and validation as had been developed by the Roman Catholic Church but through a process similar to public acclaim and manifested in veneration.

Rather than inquiring into Sufism as the theoretical foundation of sanctity, I seek an explanation for the attainment of saintly recognition and the growth of the shaykh's following in the practice of Sufism—the norms that the Sufi charismatic shaykh embodied and the messages that he spread. My underlying assumption is that Muslim believers in all segments of society generated and nourished an idealized type of a Sufi friend of God who embodied Sharʿī-Sufi norms and values and was suited to meeting their spiritual and social needs and expectations.[7] Here I adopt Max Weber's definition of *charisma* as a certain quality of personality by virtue of which an individual is set apart from ordinary men and treated as endowed with supernatural or superhuman—or at least specifically exceptional—qualities. It is essential that the charismatic individual *be recognized or regarded as such* and that this recognition be a matter of complete personal devotion arising out of enthusiasm coupled with despair and hope.[8] Moreover, to be recognized by his fellow believers (either in his lifetime or after his death) as God's favorite and become the focus of their veneration, the *walī*'s extraordinary traits and gratuitous marvels *(karāmāt)* must have been embodied within his specific community and publicly manifested. Similarly, the *walī* must have worked no less for the welfare *(maṣlaḥa)* of others than for his own personal perfection, enacting his spiritual and moral qualities to fulfill the religious and nonreligious needs of his fellow believers. The frameworks and modes of operation through which the Sufi-*walī* performed and diffused his charisma and enlarged his following are substantial to my discussion.

Given the rich information about the construction of complexes of Sufi lodges and saintly tombs in Ayyubid and Mamluk Palestine, these historical conjunctures offer us an ideal laboratory for analyzing the institutional dimension in the process through which Sufism expanded its horizons as it moved from the private to the public sphere. How did the Sufi shaykh's lodge become the center for followers of his spiritual path, and how did the dramatic spread of lodges contribute to the formation and expansion of an Islamic public space? What role did the endowing rulers play in this process, and how did their support for and patronage of righteous Sufis affect the discourse between the public and official spheres? These questions are of central importance for any study of Sufism and the public sphere in premodern Islamic societies.

To highlight the nexus of Sufism and society in the study of premodern Islam, throughout this book I interweave the reconstructed life stories of the subjects, an analysis of their main teachings, and an examination of the religious and social practices, sites, and spaces that developed around them. By placing the inquiry within a broad historical perspective, I hope to advance an understanding of universal phenomena and expose their concrete and distinctive manifestations.

On the methodological level, the book uses biographical and hagiographic texts as a valuable source in the study of medieval Sufism and the reconstruction of the milieu surrounding the Sufi friend of God.[9] Building on insights gained from studying the lives of the saints, I follow the methodological approach of reading the texts on their own terms and in their entirety rather than separating out those portions that are considered to be historically reliable from the rest.[10] This approach seems well suited to Islamic biographical literature, where the miraculous, while never as dominant as in Christian and other religious traditions, does play a role in the accounts and might well have represented a reality for those who recorded them and therefore be appropriately included in their historical works.[11]

Since the biographies of the Sufis who were studied for this book were composed for the most part after the periods that they describe, the accounts and anecdotes contained in them convey the image of true Sufi—a model of conduct that was to be followed as well as an ideal type of *walī Allāh*. This image was shaped after his death. In their endeavor to impose a normative homogeneity on the definition of the Muslim ascetic, mystic, and Sufi or non-Sufi holy man, biographers presented his figure in terms accepted by universal Islamic standards. Often jurists or orthodox-Sharʿī minded-Sufis, they modeled a Sufi's biography after those that were written by *ʿulamāʾ* for other *ʿulamāʾ* and were preserved in the standard biographical compilations. Chains of reliable reporters (*isnād*s) convey accounts of the Sufi's professional life from cradle to grave and tying him to earlier generations of leaders in religious learning and piety. This historical narrative was probably designed to shape the Sufi friend of God in accordance with a recognized cultural model. The sacred biography, in other words, had an inner function. It supplied those who considered themselves guardians of true Islam with satisfactory explanations of how and why a person acquired the qualifications to become holy. Although never developed into formal procedures of canonization, the recording, selection, and shaping of the traditions that surrounded elevated and saintly figures were a vital means employed by Muslim biographers who sought to form a widely accepted reservoir of role models. While the reconstruction of history was not their central goal, they provided historical evidence about the biographee's lives and activities.

However, other considerations must have influenced the composition of the biographies as well. For one, the tales and the messages conveyed had to appeal to different audiences of readers or listeners. The presentation of the Sufi, especially when believed to be endowed with divine grace, is thus no less concordant with the beliefs and expectations of the society that generated him than with normative standards. In many cases, biographers departed from the general designations in the introductory formula of the biography—such as *al-ṣāliḥ, al-zāhid,* or *ṣāḥib al-karāmāt* (the virtuous worshiper, ascetic, and miracle worker). Accordingly, they did not limit their historical narratives to the major stages on the path to perfection that link the biographee to a universally accepted category of elevated figures. The need to uphold the norm and at the same time be attentive to the popular voice may explain why the tales about the Sufis' extraordinary traits and deeds are not presented separately but instead are intertwined with accounts attesting to his great piety, his wisdom, and above all his commitment to disseminating righteous religious knowledge and practice *(al-ʿilm wa-l-ʿamal)*.[12]

Moreover, only by locating the universally accepted cultural model within a specific community of fellow believers could the norm become effective and the memory of its representative be commemorated. The biographee's persona must have been concrete, and the description of his life and activities must have been placed within a particular temporal and spatial frame.[13] Medieval authors carefully recorded accounts of the "true" Sufis who are studied in this book, providing eyewitness details about their lives and activities—the public practices of their heroic virtues, their networks and following, the dissemination of their knowledge and guidance throughout society, and their engagement with the world around them. Embedding these models of piety and virtue within their concrete milieu must also have served the authors' goal of conveying the splendor of cities and landscapes. This motivation is expressed in the seminally important history of Jerusalem and Hebron—*al-Uns al-jalīl bi-ta'rīkh al-Quds wa-l-Khalīl* by the Ḥanbali judge of Jerusalem, Mujīr al-Dīn al-ʿUlaymī (d. 928/1521). *Al-Uns* is used extensively in this book. Covering the history of the two sacred cities from the first Islamic century to the late Mamluk period, a substantial part of *al-Uns* is devoted to recording and narrating the lives of their scholars, Sufis, and friends of God. Here the cities and their surroundings are placed at center stage, and the actors are those credited for creating their intellectual and spiritual climate.[14]

Duly shaped by the understandings and beliefs of the times and by the traditions and intentions of the authors themselves, the biographies of the Sufis are nonetheless a valuable resource. Regardless of their apparently idealized and imaginary dimensions, the stories encompassed in the biographies studied for this book afford insights into the concrete manifestations—sometimes universal, sometimes distinctive—of an important dynamic of religious and social evolution that had an enduring impact on the history of Palestine.

NOTES

1. Broadly defined as the area that stretches from the Litani River (north to Tyre) to Rafih (on the edge of the Sinai Desert) and from the Mediterranean Sea to the western slopes of the Golan heights and Gilʿad Mountains and that falls within the Umayyad districts (junds) of Filasṭīn and Urdūn. At times, this area is referred to as the Holy Land *(al-arḍ al-muqaddasa),* a name that is mentioned with no definite borders in the Koran and is used to distinguish the land of Israel from the rest of Bilād al-Shām.
2. The term *Islamic middle periods* is borrowed from Marshall G. S. Hodgson. It is tied to the peculiarities of Islamic history in general and of Sufism in particular. See Marshall G. S. Hodgson, *The Venture of Islam: Conscience and History in a World Civilization,* Vol. 2, *The Expansion of Islam in the Middle Periods* (Chicago: Chicago University Press, 1974), esp. 3–11. Throughout, I adopt Hodgson's periodization and divide the period from the eleventh to the early sixteenth centuries into the earlier and later middle periods. Following Jonathan Berkey and others, I use the term *medieval* in its adjective form only. See Jonathan Berkey, *The Formation of Islam: Religion and Society in the Near East, 600–1800* (Cambridge: Cambridge University Press), 181–83, for a discussion of the question of periodization.
3. For general discussions of the prominence of Sufism and the fascination that was exerted by holiness in the entire Muslim world of the middle periods, see especially Albert Hourani, *A History of the Arab Peoples* (Cambridge, MA: Harvard University Press, 1991), 153–57; Berkey, *The Formation of Islam,* 231–57. Richard W. Bulliet, *Islam: The View from the Edge* (New York: Columbia University Press, 1994), 174, pinpoints the twelfth century as a period of special significance in this development. Boaz Shoshan, *Popular Culture in Medieval Cairo* (Cambridge: Cambridge University Press, 1993), chap. 1, focuses on a particular historical context

and sheds some light on the mechanisms by which Sufism rose to a prominent position and influenced the ordinary Cairenes.

4. Spencer J. Trimingham, *The Sufi Orders in Islam,* new ed. *The Formation of Schools of Mysticism,* (Oxford: Oxford University Press, 1998), 1–66. On critiques that were voiced in reviews when the book was first published (in 1971), see especially Frederick De Jong, Review of *The Sufi Orders in Islam,* in *Journal of Semitic Studies* 17:2 (Autumn 1972): 279. See also John O. Voll's foreword for the new Trimingham edition. Among recent studies that directly challenge Trimingham about the history of specific orders and regions is Carl W. Ernst and Bruce B. Lawrence, *Sufi Martyrs of Love: The Chishti Order in South Asia and Beyond* (New York: Palgrave, 2002), esp. chap. 1, "What Is a Sufi Order?" Trimingham's observations regarding the shift to what he calls the *tarīqa stage* are discussed in chapter 3 in the section titled Diffusing the Tradition.
5. Probably the most comprehensive study that examines both the doctrinal and social dimensions of medieval Sufism is Éric Geoffroy, *Le Soufisme en Égypte et en Syrie sous les Derniers Mamelouks et les Premiers Ottomans: Orientations Spirituelles et Enjeux Culturels* (Damascus: Institut Français, 1995).
6. The most recent and comprehensive contributions are Bernd Radtke and John O'Kane, *The Concept of Sainthood in Early Islamic Mysticism: Two Works by al-Ḥakīm al-Tirmidhī* (Richmond, UK: Curzon, 1996); Richard J. A. McGregor, *Sanctity and Mysticism in Medieval Egypt: The Wafā' Sufi Order and the Legacy of Ibn 'Arabi* (Albany, NY: SUNY Press, 2004). McGregor takes up *walāya* as his central theme and explores the development of the concept of sainthood after al-Shaykh al-Akbar, specifically in Egypt.
7. See Josef Meri's conclusion that the cult that emerged around the "historical saints" (as opposed to the "traditional saints" such as prophets and patriarchs) arose for social reasons and in practical terms had little to do with the formulation of doctrines of sainthood. Josef Meri, *The Cult of Saints among Muslims and Jews in Medieval Syria* (Oxford: Oxford University Press, 2002), chap. 2. The social impetus for the genesis of the "historical saint" is nevertheless obscure. See Richard J. A. McGregor's review in *H-Mideast-Medieval@H-net,* June 2004.

8. Max Weber, *Theory of Social and Economic Organization,* trans. A. M. Henderson and Talcott Parsons, ed. with an introduction by P. Talcott (New York: Free Press, 1947), 359.
9. Important as an implementation of this approach in the context of medieval Sufism and sanctity in the Islamic Near East is Denis Gril, *La Risāla de Ṣafī al-Dīn ibn al-Manṣūr ibn Ẓāfir: Biographies de maîtres spirituels connus par un cheikh égyptien du VIIe/XIIIe siècle* (Cairo: Institut Français d'Archéologie Orientale, 1986), 1–79. See further the suggestions and ample examples in R. Chih and D. Gril, eds., *Le saint et son milieu: ou comment lire les sources hagiographiques?* (Cairo: Institut Français d'Archéologie Orientale, 2000). For a different interpretation, see Jawid Mojaddedi's argument that as products of the "labour and savoir faire" of the individuals and school traditions that compiled them, the *ṭabaqāt* works are an invaluable source for the time in which they were produced rather than for the past they describe: Jawid A. Mojaddedi, *The Biographical Tradition in Sufism: The ṭabaqāt genre from al-Sulamī to Jāmī* (Richmond, UK: Curzon, 2001), esp. 181.
10. See especially Evelyne Patlagean, "Ancienne hagiographie byzantine et histoire sociale," *Annales esc.* 23 (1968): 106–26; Stephen Wilson, ed., *Introduction to Saints and Their Cults: Studies in Religious Sociology, Folklore and History* (Cambridge: Cambridge University Press, 1983), 1–2 and the annotated bibliography on this field at 309–417.
11. See the comments of Geoffroy in *Le Soufisme,* 37–38, with regard to the place of hagiographic material in the biographical literature about the Sufis that was composed from the twelfth century onward.
12. Charles Alman, "Two Types of Opposition and the Structure of Latin Saints' Lives," *Mediaevalia et Humanistica* n.s. 6 (1975): 1–11, represents an important contribution to the approach that highlights the significance of structure and techniques applied in the composition of sacred biographies in medieval Western Christianity.
13. For the notion of persona and its performing character, see E. Goffman, *The Presentation of Self in Everyday Life* (New York: Doubleday Anchor Press, 1959), 17–76; M. Mauss, "La Notion de personne, celle de moi," in *Sociologie et Entropologie,* 6th ed. (Paris: PUF, 1995), 333–62. For charismatic performances in con-

temporary Sufi communities, see Paulo G. Pinto, "Performing *Baraka:* Sainthood and Local Spirituality in Syrian Sufism," in *On Archaeology of Sainthood and Local Spirituality in Islam: Past and Present Crossroads of Events and Ideas,* Yearbook of the Sociology of Islam 5, ed. G. Stauth (Bielefeld: Transcript Verlag, 2004), 195–211. I would like to thank Paulo Pinto for introducing me to these works.

14. For details about Mujīr al-Dīn and his work, see Donald P. Little, "Mujīr al-Dīn al-ʿUlaymī's Vision of Jerusalem in the Ninth/Fifteenth Century," *Journal of American Oriental Society* 115:2 (April–June 1995): 237–47.

· ONE ·

Beginnings

Sulīmān b. Ṭarkhān al-Haythamī al-Tamīmī . . . said, "Whenever I entered al-Bayt al-Muqaddas, my nafs *[the lower self, seat of selfish lusts and passions] parted from me."*

—*Mujīr al-Dīn,* al-Uns al-jalīl, *1:292*

Sarī al-Saqaṭī b. al-Mughilis said, "On my way from Ramla to Bayt al-Muqaddas al-Sharīf, I passed a hill with rain water and herbs. Sitting to eat the herbs and drink the water, I said to myself that never before in my life had I had such ḥalāl *[pure and lawfully acquired food and drink]."*

—*Mujīr al-Dīn,* al-Uns al-jalīl, *1:295*

My discussion of the early phase in the history of Sufism in Palestine begins by examining how and in what historical circumstances the stage was set for the diffusion of Sufism in the Holy Land and its incorporation into the worldwide networks that were forged by Muslim ascetics and mystics. The focus then shifts to the early ascetics (the *zuhhād*) who are connected with Palestine during the early Islamic period—their mode of life and devotional practices, the message they spread, and the construction by the authors of standard biographical dictionaries of certain figures among them as role models of piety and moral uprightness for generations to come by. Related broad issues that are raised and addressed are the typical features and various nuances of nascent Islamic asceticism, the foundations of the Sufi mainstream tradition, and the relationship between ascetic piety and mysticism. Chapter 1 concludes with an examination of the formative period of Sufism in Palestine. It centers on the figure of Ibn al-Jallā', the great shaykh of al-Shām, who lived in the city of Ramla in the late ninth and early tenth centuries before moving to Damascus. A diagram of his lines and networks illustrates the formation of the cosmopolitan elite of mystical wayfarers and contextualizes the teachings and precepts that were imparted and circulated within its circles. The teachings of those who belonged to the wayfaring elite under study offer insights into the genesis as early as the formative period of small circles of wayfarers who crystallized around mystic mentors and eventually constituted the core of local Sufi congregations.

SETTING THE STAGE

In one of the biographical entries preserved in *al-Uns al-jalīl bi-ta'rīkh al-Quds wa-l-Khalīl,* Mujīr al-Dīn al-ʿUlaymī narrates the ascetic habits and precepts of Bishr al-Ḥāfī (the barefooted) (d. 226–227/842). An outstanding early representative of the ascetic and mystical movement of Baghdad that in time came to be known as Sufism, Bishr al-Ḥāfī is praised by later Sufi and non-Sufi authors for his constant spiritual quest and scrupulous life. He considered even food to be a "veil" on the path to God.[1] In selecting his quotations, Mujīr al-Dīn probably intended to bind the renowned Sufi figure tightly to the history of Jerusalem:

> Bishr al-Ḥāfī, one of the "people of the Path" *(ahl al-ṭarīqa),* was one of the most virtuous and outstandingly pious worshipers. His origins were in Merw [in eastern Iran], but he settled in Baghdad, where he died in 227/841.
>
> The reason he was called "al- Ḥāfī" is that one day when he was already living a life of renunciation, he went to a shoemaker to ask for a strip of leather for his shoe. The shoemaker questioned him: "What distinguishes your efforts from those of other

human beings?" At that moment, he threw away the shoe, and thereafter he remained barefooted.

When people asked him, "Why are the virtuous worshipers *(ṣāliḥūn)* happy in al-Bayt al-Muqaddas?," he would reply, "It is because staying there is accompanied with spiritual intention *(himma)*, and the human soul is directed there to him alone." And he said: "Nothing is left to me of the pleasures of this world but lying down on my side under the heavens in the Dome of the Rock."[2]

By Bishr al-Ḥāfī's lifetime, visits to Jerusalem had become commonplace among early Muslim ascetics (the *zuhhād* or *nussāk*) and mystics (later to be known as Sufis) who developed and circulated the notion of the special sanctity of Jerusalem in particular and the Holy Land in general.[3] Almost all other great ascetics and mystics of his time from the eastern and western lands of the Arab caliphate—such as Sufyān al-Thawrī, Ibrāhīm b. Adham, Abū Yazīd al-Bisṭāmī, Sarī al-Saqaṭī, and Dhū l-Nūn al-Miṣrī—are reported to have visited Jerusalem.[4] The accounts of their visits are expressive and reflect the city's image as an ideal site for seeking perfection in the worship of God and attainment of the Sufi goal of purity and faithfulness. The same image applies to the Holy Land as a whole.

Ibrāhīm b. Adham (d. 160/777), a native of Balkh (in present-day Afghanistan) who settled in Syria on the border of Byzantine and lived there a life of extreme world-renouncing piety, advised his friends to leave "this world" and direct their steps to the Holy Land *(al-arḍ al-muqaddasa)* and the mountains of Jerusalem.[5] Several historians suggest that ascetic monks in the mountains of Syria-Palestine might have helped to create a positive attitude about Palestine among counterpart Muslim ascetics.[6] "I have immigrated to al-Shām in order to eat there food free from religious taint," says Ibrāhīm b. Adham, who earned his livelihood in the Holy Land as a porter or guard.[7] In a similar vein, the famous Sarī al-Saqaṭī (d. 253/867) of the early Baghdad school of mysticism, who on his way from Ramla to Jerusalem ate herbs and drank rain water, is quoted as saying that he had never before had such *ḥalāl* (second chapter quotation above). An earlier tradition (dating from the early eighth century) tells of a contemporary ascetic worshiper of Basra whose *nafs* parted from him whenever he entered al-Bayt al-Muqaddas (first chapter quotation above).

Historical evidence is too scarce to allow us to draw even a partial demographic picture of nascent Islamic asceticism *(zuhd)* and mysticism *(taṣawwūf)* in medieval Palestine. Nor do any accounts provide precise information about pilgrimages and sojourns in its sacred cities during this period—such as the number of pilgrims and visitors, the places from which they set out, their final destinations, and the duration of their stays. The best available sources indicate that Jerusalem was part of the *ḥajj* route and a magnet for ascetics and mystics from the entire Muslim world. It may be surmised that some directed their steps to Hebron as well. It is also probable that Muslims in general, who combined the *ḥajj* with a visit to Jerusalem, passed through Hebron and took the opportunity to visit its holy sites. However, a number of precise testimonies from the early tenth century indicate pilgrimage and visits to Hebron—not only from various places in Palestine but also from other regions, such as Syria and Iraq. Taken together, these testimonies suggest the beginning of a tendency to sojourn frequently in the city. The volume of visitors *(zuwwār)* necessitated the building of guesthouses around the city's congregational mosque.[8]

In contrast, the literature in praise of Jerusalem supplies many testimonies concerning early ascetics and mystics from all corners of the Muslim world who either resided in Jerusalem or made visits to its holy sites from the very early first Muslim century. Some seem to have sojourned for long periods, while others apparently stayed only a short time—for even "he who directs his steps to Jerusalem if only in order to recite there the five ritual daily prayers will be as purified as a baby on his day of birth."[9] Sanctification of the *ḥajj* and the *ʿumra* (the "minor *ḥajj*," which need not be performed at a particular time of the year) from Jerusalem, extolled by traditions that can be traced back to the early eighth century, must have further motivated visits to the city. Before setting off on the pilgrimage to Mecca in the season of the *ḥajj,* some pilgrims would come to Jerusalem to sanctify themselves and prepare themselves for the *ḥajj* and the *ʿumra.*[10] In the eighth century, the holiness of Jerusalem and the holy places there, especially the Rock, is contested, and the primacy of Mecca is unchallenged. The visit to Mecca is the *ḥajj* or pilgrimage, while a journey to Jerusalem is simply a visit, *ziyāra,* even though, as early as the late first and early second Islamic centuries, a general agreement developed regarding the sanctity of Jerusalem. Several traditions—some extolling visits to Jerusalem, others contesting the city's position as the object of *ziyāra*—testify to this tendency. The most famous of all is the tradition that combines the pilgrimage to Mecca and the visit to al-Medina with a visit to Jerusalem, praising and recommending prayer in the three mosques of these cities during the same year.[11]

The first of the early traditions contained in *al-Uns al-jalīl* about the *zuhhād* and scholars of religion—the *ʿulamāʾ,* who entered Jerusalem and Hebron following the Muslim conquest—concerns one of the Prophet's companions. Having met the caliph ʿUmar b. al-Khaṭṭāb (634–644) at Mecca during the pilgrimage season, the companion said to him: "I have already performed the *ḥajj* and the *ʿumra* and have already prayed at the Prophet's mosque. It is my wish now to pray in al-Aqṣā mosque." After hearing this wish, the caliph immediately furnished the Prophet's companion with the best provisions for the journey.[12]

The visit to Jerusalem was often combined with visits to the coastal towns (the *ribāṭāt*) in Palestine and other parts of the Muslim world.[13] The coastal towns along the Mediterranean are frequently associated in the literature in praise of Jerusalem with the figures of *zuhhād* who either settled or sojourned there. Among those are Acre and Caesarea. However, Ascalon, above all, attracted the attention of the compilers; its merits far outweighed those of any other coastal town in Palestine.[14]

Arabs—either Syrian natives or immigrants from among the conquerors—were the first to settle in the garrison towns and fringe areas along the Byzantine-Muslim frontier in Syria-Palestine and upper Mesopotamia to protect them from Byzantine attack. Other newcomers soon augmented those first Muslim settlers. Among them were pious ascetics as well as learned men. A unique form of asceticism evolved along the Arab-Byzantine frontier, where scholar-ascetics came to fight the enemies of Islam. A fervid atmosphere of self-denial and martyrdom characterized life on the frontier. It was there that the piety of the fighters of faith reached its peak with supererogatory acts of worship, self-imposed mortification and poverty, and an incessant search for purity, especially in dietary matters. The Umayyad regime encouraged the *jihād* fervor of the ascetics and settlement in the garrison towns in general. For the ascetic, in addition to holy war, life in the *ribāṭ* might have offered a space away from the "impious" and "corrupted" surroundings of the powerful.[15] Thus, the coastal towns of Syria-Palestine constituted a refuge or place of retreat for world-renouncing ascetics long after these towns lost their strategic significance, as the mountains of al-Shām served from earliest times.[16]

The biographical literature provides additional testimonies of early ascetics and mystics in the sacred cities of Jerusalem and Hebron, the coastal towns, and other Palestinian cities and towns (notably Nablus and the Umayyad provincial capital of Ramla) as far south as Eilat. Descriptions in biographical entries further reflect the desire of ascetics and mystics to be in the immediate vicinity or under the aegis of the sacred city. This seems to have continued to inspire visits of ascetics and mystics to Jerusalem long after the erosion of its political and economic position following the ascendancy of the ʿAbbasid caliphate and the shift of the center of government from Damascus to Baghdad (in the mid-eighth century). The ʿAbbasids might have had no political plans for Jerusalem, but they neither denied nor denigrated its sanctity. The biographies drawn on during research for this book also suggest that the majority of Muslim ascetics and pious worshipers lived in Palestinian urban and rural areas in later periods from the third century of Muslim rule onward.

Early *zuhhād*—seeking to implement the ideal of pilgrimage to the holy sites of Palestine, to reside in the sanctuary's surroundings, or to lead a pious and austere life in coastal towns, in the mountains, or in other isolated spots—set the stage for the diffusion of ascetic and Sufi piety in Palestine. Transients and immigrants, disseminating the teachings of the early ascetic and mystical trends that had their origins in the spiritual centers of the eastern and western Muslim world, incorporated Palestinian cities and their hinterlands into the universal world of Sufism that was gradually evolving and maturing both as a spiritual path and as a social phenomenon.[17]

Placing the lives and teachings of prominent representatives of Islamic asceticism and nascent mysticism in Palestine during the early Islamic period within the broader context of the evolution of Sufism sheds light on the concrete manifestations and particular features of a diverse Sufi tradition that began at this time.

TYPICAL ASCETIC PIETY AND DIVERSITY

Among the early Muslim ascetic figures depicted in the sources is Ṣāliḥ b. Yūsuf Abū Shuʿayb al-Muqannaʿ (the Veiled). Born in the town of Wasit in southern Iraq, he moved to Ramla at one point, where he lived during the Tulunid period until his death in 282/894–895. Abū Shuʿayb's biography reveals him to be an outstanding pious and charismatic figure—if not in the eyes of his fellow believers then at least in the collective memory of the local community after his death. The following story, as narrated by Mujīr al-Dīn, represents the retrospective, imaginary legacy of the renowned ascetic of Ramla as later developed and constructed by his biographer:

> It is related that he set out for the pilgrimage to Mecca ninety times on foot, and that each time he would come first to the Rock of Bayt al-Muqaddas, where he would perform the *iḥrām* [i.e., he would announce aloud his intention and readiness to enter into a

> state of sanctification]. He would then enter the desert of Tabuk (in the northern part of the Hijaz, en route to Mecca) in a state of self-deprivation *(tajrīd)* and trust in God *(tawakkul)*. . . . It is related that people would make visits to his grave [in Ramla] to pray for healing; for whoever invokes God's name while standing there, his prayer for healing will be granted. Today, however, we cannot identify his grave. This is because of the long time that has elapsed since then and the duration of the Crusader rule over this land.[18]

Abū Shuʿayb's biography is illustrative of certain prominent aspects of the piety of the early Islam's devotees, whose practices and attitudes show them to be ascetics and quietists rather than mystics. Historians of Sufism have long distinguished the early Muslim ascetic from the Muslim mystic even though both are often subsumed under the common title of "Sufis" in later Sufi treatises.[19] Their observations yield several practices that when joined may be classifiable as typical ascetic piety. Modeling his mode of life on the example of earlier generations of renowned ascetic and pious figures—beginning with the Prophet Muḥammad—the *zāhid* of Abū Shuʿayb's epoch normally emphasized personal purity and fear of God. His strivings for self-purification and self-improvement were aimed at securing God's favor and were manifested in spectacular acts of worship and abstention from worldliness. At the heart of the *zāhid*'s religious attitude and devotional life lay the principle of utter trust in God *(tawakkul)* and unquestioning resignation to divine will *(riḍā')*. In their extreme forms, trust and resignation involved the renunciation of every personal initiative and volition for whoever seeks to secure his existence through his own efforts casts doubt on God's benevolence and in his ability to provide for all the wants of humankind. Significantly, the story about Abū Shuʿayb as told by his biographer does not imply such understanding of *tawakkul*. His trust in God does not seem to have entailed dependence on others.

Strict compliance with the legal prescriptions of the divine law was a prevailing tendency among Abū Shuʿayb and his contemporaries of like mind. They did not renounce the formal legal doctrines and requirements of the Islamic rites as laid down in the divine law; rather, they internalized them. Furthermore, they did more than just fulfill their religious duties; they paid close attention to the underlying motives of their actions and sought to impregnate them with a deeper spiritual meaning. The story about Abū Shuʿayb, even when stripped of its legendary layers, exemplifies the ascetic element in the performance of the pilgrimage. He seems not only to set out on the journey repeatedly but also to have opted for hardship along the way and severed all other worldly connections. This attitude and mode of *ḥajj* performance must have inspired later generations of men and women who tread the spiritual path. Deeply embedded in Islamic ascetic tradition, the pilgrimage to Mecca continued to be a central rite of the Sufi life. While imbuing the various *ḥajj* rituals with esoteric and metaphorical meaning—viewing the pilgrimage as a journey toward God and the Kaʿba as a holy site in which God might bless the mystical wayfarer with revelations and illuminations—Muslim mystics faithfully complied with the religious obligation. Only a few totally abandoned its formalities and perceived them to be an impediment to the advancement on the path leading to closeness to God and communion with him.[20]

Recitation of the Koran appears as a desirable duty among the early *zuhhād*. Recitation of the entire Koran *(khitām al-Qur'ān)* and night prayers *(qiyām al-lail, tahajjud)* and meticulous contemplation on the Koranic revelation were a means for maintaining the constant "mindfulness"—"memorization" and "mentioning" *(dhikr)*—of God that the Koran repeatedly enjoins and also for imbuing the performance of religious practices and duties with a deeper spiritual meaning. Indeed, many pious ascetics who frequented Jerusalem are reported to have performed long vigils for prayer and recitation of the entire Koran during their visits to its holy sites. A tradition about a certain *zāhid* who lamented the loss of his ability to perform night vigil in prayer illustrates the significance of the practice as an essential part of the early Islamic ascetic lifestyle.[21] Such traditions most probably contributed to the Sufi perception of recitation of the Koran as one of the religious obligations without which mystical training would be useless and meaningless. "An aspirant who does not know the Koran by heart is like a lemon without scent," states al-Jāmī, the great fifteenth-century Persian mystic and poet.[22]

Constant mourning and weeping as a sign of repentance appear in the sources as another salient characteristic expression of early ascetic piety. The grief of the "weepers" *(bakka'ūn)* sprang as much from their fear of failing to purify their hearts and hence to secure God's satisfaction as from their fear of the last judgment. Consider, for example, Abū Ḍahr Yazīd b. Abī Sumayd (or Sumayya), the famous ascetic of Eilat (d. 208/824), who behaved in a pious manner and prayed and wept frequently. A Jewish woman who empathized with his piety wept with him. One night he called on God: "Oh God most high, this Jewish woman cried out of mercy for me, even though her religious creed is different from that of mine. Oh God, I seek mercy from you alone."[23] Another telling story is attributed to Ibn ʿAbād al-Arsūfī, an ascetic and pious worshiper from the coastal town of Arsuf-Apollonia (d. unknown). He tells of his encounter with a certain overzealous shaykh while visiting Bayt al-Muqaddas:

> The shaykh seemed to be burning with flame. His garment and turban were pitch black, his hair long, and his whole look gloomy and dreadful. I turned to him and said, "May God have mercy upon you, only if you changed this clothing of yours could you know the significance of whiteness." The shaykh wept, "This clothing is similar to that of the time of calamity; we are not in this world but in garments of mourning."[24]

The basic attitudes and actual practices of early Muslim ascetics—such as humility, repentance, long vigils, and fasting—might have developed independently. Still, the impression is that non-Muslim pietistic and ascetic traditions in some instances inspired an Islamic tendency and helped give it shape. Some of the Muslim pious ascetics of the Holy Land must have been in close contact with friendly Jewish circles, and this is reflected in the many reminiscences from rabbinical literature. But it seems that they received their main impetus from the example of Christian monks and anchorites of Palestine; monastic asceticism was deeply rooted in the environment in which the early *zuhhād* of the Holy Land lived.[25] Long after the Muslim conquest of Jerusalem, the city remained predominantly Christian, and the hills, ravines, and little plains of the barren landscape, which lies between the Judean hills and the Dead Sea—the Great Laura in particular—continued to contain a vigorous monastic life.[26] Given the rich tradition of Christian monasticism and the presence of thousands of monks inhabiting the Palestinian landscape, one can easily imagine that some of the early *zuhhād* were influenced by monks and hermits and sought to emulate them. Muslim ascetics became acquainted with Christian monastic practices through observation, casual meetings, and dialogues with monks. Reports clearly show that Muslims in Jerusalem, for example, were well acquainted with the phenomenon of Christian monasticism. On the most basic level, the confluence of Eastern Christian monasticism and the world of *zuhd* occurred where individuals of both groups lived or sojourned in the same places.[27] For all their scarcity and fictional elements, descriptions of direct meetings between *zuhhād* and Christian monks in Jerusalem during the first centuries of Islamic rule yield the notion of a certain commonality. The following stories portray the Christian monk as a model for the typical ascetic seeking inspiration and guidance:

> Qāsim al-Zāhid related, "I saw a monk standing at the gate of Bayt al-Muqaddas. He did not cease from shedding tears. His state concerned me, and I asked him to grant me some piece of advice, which I promised to uphold to and transmit from him thereafter. The monk said, 'Be like a man rounded up by beasts of prey. He fears that if his mind is distracted, he will fall prey to them.

Therefore, his night is full of dread while the misled are confident, and his day is full of pain and agony while those who take pleasure in the vain of this world are full of delight.'"[28]

'Abd Allāh b. 'Āmir al-'Āmirī related, "I questioned a monk *(rāhib)* in Bayt al-Muqaddas about the first step of entering the [path of] worshiping. He replied, 'Hunger.' I then asked, 'What is the indication for this?' He replied, 'The human body is created out of dust, while the source of his spirit is the kingdom of heaven. When the human body is satiated, it relies on the earth, but whenever it is not satiated, it yearns for the kingdom of heaven.' I asked, 'What provokes hunger?' He replied, 'Persistence in the invocation of God *(dhikr)* and in humility.'"[29]

Despite being indicative of the closeness between the monk and the Muslim ascetic seeking his advice, this last story also hints at certain dissimilarities in their ascetic outlooks and practices. Although the typical early Muslim ascetic, as depicted by his biographers, shared with the monk the practices of fasting, eating frugally, and abstaining from food that did not come from pure sources, the ascetic would not normally indulge in harsh self-deprivation or extreme self-inflicted suffering—practices that are frequently encountered in the *lives* of the "servants of God."[30] Indeed, few in the sources are depicted as living a life of constant mortification of the flesh *(taqashshuf)*. Nor do the sources suggest that the *zāhid*'s contempt for the life of "this world" and abhorrence of its delights necessarily imply retreat *(khalwa)* from society or exile in some isolated spot, on a mountain, or in a desert.[31] The Muslim ascetic, like the typical Christian monk in the cities, towns, and villages of Palestine or in the "Desert City," was part of his natural and social environment, living in a landscape where barren mountains and cultivated land intermingled and in a society where spiritual, social, and political lives belonged together.[32] Closely associated with devoting one's life to worship *('ibāda)* and contemplation, withdrawal from life *(inqibād)* simply meant, for many, distancing themselves from the spaces that surrounded the powerful and wealthy. Accordingly, they would limit their world-renouncing piety to renouncing the patronage of the rulers—in the form of gifts or paid positions in the state administration.[33] An example is Hānī b. Kulthūm, an ascetic worshiper from the city of Ramla (d. unknown) who refused the position of provincial governor when it was offered to him.[34] But although he was critical of materialism and avoided worldly delights, the typical ascetic of the early Islamic period, like his successor in later times, led a pious life within the world. Consider Thawr b. Yazīd, an ascetic worshiper who lived in Jerusalem. Some worshipers from the villages surrounding Jerusalem came to the city every day to join him in the performance of the five daily prayers at the holy sites, and he led them in prayer and related prophetic traditions to them.[35]

Medieval Muslim authors, although referring to extremely devout figures collectively as *zuhhād* and *ʿubbād* (pious worshipers) or as Sufis, distinguish at least two different forms of Islamic asceticism. Thus Ibn Rajab, the fourteenth-century scholar and historian, distinguishes an extreme ascetic from another, more moderate type that is by far the most frequently encountered and the most admired in biographical literature that is not directly affiliated with Sufism. The former type renounces the world and his troubles. In his words: "He is pious, keeps to his home and mosque, holds his tongue, and avoids trouble."[36] What is more, from the early beginnings of Islamic asceticism and mysticism, learned and pious men, among them famous ascetics and mystics, were critical of the extremes of *zuhd* practiced by some of their overzealous contemporaries. Their criticism seems to have been no less vigorous than that of Christian thinkers who, from late antiquity and throughout the Middle Ages, urged a moderate form of asceticism and condemned extreme practices of self-deprivation.[37] Their polemics were based on the prophetic model displayed in the *ḥadīth,* which they recognized as the chief source of religious authority alongside the Koran. In particular, they condemned the extremes of trust in God.

The reaction of the early traditionalists, the so-called Hadith folk, to *tawakkul* stemmed from their moralistic conception of the community. If the overzealous ascetic wanted to leave the world and renounce every personal initiative and volition out of complete trust in God's benevolence, then those who live within the community would have to cater to his needs.[38] Noteworthy in this regard is ʿAbd Allāh b. al-Mubārak, the leading ascetic of eighth-century eastern Iran and author of *Kitāb al-zuhd* (The Book on Renunciation)—a collection of the *ḥadīth* and pious dicta that emphasize the world-renouncing attitude of the Prophet, his family, and the companions and the successors. One of the earliest critics within the circles of the *zuhhād* themselves, he exemplified inner-worldly ascetic piety both in his own lifestyle and in preaching to others and disapproved of the apathetic ascetics that he had met while in Baghdad. He urged his numerous admirers to be actively involved in the affairs of this world and the life of the community by engaging in gainful employment.[39]

Some critics even deplored excessive religious devotion as vainglory and hypocrisy, setting an alternative model for pious behavior. These were the Malāmatiyya (or people of "the Path of Blame") in the eastern lands but also in Syria. From the beginning of their movement in ninth-century Nishapur, the Malāmatiyya represented an extremely introverted reaction to extroverted and ascetic forms of spirituality. During the formative period of their movement, they called for abandoning all outward marks of distinction and all inward claims to spiritual superiority.[40] Their sharp reaction against individuals and movements known for their extreme asceticism was itself a continuation of an Islamic trend that began in the very early days of Islam in opposition to the Christian mode of extreme self-denial as the perfect path to salvation.[41] The deliberate concealment of their piety came as a reaction mostly against the ostentatious asceticism of the Karrāmiyya, the movement that formed around the charismatic ascetic, public preacher, and theologian Abū ʿUbayd Allāh Muḥammad b. Karrām (d. 255/869–70) and that flourished in Transoxania, Khurasan, and Jerusalem from the ninth century to the Mongol conquest.[42] Ibn Karrām's preaching aimed to instill in his audience a fear of God and a desire for paradise. To obtain God's favor and draw nearer to him, he taught the large crowd flocking around him a way of life that was based on mortification of the flesh, holy poverty, and utter dependence on God in all aspects of life.[43] So powerful were these sentiments that they were transformed into a mass movement.

Repeatedly persecuted by governors of Iranian provinces who were irritated by the effects of his public sermons and the enthusiasm caused by his mere presence, in 865 Ibn Karrām retired to Jerusalem, where he lived until his death. His fiery sermons in the courtyard of the Dome of the Rock drew large crowds; according to an anonymous source, he had some 20,000 followers in Jerusalem. After his death, his tomb near the Jericho gate and close to the graves of the prophets became a gathering place for his numerous disciples and the prototype of a special hermitage in Jerusalem. Long after Ibn Karrām's demise, the pious inhabitants of this hermitage were engaged in preaching and begging. A century after his death, the Arab geographer al-Muqaddasī reported on a sect of his followers in Jerusalem where they had lodges (*khānaqāh*s) and meeting places *(majālis)*. From Muqaddasī and other writers, we learn of the popularity and tremendous influence of the Karrāmiyya, especially among the lower classes of eastern Iran. His disciples there established the *khānqāh* as the first missionary center and quasi-monastic institution. They would distribute a *hadīth* in the name of the Prophet: "At the end of the days, there will appear a man named Muḥammad b. Karrām, and he will cause the Islamic law and community *(al-sunna wa-l-jamāʿa)* to rise again; he will have a *hijra* similar to my *hijra* from Mecca to Medina."[44] Despite their obvious ascetic credentials and the great appeal of their founder's teachings, the Karrāmiyya did not survive the expansion of the ascetic and mystical school of Baghdad and are never described as Sufis in contemporary sources. The movement that came to be known as Sufism remained staunchly opposed to Ibn Karrām's version of ascetic piety.[45]

Discernible in the lives and teachings of early generations of *zuhhād,* internal differences and tensions continued to characterize the world of *zuhd* throughout its history, resulting in a variety of trends in and attitudes toward religious, social, and political issues. However, to divide the Muslim ascetics who were connected with medieval Palestine and their contemporaries in other Islamic regions into clear-cut categories of extreme versus moderate asceticism or of demonstrative versus modest piety would be to oversimplify. Similarly, it would be overgeneralizing to accept the dichotomy proposed by Max Weber in his *Sociology of Religion* between "inner worldly" *(innerwelttliche)* ascetics who are aware of their responsibility toward their fellow believers and therefore participate in the life of the community and "world rejecting" *(weltablehnende)* ascetics who withdraw from all creaturely interests and are oblivious to the society around them.[46]

A close examination of accounts and narratives by medieval Muslim authors about the actual ascetic practices of those designated as *zuhhād* and *ʿubbād* reveals various degrees of withdrawal from life and society and different nuances of ascetic habits in each of the supposedly distinctive extreme and moderate forms of premodern Islamic asceticism. Historically and conceptually, *zuhd* remained highly heterogeneous in nature.[47] At the same time, in the world of the medieval Muslim authors whose works are studied here, the term *zuhd* implied a way of life and a mode of conduct whose characteristics were very specific. To warrant its application, the ascetic practices had to be manifested in detail.

EARLY ROLE MODELS

Nothing better manifests the inner-worldly outlook shared by many early Sufi ascetics than the accounts of their role as collectors and transmitters of the prophetic traditions, the *ḥadīth*—the common legacy of Muslim believers and their ultimate source of guidance and inspiration.

The standard biographical dictionaries on the renowned men of religious learning and piety that were consulted during research for this book include the names of many early *zuhhād* who were designated as scholars of *ḥadīth (muḥaddīthūn)*. Significantly, biographies of the same figure by different authors differ in the elements of the persona that they highlight. While some authors present the figure of the *zāhid-muḥaddīth* as ascetically minded, others play down his ascetic habits and emphasize instead his trustworthiness as a collector and transmitter of prophetic traditions. Moreover, some authors of standard biographies of the *muḥaddīthūn* express doubts about the authenticity of this or that *zāhid*'s collection of prophetic traditions and pious dicta, accusing him of a lack of care in scrutinizing traditions and even of falsifying them. The differing presentations of the same individuals probably stem from the biographers' different school traditions and the distinctive intent of their work—a point that I return to later in this section.

From the beginnings of Islam, the transmission of *ḥadīth* concerning the sayings and deeds of the Prophet had a clearly edifying dimension. Through his transmission of the prophetic legacy, the *ḥadīth* scholar imparted to his fellow believers the exemplary ethos and practices ascribed to the ultimate model of religious virtue as well as to his closest disciples and companions. The prophetic traditions furthermore constituted the primary ingredient of *ʿilm,* the knowledge that characterized the scholars of religion (the *ʿulamāʾ*), at least during the first four centuries of Islam.[48] As one of the *ʿulamāʾ*—guardians of the prophetic legacy and its disseminators in a chain of authorities *(isnād)* extending back to the earliest generations—the ascetic *ḥadīth* scholar must have helped shape and model the life of his community in light of the norms and values laid down in the Sunna of the Prophet. At the same time, his activity in the field of *ḥadīth* may well have contributed to the spread of *zuhd* ideals, particularly by helping create and disseminate models of *zuhd* behavior for the larger Islamic community. It is not surprising that the *zuhhād* and *ʿulamāʾ* drawn to Jerusalem and Hebron from the early days of Muslim rule to the Crusader conquest appear under the same title in Mujīr al-Dīn's famous history of the two holy cities.

Among the early *zuhhād* of Palestine who were praised for their trustworthiness as *ḥadīth* transmitters was the abovementioned, Abū Ḍaḥr b. Abī Sumayd. His extensive biography appears in *Tahdhīb al-tahdhīb* (Refinement of the Refinement), the vast biographical collection on the noted *muḥaddīthūn* that was written by Ibn Ḥajar al-ʿAsqalānī, the famous fifteenth-century Egyptian *ḥadīth* scholar, judge, and historian whose life's work constitutes the final summation of the science of *ḥadīth*. Ibn Ḥajar ascribes to Abū Ḍaḥr a prominent role in the collection and transmission of *ḥadīth* extending back to such pious figures as the Umayyad caliph ʿUmar b. ʿAbd al-ʿAzīz (r. 717–720). As his trustworthiness became established, people from his hometown of Eilat directed their steps to wherever he sat—whether in his home or in a mosque—to hear traditions from his lips.[49] The story about his constant mourning and weeping, which showed him to be a model of simple ascetic piety, is contained in *Ṣifat al-ṣafwa* (The Nature of the Elect) by Ibn al-Jawzī, the famous jurist, *ḥadīth* expert, preacher, and prolific author of twelfth-century Baghdad.[50] Ibn al-Jawzī tells how a group of people used to join Abū Ḍaḥr annually for the *ḥajj* and how along the way he would remind them of the day of judgment. This presentation of the ascetic *muḥaddīth* must have been intended to serve the author's aims. An ardent opponent of Muslim mystics, whom he considered to be responsible for having introduced into the dogma of Islam negative innovations *(bidʿa)*, Ibn al-Jawzī's main concern in compiling his treatise was to demonstrate that the true Sufis of Islam were those who set themselves to follow faithfully the teachings of the great companions. Therefore, they were entitled to disseminate the fundamentals of the Islamic creed alongside other renowned learned and pious men and women.

Abū ʿUnayr ʿIsā b. Muḥammad b. Ishāq b. al-Naḥḥās (son of a coppersmith) from Bayt Ma'mūn, a village in the Ramla area, was another ascetic who gained recognition as a *ḥadīth* expert. Ibn Ḥajar depicts him as one of the most pious and trustworthy *muḥaddīthūn* of his time and locates him in a vertical chain of transmitters of religious lore. Traveling in search of religious knowledge *(ʿilm),* he used to set out on a journey dressed only in a *khirqa,* the coarse cloak that was identified with the pious ascetic as a symbol of his modesty and poverty. His education in *ḥadīth* started at a early age. Having heard prophetic traditions from his father and the most renowned *ḥadīth* scholars of his hometown of Ramla, he later transmitted *ḥadīth* to the keen seekers and admirers who flocked to his house until his death in 256/869. He was well versed in *ḥadīth* and famous as a trustworthy transmitter, and several of the compilers of the six genuine *ḥadīth* collections that were produced in the late ninth century cited traditions imparted on his authority.[51]

The inner-worldly outlook of the typical early *zāhid* found expressions in another way as well. Some *zuhhād* lived an ascetic life but also cared for the needy and poor among the community of believers, combining ascetic piety with service to others. Asceticism, humility, and generosity were brought together and manifested in practice.[52] A story imparted by Muḥārib b. Dithār, whom Mujīr al-Dīn lists among the early *zuhhād* and *ḥadīth* transmitters who frequented Jerusalem (d. unknown) provides a telling testimony of the intertwining of ascetic piety with the practice of moral uprightness. Ibn Dithār relates, "We used to accompany the *zāhid* worshiper al-Qāsim b. ʿAbd al-Raḥmān on his way to al-Bayt al-Muqaddas. He surpassed us in three matters: performing prayer by night, providing generous charity to the needy, and preventing maltreatment of the people."[53] Several traditions call not for giving charity as such but for seeking the company of the poor and unprivileged. Closely related to the *zāhid*'s humility and glorification of poverty, these traditions apparently reflect a real custom among the early ascetics. An early testimony concerns the famous female ascetic and *ḥadīth* transmitter Umm al-Dardāʿ (d. unknown), a wife of the Prophet's companion Abū al-Dardāʿ, who used to spend half the year in Damascus and half in Jerusalem. In Jerusalem, she would spend her time in the company of the poverty-stricken.[54] Another example relates to Ibrāhīm b. Adham. While in Jerusalem, he called on Sufyān al-Thawrī, who at the time was occupied in constant prayer and recital of the Koran at the city's holy sites, to talk to the poor as proof of his humility.[55] Such expressions of benevolence and moral uprightness must have contributed to the view of the *zāhid* as a model of virtue. Seen in the broader context of the evolution of Sufism, the *zāhid*'s example of caring for others undoubtedly inspired the Sufi rule of *īthār.* Altruism or giving preference to others over oneself came to be one of the first stages in the preparatory steps of the path and the Sufi's duty throughout his life.

Modeled on the Prophet Muḥammad, inner-worldly *zuhd* over time came to be a hallmark of the Sufi tradition and profoundly influenced other trends in Islam. Most notably, the form of *zuhd* that brought together moderate asceticism and community-oriented piety was embraced and implemented by adherents to Ḥanbalīsm, which more than any other Sunni school of law and thought developed into an activist social organization.[56] Moreover, numerous individuals who did not live in accordance with its stringent standards did revere the ascetic ethos. As pointed out by Roy Mottahedeh, in the view of a multitude of Muslim medieval authors, the only lasting *ḥasab* (honor acquired through deeds) was *tawqā*—literally, "fear of God" or, more loosely, "piety."[57]

At times, the esteem that was accorded to men and women of recognized ascetic piety created a circle of local admirers around them during either their lifetime or, more often, around their tombs. Such, according to Mujīr al-Dīn, was the circle around the tomb of Abū Shuʿayb in Ramla. In his days, circles of admirers of a charismatic *zāhid* or *ʿabīd* were of a loose nature, and ceasing to admire that figure did not necessarily mean leaving a certain following or association. This is probably why (except for the Karrāmiyya, who faithfully disseminated the teaching of the founder long after his death, utilizing the *khānqāh* as their center of operation) the ascetic schools that evolved in Basra and Khurasan during the ninth and tenth centuries did not transform from small circles into structured movements.

By the turn of the tenth century—on the eve of the ascendancy of the Baghdad school and the beginning of the incorporation of regional ascetic and mystical schools into the ethical-mystical movement known as Sufism—a moderate type of ascetic piety was making its presence felt throughout the Muslim world and was assuming a variety of nuances and local expressions.[58] By then, *zuhd* had evolved as a distinctive, albeit internally diversified current of Islamic belief and practice that was embraced, in one form or another, by virtually the whole of the *ʿulamāʾ* class, as attested in biographical literature devoted to the most renowned Muslim intellectuals at the time.[59]

Historians of Sufism tend to ascribe to the early *zuhhād* a great degree of separateness from the society around them.[60] While normally practicing the spiritual path to perfection and salvation individually, many *zuhhād* connected with Palestine during the early Islamic period seem to have pursued an innerworldly outlook and mode of life. No matter how limited their practical influence might appear, they must have played a prominent role as one among the various groups that were disseminating the truth of Islam and shaping the religious and social life of the local communities.

Imparted orally and committed to writing by the biographers, the stories about the early *zuhhād* of Palestine—sometimes authentic, sometimes imaginary—commemorated them and constructed role models for later generations of local Muslim believers. As the tales about these figures spread, their tombs came to be objects of pilgrimage—public spaces that with the mosques were the focus of common rituals. Gradually influenced by these role models, a new cultural landscape filled with Islamic landmarks was emerging.

THE WAYFARING ELITE

Sufi authors of the late fourth to twelfth centuries who endeavored to impose a uniform spiritual tradition have shaped much of our knowledge and understanding about the formative period of Sufism *(taṣawwuf)*—often referred to as *Islamic mysticism*—in the ninth and early tenth centuries. This tradition had to be based on a reconciliation between the normative exoteric dimension of Islam and the experimental vision of its true reality—that is, between *sharīʿa* and *ḥaqīqa*. Sufi authors' understanding of the "correct" creed and behavior of Sunni Islam and their definitions of Sufism were determined by the theological school or faction that they were affiliated with and that they sought to nourish and propagate.

Whatever the differences, this was a period during which many legal scholars still regarded Sufism with suspicion, and yet Sufi authors shared the goal of legitimizing the Sufi path and justifying Sufism's rightful place in Islamic practice. As a corollary of this endeavor, authors of normative Sufi treatises tended to omit controversial aspects of the Sufi's life and teaching or excluded certain biographies altogether. Most glaring is the exclusion of Islam's famous tenth-century mystic and martyr al-Ḥallāj from the biographical section of al-Qusayrī's *al-Risāla*.[61] Yet underneath the thick layer of uniformity and conformity, the accounts and narratives of the spiritual centers, teachers, and teachings and the lines and circles of the great Sufi mentors allow scholars to reconstruct the lives and legacy of renowned mystics connected with Palestine, in one way or another, during the formative years of Sufism.

Few men and women who may be classifiable as Sufis or mystical wayfarers (designated in the sources as *mutaṣawwifa, ahl al-taṣawwuf,* or *sālikūn*) lived in Palestine for any length of time in the ninth and early tenth centuries. This is not surprising given that most of the representatives of nascent Islamic mysticism originated in the eastern provinces of the Muslim world and that most of the great early Sufis were itinerants. Though they included the sacred cities of Palestine in their wanderings, many continued their travels or returned to their homelands. Added to the cosmopolitan character of many was the universally shared elitist approach of early Sufis that severely limited access to their circles.

Among the forerunners of Sufism in Palestine, Lubāba al-Mutaʿabbida (the Devotee) (d. unknown) is noted as being a resident of both Syria and Jerusalem. Her sayings were selected and recorded by Abū ʿAbd al Raḥmān al-Sulamī (d. 412/1021) in *Dhikr al-niswat al-mutaʿabbidāt al-ṣūfiyyāt,* the earliest work on Sufi women saints.[62] Preceded by a chain of conveyance that proves their veracity, the following selection of her sayings presents her as a specialist in the ways of gnosis *(maʿrifa)* and of inner struggle against human passions and drives *(mujāhada):*

> Aḥmad [ʿAbd Allāh] b. Muḥammad of Antioch reported from Aḥmad b. Abī al-Harawī that Aḥmad b. Muḥammad related that Lubāba the Devotee said, "I am ashamed lest God see me preoccupied with other than Him after having known Him."
>
> He also related that she said, "Knowledge of God bequeaths love for him; love for Him bequeaths longing for him; longing for him bequeaths intimacy with him; and intimacy with him bequeaths constancy in serving him and conforming to his laws."
>
> A man said to her, "This is the question: I want to perform the pilgrimage to Mecca, so what invocation should I make during this period?" She said, "Ask God Most High for two things: that he will be pleased with you so that he will make you attain the station of those who find their satisfaction in him, and that he will magnify your reputation among his friends *(awliyāʾ).*"[63]

The full doctrinal history of Sufism in Lubāba's epoch lies well beyond this discussion. Still, secret and intuitive knowledge (*maʿrifa,* as opposed to *ʿilm*) and ardent love of God *(maḥabba)*—whether considered complementary or placed one above the other (as in her sayings)—were clearly key themes of the forerunners of Sufism who developed the groundwork for a mystical approach to religious understanding. There is no doubt that from earliest times, Muslims strove to gain nearness to God and did so through devotional and ascetic practices and through love and knowledge of him. But while merging traditional mystical and ascetic elements, many Muslim mystics of the formative period seemingly considered asceticism to be a stage, important as it was, in a mystical journey *(sayr)* or path *(ṭarīqa)* that leads far beyond the ascetic ideal.[64]

Reflected in Lubāba's sayings is the perception that mystical experiences are the highest stage of spiritual progress, which lies at the heart of the evolution of an early Sufi tradition in the form of a religion of the elite. Those who attain intuitive knowledge of God *(al-ḥaqq)* and intimacy with him become his *awliyā'* (friends or intimates). As saints in other religious traditions, the *awliyā'* are not necessarily sacred themselves but are connected to the sacred in a special manner and are thus close to sacred reality. This concept of deep intimacy with God *(parresia)* must have been deeply embedded in the culture and society of medieval Palestine. Developed in church literature from Asia Minor, it was adapted by sixth-century Syrian authors to apply to the spiritual ascent of monks.[65] But despite the similarities between the notion of the sacred in the Islamic and Christian faith, the position of the Muslim *awliyā'* as formulated in classical Sufism did not correspond exactly to that of the Christian saint. It was connected to the theory of advancement along the Sufi path leading to spiritual perfection.

From the early times in the evolution of Islamic mysticism, Sufi shaykhs drew their inspiration and legitimacy from the idea of a path *(ṭarīqa)* by which to approach God that implied that human beings were the creatures and servants of God and yet could also become his *awliyā'*. Their special link to the divine makes the *awliyā'* the elevated "others." They were superior to the masses of Muslim faithful and also to the scholars of religion, the *'ulamā'*, who possessed traditional or transmitted knowledge as opposed to the intuitive, supersensory perception of the Muslim mystic.[66] By the early tenth century, this notion had become dominant within Sufi circles. Cosmopolitan elites of mystical wayfarers emerged that were tied together spiritually and intellectually in networks of masters, companions, and disciples. By that time, mystical trends originating in other parts of the Muslim world had made their way to Greater Syria as a whole. Disciples of such great mystics as Abū Turāb al-Nakhshabī the Khurāsānī (d. 245/859), Dhū l-Nūn the Egyptian (d. 245/860), and the above-mentioned Sarī al-Saqaṭī the Baghdadi disseminated their masters' teachings about the path and made their own contributions to the growth and sophistication of the old tradition of ascetic spirituality. The teachings of these and other early great spiritual masters reflect a doctrinal and experimental evolution from the typical ascetic to a true mystic who is conscious of having entered into a uniting love with God and who has been immersed in his contemplation. They lived an extremely ascetic life and stressed both by their living example and in their teachings the contribution of traditional ethical and practical ascetic values to a person's spiritual ascent.[67] In other words, rather than marking a decisive shift from ascetic to mystical piety, their lives and works display the gradual growth of Islamic mysticism out of simple ascetic piety.

Aḥmad b. Yaḥyā' Abī 'Abd Allāh, known as Ibn al-Jallā', was undoubtedly the foremost representative of the formative period of Sufism in Syria-Palestine (figure 1.1). A native of Baghdad, Ibn al-Jallā' at some point settled in Ramla and then moved to Damascus, where he died in 306/918–919. Biographers routinely designate him as one of the great Sufi shaykhs of his time, even the greatest shaykh of Bilād al-Shām. Contemporary admirers would say, "There are in this world but three peerless Sufi leaders. These are Abū 'Uthmān [al-Ḥīrī] in Nishapur, al-Junayd in Baghdad, and Abū 'Abd Allāh b. al-Jallā' in al-Shām."[68] His sayings are documented in classical Sufi manuals, beginning with *Kitāb al-luma' fī l-taṣawwuf* (The Book of Flashes) by al-

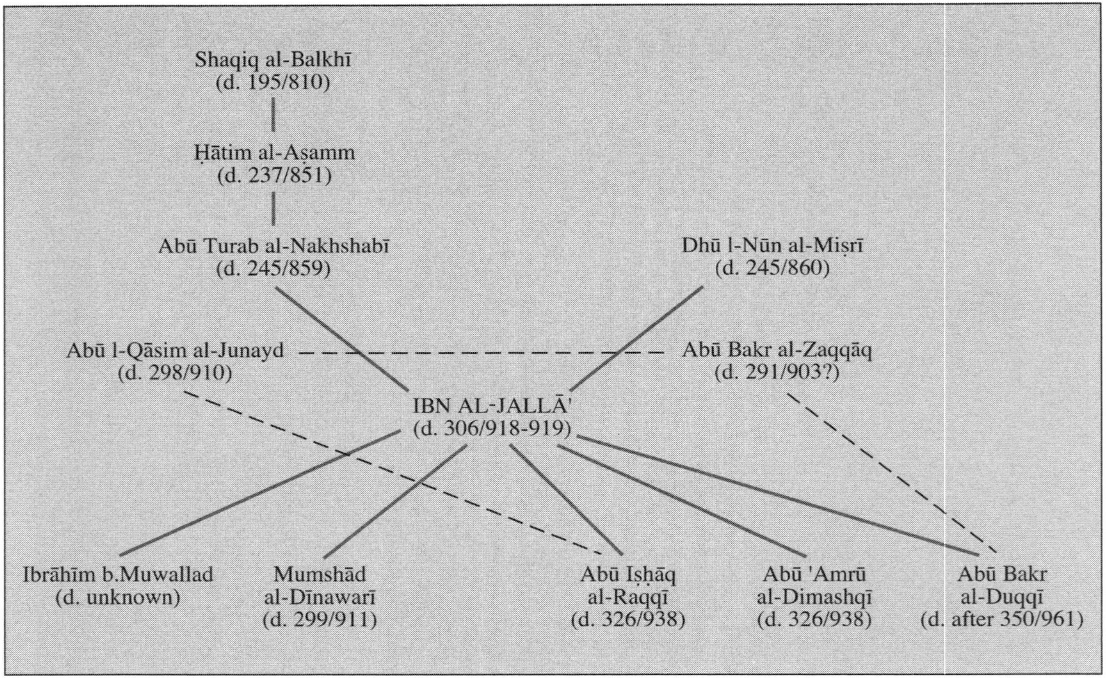

Figure 1.1. The lines and circle of Ibn al-Jallāʾ (d. 306/918–919)

Sarrāj (d. 378/988), and his biography is included in works constituting the main tradition of Sufi historiography, beginning with *Ṭabaqāt al-ṣūfiyya* (Classes of the Sufis) by al-Sulamī. Even biographers not directly affiliated with Sufism devoted long entries to him; the most extensive biography of Ibn al-Jallā' is contained in *Ta'rīkh madinat dimashq,* the voluminous history of Damascus by Ibn 'Asākir.[69]

The accounts about Ibn al-Jallā''s lines and circle of disciples and companions provide a lively testimony of the spiritual centers at the time, the networks forged between the great spiritual masters, and the spread of their teachings. In Baghdad, he associated with Abū l-Qāsim al-Junayd (d. 298/910), his associate Nūrī (d. 295/907), and other local and transient great shaykhs. It was probably also during his days in Baghdad, where a convergence of various ascetic-mystical strands took place, that he became a close disciple *(ṣāḥib)* of both Dhū l-Nūn al-Miṣrī and Abū Turāb al-Nakhshabī, whose wanderings enabled them to carry their teachings far beyond their places of origin. Through Abū Turāb al-Nakhshabī, Ibn al-Jallā' was connected with the eastern tradition of ascetic spiritually and the line of Shāqiq al-Balkhī (d. 195/810), who was not only an expert on the doctrine of absolute trust in God but also the first to discuss the mystical states.[70] The young Ibn al-Jallā' seems to have been initiated into the path by his own father, Yaḥyā' al-Jallā' (d. 258/871), himself a close associate of Ma'rūf al-Karkhī, Bishr al-Ḥafī, and Sarī al-Saqaṭī, who played prominent roles in the formation of the ascetic-mystical tradition that flourished in Baghdad in the second part of the ninth century. When asked about the meaning of his father's name, Ibn al-Jallā' explicated: "The reason he was called 'al-Jallā'' is that whenever he spoke about the hearts (*qulūb,* pl. of *qalb,* the organ of spiritual communication that knows God), he cleansed *(jalā)* them from the blackness of the sins."[71]

Legend has it that when Ibn al-Jallā' was young, he asked his parents to "give him to God," and they agreed. He then left his home for a considerable time, but when he wished to return, they would not let him enter the house even though it was raining heavily: "We gave our son to God," they said, "and we are Arabs. We do not take back what we have given."[72] The legend, which exemplifies an extreme self-sacrifice that is made out of love of God and a yearning for self-annihilation in the divine, appears first in the voluminous *Ḥilyat al-awliyā'* (Decoration of God's Friends) by Abū Nuʿaym al-Iṣfahānī (d. 430/1038–1039) and thereafter is included in most Sufi biographical and hagiographic collections. By placing under the same rubric of the friends of God such well-known Sufis as Ibn al-Jallā', his masters, companions, and disciples, and outstanding virtuous and pious non-Sufi authorities from the time of the Prophet, Abū Nuʿaym probably sought to legitimize the figure of the Sufi-*walī* as one among the other God's friends. In other words, he sought to place him within a normative mode that was accepted by universal Islamic standards. At the same time, "The Decoration" contains legends about the Sufi *awliyā' Allāh* that reflect the spread of belief in their extraordinary virtues among their communities of fellow believers.

Significantly, Abū Nuʿaym, followed by a number of later biographers and hagiographers, designates Ibn al-Jallā' as one of the *abdāl*, a high rank in the Sufi hierarchical order of *awliyā'*. Numerous legends were told about these holy men and women, usually forty in number, without whom the world could not subsist. Due to their very existence, the *abdāl* assure their fellow believers that rain, food, and victory over their enemies will be theirs. Mentioned together with ascetics in a number of early Sufi texts, gradually the *abdāl* assumed high spiritual meaning: the term was used to designate a Muslim holy man who, after his death, would be "substituted" for *(badala)* by another.[73] Many among these figures were connected with Syria-Palestine, the "mine" of the ascetics and holy men. S. D. Goitein draws attention to the relationship between the idea of the *abdāl* and the rabbinical theory of the sixty-six (or thirty or forty-five) hidden "just" who through their piety save the world.[74] Yet an additional explanation of the word and hence of the place and role of the *abdāl* in Islamic piety circulated within Sufi circles. Those who have assumed the rank of *abdāl* have transformed *(baddalū)* their *nafs,* the inferior aspect of the human physiological constitution.[75]

Ibn al-Jallā' does not seem to have attempted to convey to his listeners a detailed account of the spiritual attainment that he had experienced, the mystery of his initiation, or his progress along the mystical path. Nor does he seem to have devised a systematic formula for teaching about the stages or "dwelling stations" of the path. Nevertheless, the citations of his mystical statements and the tales about his lifestyle that are scattered throughout Sufi manuals and biographical literature cast light on his mystical visions and goals, featuring an intricate combination of mystical elements and extreme ascetic outlook. This combination is well attested in Ibn al-Jallā''s definition of the Sufi:

> Ibn al-Jallā' was asked, "Who is called 'Sufi'?" He answered, "We do not know him by the conditions set in learning. But we do know that he is one who is poor, stripped of worldly causes. He is with God without being tied to a place, but God (may he be exalted) does not bar him from knowing all places. This is the one called 'Sufi'."[76]

Endowed with esoteric knowledge of the true reality, the Sufi friend of God is raised far above all other believers. In Ibn al-Jallā's words:

> God *(al-Ḥaqq)* singled out from among his companions some people for speech *(kalām)* and others for friendship *(khulla)*. He then inflicted various severe trials on those whom he had elected to be his companions for the meaningful, exalted cause. Therefore, each one of you should beware of aspiring to the spiritual stage *(rutba)* of the grandees.[77]

Seemingly, the legacy of his master Dhū l-Nūn constituted the main source of inspiration for the exclusive-elitist approach that Ibn al-Jallā' embraced and disseminated to the few who sought his instruction in the secrets of Sufism. Credited by later Sufi authors with formulating the first theory of *maʿrifa* and repeatedly associated with the Hermetic traditions of late antiquity and Hellenistic philosophy, Dhū l-Nūn distinguishes three kinds of knowledge—"that of the ordinary Muslims; that of scholars and sages, the *ʿulamāʾ*; and that of God's friends, who 'see God with their hearts.'"[78]

The notion of the supremacy of the Gnostic *(ʿārif)* over the scholar of religion *(ʿālim)* found explicit expression in the teachings of some of Ibn al-Jallāʾ's disciples. Ibrāhīm b. Muwallad (d. unknown)[79] said, "He on whom Providence rests [is elected to be God's friend] is far more exalted than the one who is educated by way of scholastic learning *(ʿilm)*."[80] When Abū Bakr al-Duqqī (d. 360/970)[81] was asked about bad conduct among "the poor" (*fuqarāʾ*, the Sufis) in their affairs, he said, "It consists in their descending from [seeking] inner truths to scholastic learning *(ẓāhir al-ʿilm)*."[82] And he also remarked: "There is no real, true life but that of the people of *maʿrifa*."[83] As the sole repository of truth in the fullest sense (being concerned above all with the absolute, the infinite, and the eternal), Sufism has the right to be inexorable, exacting, and aloof.

Another distinction is made by Ibn al-Jallāʾ among three kinds of worshipers. Here the Gnostic is set apart from the pietistic and the ascetic due to his attainment of the ultimate realization of God's unity and oneness *(tawḥīd)*:

> He for whom praise and condemnation are equal is *zāhid*, and he who performs the religious duties *(farāʾiḍ)* at their appointed time is *ʿābid*, and he who realizes that all deeds generated from him, is a *muwaḥḥid*.[84]

Closely linked to the belief in divine unity is Ibn al-Jallāʾ's teaching about the principle of trust in God, *tawakkul*. Al-Sulamī—who defines the Sufis as "those who have mystical states *(aḥwāl)* and speak about isolation *(tafrīd)*, the truths of unity *(tawḥīd)* and the application of the methods of detachment *(tajrīd)*"[85]—is greatly concerned about highlighting the absolute dependence of *tawakkul* on the doctrine of *tawḥīd* in the teaching of Ibn al-Jallāʾ. Trust in God in its interiorized sense means the realization of *tawḥīd* for it would be "hidden partaking" *(shirk khafī)* to rely on or be afraid of any created being. Accordingly, attempts to secure one's livelihood amount to a lack of a sincere belief that God is the lord and sustainer of all things: "Your concern about livelihood diverts your mind from God and makes you in need of human beings," states Ibn al-Jallāʾ.[86] As he is the only one who benefits or harms you, every feeling and thought must turn in perfect sincerity exclusively to him: "Since there is no God except him, the mystical wayfarer *(sālik)*, in his entirety, should be devoted to him alone. . . . God is the ultimate endeavor *(himma)* of those who possess divine gnosis. They devote themselves to nothing but him."[87] "Perfect sincerity *(ilkhlāṣ)* in reliance on God's beneficence embraces the whole object of *maʿrifa,*" declares one of Ibn al-Jallāʾ's celebrated disciples, Mumshād (or Mamshād) al-Dīnawarī (d. 299/911),[88] who embraced his master's doctrine of *tawakkul* and further imbued it with the notion of the mystic's supremacy over all humankind. He is reported to have said: "Even if you accumulate the wisdom of the first and last sages and claim to have attained the spiritual states *(aḥwāl)* of God's favorites, you will not attain the ranks of the *ʿārifīn* until the inmost ground of your soul *(sirr)* contemplates him. Only then you be absolutely certain of what he promised and allotted to you."[89] Once this stage of ultimate realization and devotion is reached, no one can harm the mystic, and his hope for God's benevolence can overcome his fear of the last judgment. In the words of Ibn al-Jallāʾ's disciple, Abū Bakr al-Duqqī, "He who knows God, his hope for his mercy *(rajāʾ)* never ceases."[90]

Ibn al-Jallāʾ probably acquired his stringent ascetic version of trust in God mostly from his other master, Abū Turāb al-Nakhshabī, who disseminated the ideas of *tawakkul* of his own master Ḥātim al-Aṣamm (d. 237/851), the disciple of Shaqīq al-Balkhī, the earlier exponent, if not the founder, of the doctrine. According to later Sufi authors, only two of Abū Turāb's 120 students were able to endure the rigors of ascetic training and become established Sufi masters.[91] One of these was Ibn al-Jallā'. When asked about divine love, he said, "What have I to do with it? My quest is to learn how to attain the stage of repentance *(tawba),*"[92] thereby inferring that he had not yet fully interiorized the ascetic ethics and practices that the mystical wayfarer needs before attaining the highest stages of spiritual ascent. His extreme ascetic outlook is displayed in his utterances and tales about abstinence and poverty.

Al-Qushayrī in his "Epistle"—most probably drawing on the classical Sufi textbooks by al-Sarrāj, al-Makkī, and al-Kalābādhī that gave Sufism its final shape and orthodox tone—was the main collector and recorder of Ibn al-Jallā's teachings relating to the various principles of asceticism. Classifying the forerunners of Sufism in the *Ṭabaqāt* section of his treatise as pious traditionalists rather than mystics,[93] the material that al-Qushayrī selected emphasizes the overzealously ascetic over the mystic element of the persona. The theories and practices of the path relating to purity in dietary matters, poverty, and humility are here brought together:

> Ibn al-Jallā' related, "I know someone who lived in Mecca for thirty years without drinking the water of Zamzam except for what he drew with his own bucket and rope, and he did not eat food that was brought there from other cities."[94]
>
> Ibn al-Jallā' declared, "One who does not associate God-fearing with his poverty eats the manifestly forbidden."[95]
>
> Ibn al-Jallā' commented, "Renunciation is to regard the world with the eye of extinction so that it becomes inferior in your eyes. Then turning away from it will become easy for you."[96]
>
> Ibrāhīm b. Muwallad said, "I asked Ibn al-Jallā', 'When does the poor one deserve the name?' He replied, 'When nothing of it remains for him.' I inquired, 'How is that?' He answered, 'When he possesses it, he does not have it [poverty]. And when he no longer possesses it, then he has it.'"[97]
>
> Ibn al-Jallā' remarked, "If it were not for the [higher] noble pur-

pose of being humble before God, it would be the way of the poor one to strut proudly when he walks."[98]

Love of God is the ultimate driving force behind all acts of self-denial and behind the contemplation of nothing but him. The mystic as God's lover *(ḥabīb)* and the perception of intimacy with the divine as the uppermost mystical stage, often attributed to such intriguing figures in the history of early Sufism as Shaqīq al-Balkhī and Dhū l-Nūn, were notions disseminated among successive generations of disciples. The repeated theme is beautifully expressed by Ibn al-Jallā''s disciple, Ibrāhīm b. Muwallad:

> If it were not for the tears and longing of those whose hearts are filled with passion for God *(ʿushshāq)*, then the might of fire and water would not have manifested themselves to the people. This is so because all fire is ignited in the souls of lovers and all waters shed from their eyes.[99]

For one whose heart is filled with passionate divine love and experiences proximity to God, to be parted from him is conceived of as the most painful affliction. Ibn al-Jallā''s other disciple, Abū Bakr al-Duqqī, is said to have spent the night upright in solitary meditation. When he woke up, he wept: "Oh Lord, return the heart of the depressed man who was left with no trace of his beloved one, and the people around him are weeping."[100] He then recited:

> If the nights had been punished by [the grief of] our separation,
> their tears would have wiped the stars' light.
> If the days had been watered with the bitter cup of our separation, they would have dissolved.[101]

Only those of exceptional spiritual talent were able to adhere throughout their lives to such stringently ascetic ethics and practices as those propagated by Ibn al-Jallā' and his masters, disciples, and companions. Similarly, mystical experiences of ardent divine love and total immersion in the contemplation of God, which prepare the soul for its spiritual ascent, remained the domain of the few.

But in spite of the highly elitist and inclusive character of early Islamic mysticism, during the formative period in its history the theoretical and experimental foundations were laid for the association that came to be known as "the people of the way" (*ahl al-ṭarīqa,* or *ahl al-ṭarīq*) and which gathered around mystic mentors. The genesis of first core circle of this association—as reflected in accounts of the famous mystic of Ramla, his own master, and their companions and disciples—is the subject of the next section.

THE GENESIS OF THE SUFI CIRCLE

The formulation of the doctrine of the path soon gave birth to the concept of guidance along its "states" and "stations." Whatever the steps of spiritual progress that might lead to a union with or vision of God, "Sufism *(taṣawwuf)* has always a beginning, a culmination, and intermediary stages," states al-Sulamī.[102] The first station at the very beginning of the path is always *tawba* (repentance or conversion)—a term that within Sufi circles entails not only the usual meaning of turning away from sin and subduing natural desires but also a deeper psychological transformation of the self.[103] Once the preparatory stage of radical change in one's life is attained, individual effort in the pursuit of the mystical path is no longer sufficient; the aspirant must seek the guidance of someone called variously a "master" *(shaykh),* an "elder" *(pīr),* or a "guide" *(murshid)*—a wise and experienced person who has attained the goal of mystical striving. By the eleventh century, it had become common for the aspirant to call on a shaykh rather than tread the spiritual path alone. Sufi writers living in the late tenth and early eleventh centuries repeatedly insisted on the need of a guide along the path. Al-Sulamī, followed by others, urged the aspirant to seek a guide and mentor who possessed wide knowledge and experience to lead him on the right course, warn him of the pitfalls along the path, and teach him to distinguish his sinful from his virtuous deeds.[104]

The general need for an authoritative guide had long been acknowledged in Sufi circles, where novices, like students of the Islamic sciences, were encouraged to seek authoritative masters to guide them. "Whoever attains a stage *(rutba)* through individual efforts, lapses from it; whoever is led to attain it, stands firm in it," states Ibn al-Jallāʾ.[105] No matter how informal and unstructured the ties that bound seekers of the path to masters may appear, references to wayfarers who attached themselves in one way or another to superior mystic-masters in their quest for spiritual development are indicative of the birth of circles of companions and aspirants around them.

Following the lead of the fourteenth-century Moroccan Sufi Ibn ʿAbbād al-Rundī, Fritz Meier points out a universal transformation of the teaching shaykh *(shaykh al-taʿlīm)* into the directing shaykh *(shaykh al-tarbiyya)*. Beginning in Khurasan, the new model matured and spread throughout the Muslim world in the course of the eleventh century. The *shaykh al-taʿlīm*'s instruction was oriented toward the elucidation of textual exegesis, and the shaykh was relatively uninvolved in the private, inner life of his disciple. The *shaykh al-tarbiyya* took on a new and a far more encompassing role in the education of his disciples. In his position of unquestionable authority, he would closely monitor their progress and supervise all their actions.[106] This shift signaled a new theoretical dimension as well. A model was formulated in which the *walī Allāh* exercises complete authority over his followers; he becomes a patron rather than a simple teacher.[107]

However, as Meier argues, "One is suspicious of the assertion that the earliest Ṣūfiyya did not yet have need of training and therefore did not engage in it. . . . Training in Sufism cannot be sharply separated from teaching since Sufism naturally had to address questions of training."[108] This last observation may be generally applicable to the early mystics under study here. A thorough investigation of narratives that cast light on the genesis of their circles challenges the repeated assumption that the early shaykhs were lecturers on Sufi wisdom—teachers rather than guides on the spiritual path.[109]

Little is known about the content of the early Sufi master's guidance, the practices that he applied in training his few select disciples and intimates, or the ways that he interacted with them. Nevertheless, a few rare testimonies that relate to the early mystics whose biographies were studied for this book infer that as early as the formative period of Sufism, the shaykh would equip those who called on him with the knowledge of the essentials of Sufism and the sacred law, with generalized instructions on spiritual etiquette, and with behavioral training by means of definitive instructions and supervision. The example of Dhū l-Nūn is instructive in this regard. The following story about his method of imparting the principles of *tawakkul* and abstinence to the circle of disciples orbiting around him during their stay in Mecca is told by his committed disciple, Ibn al-Jallā':

> I spent many days in Mecca in the company of Dhū l-Nūn and a group *(jamā'a)*. God provided us with nothing. One day, Dhū l-Nūn directed his steps to the mountain [of 'Arafat] to perform the prayer-ablution there. As I followed him, I saw a fresh banana peel thrown in the valley. I picked it up and hid it in my sleeve. When we reached the mountain, the shaykh turned to me and ordered, "Throw away the unlawfully seized and hidden thing you have in your pocket." Ashamed, I did so. We then returned to the mosque for the performance of the five daily prayers. After the last prayer, a man came by carrying food in a covered pot. He stood still looking at the shaykh. Dhū l-Nūn said, "Hand it over to me." I expected the shaykh to eat it, but he stayed still in his place. He then ordered me to eat. I asked, "Should I be the only one to eat?" He said, "Yes, for it was you who sought food, while we sought nothing. Those who seek food should eat." Deeply ashamed, I complied with the order.[110]

To achieve compliance with the master's entire instructions, his image as a charismatic model of virtue was shaped and disseminated among later generations of companions and aspirants. Eyewitness accounts of the actual manifestations of his heroic virtues must have been pivotal in this process. The values and norms that such stories conveyed must have appealed to listeners, who further shaped the master's image as a charismatic figure. Ibn al-Jallāʾ related to his disciples a miraculous deed that had been performed by his venerated master. While in the Hijaz for the purpose of the *ḥajj*, he accompanied Dhū l-Nūn to the shore of the Red Sea, where the encountered a woman who was weeping bitterly. When Dhū l-Nūn inquired the reason for her mourning, she told him that a crocodile had come out of the sea and seized her son. Dhū l-Nūn prayed for her, and at that moment the crocodile came by and threw the child onto the shore.[111]

Sometime later on a pilgrimage, Ibn al-Jallāʾ took the opportunity to instill in his disciples the lessons of generosity and caring for the needy. His disciple Abū ʿAmrū al-Dimashqī relates that while journeying to Mecca and suffering from hunger, the group tried to buy a sheep from a woman. First she asked for fifty coins, and then she reduced the price to five coins. When they accused her of mockery, she said that she would have been pleased if she could have given them the sheep for nothing in return. Ibn al-Jallāʾ then ordered his disciples to give the 600 coins that they were carrying to the woman and to leave her the sheep as well. "And this was the finest journey we ever made," concludes Abū ʿAmrū.[112]

This is how the doctrinal shaping of disciples was interwoven with their spiritual formation: the master stimulates the aspirant's quest for advancement on the path through tales *(ḥikāyāt)* that clarify the doctrine and create role models for imitation. Accounts that describe training in Sufism furthermore convey the idea that the shaykh shapes his disciples more through the impact of his mystical state *(ḥāl)* and spiritual virtues than through his speech *(maqāl)*. The shaykh, in other words, must be the living example of the principles he preaches—above all, confidence in God, veracity *(ṣidq)*, and poverty *(faqr)*—and must impart them through his personal example rather than through lessons on these principles. No anecdote illustrates Ibn al-Jallā''s teaching by personal example more clearly than that related to the Sufi principle of poverty:

> Abū Muḥammad Yāsīn related, "I asked Ibn al-Jallā' about poverty. He fell silent. Then he withdrew and went away. He returned a short time later and said, 'I had four coins and was ashamed before God [glorious and majestic] to speak about poverty until I had gotten rid of them.' Then he began to speak about poverty."[113]

The teaching-training might have involved a single disciple or a whole circle of companions and aspirants who clustered around the master. The master seemed to transmit knowledge and guidance on more or less random occasions rather than in regularly organized meetings. He and his small circle would gather wherever he dwelt and traveled or in a mosque that served them as a place of retreat, devotion, training, and residence—at least before the advent and spread of the organized Sufi lodge.[114] On one occasion while sitting in the mosque surrounded by a group *(jamāʿa)*, Ibn al-Jallā' took the opportunity to train his disciples in the ways of self-control and austerity. He ordered one of them to remove a piece of fig peel that he had on his cheek and throw it on the floor of the mosque. He then picked up the peel, left the mosque, and threw the peel outside the gate. Returning to his seat in the mosque, he exclaimed, "*Zuhd* is viewing the world as ephemeral and meaningless. Once seen in this fashion, it may become easier for you to renounce it."[115]

After a Sufi attained the quest for enlightenment, he enjoyed and deserved veneration. In the words of Mumshād al-Dīnawarī, one of Ibn al-Jallā''s closest disciples:

> The rules of proper conduct *(adab)* of the aspirant *(murīd)* consist of commitment to the veneration of the shaykhs. . . . I never sought out any of my shaykhs before freeing myself from all my

possessions. For he who comes to the shaykh with his possessions is deprived of the blessing *(baraka)* of his vision and his words and the sitting in his company.[116]

Every opportunity to receive the shaykh's guidance must be seized. While in Damascus, ʿAlī b. Bundār of Nishapur was asked by Ibn al-Jallāʾ where he had spent the three days he had already been in the city. ʿAlī b. Bundār replied that he had written down traditions at the dictation of the *ḥadīh* expert Ibn Jawṣā. Ibn al-Jallāʾ then scolded him, saying, "So what is merely recommendable *(sunna)* withheld you from what is duty *(farīḍa)*."[117]

However, merely to follow a Sufi master and his path intensively and faithfully and to align one's own will with his authoritative guidance are not enough. Emotional trust must be instilled and cultivated. It was probably this need that in time generated the characteristic image of the shaykh as a paternal guide who knows everything about his disciples, even their innermost secret thoughts, and who, more important, cares about them. Somehow, this psychological aspect, which later Sufi shaykhs applied to constitute their community of followers as a fraternity *(ṭarīqa)*,[118] can be traced back to the formative years of the Sufi tradition.

The case of Abū Bakr al-Duqqī, the close disciple of Ibn al-Jallāʾ, illustrates the above point. One day he asked his master, the great shaykh Abū Bakr al-Zaqqāq (d. 291/903?), which spiritual mentor he should follow or associate himself with *(ṣaḥiba)* while treading the path. The shaykh responded: "Him with whom there is no reason for mistrust between you." When he posed the same question again, the shaykh said, "Follow him whom you trust to know about you what God knows about you."[119] Although al-Duqqī followed many shaykhs, it was to Ibn al-Jallāʾ that he fully entrusted himself. The term that al-Sulamī uses to describe this bond is *intamā ilā* as distinct from the more general *ṣaḥiba*.[120] A later author extols al-Duqqī as the most excellent of all the shaykhs in companionship *(ṣuḥbat li-l-mashāyikh).*[121]

Accounts of the mystics who are under consideration here do not provide examples of disciples who pledged their sole allegiance to one spiritual guide, spent many years in his company, and entered a life that was dominated by his guidance. Disciples were bound to mystic mentors by ties of deference and affection, but these ties were relatively unstructured. Nor do the accounts suggest the existence of any local group of companions and aspirants who orbited around one specific individual in his home or in a mosque. Rather, in common with their contemporaries throughout the Muslim world, companions and aspirants who belonged to the lines and circle of Ibn al-Jallāʾ would travel freely among many Sufi shaykhs, sharing companionship while learning and cultivating interior practices.

Abū Iṣhāq al-Raqqī (d. 326/938), one of the greatest shaykhs of Syria, is said to have shared companionship with both Ibn al-Jallāʾ and his famous contemporary al-Junayd and to have had many disciples.[122] Mumshād al-Dīnawarī, who seems to have traveled frequently, related, "In the course of one of my journeys *(siyaḥa),* I met a shaykh whose blessing and moral advice I sought. He said to me, 'Persist with your sincere intention *(himma),* for he who is sincere and righteous in his intention will be held true for all the deeds and mystical states *(aḥwāl)* that come after.'"[123] The following story, attributed to Mumshād al-Dīnawarī, further confirms the impression of a free-floating mystical wayfarer who seeks guidance from those who seemed to have advanced on the path:

> There was a man among us who increasingly reduced his subsistence until he had just a fruit kernel and finally only water. We asked him, "What should the Sufi *(faqīr)* do if he suffers from hunger?" He answered, "He should pray." We asked, "What should he do if he cannot pray?" He replied, "He should sleep." We asked, "And if he cannot sleep?" He replied, "God never deprives the *faqīr* of any of the following: strength, nourishment, and a source from which he can derive them."[124]

The search for different shaykhs as sources of blessing and guidance was regarded as meritorious, as is attested in accounts of some celebrated Sufis who allegedly had hundreds of shaykhs. An example is Muḥammad al-Duqqī, who met 300 shaykhs.[125] Traveling in search of many superior mystics apparently was regarded as necessary for deepening one's spiritual training and for developing the ability to adjust to different conditions of life and company.

As mystical wayfarers wandered from place to place, seeking from one another guidance in the secrets of Sufism and in advancement on the path, no clear-cut distinction seems to have existed among guides, disciples, and companions. Thus, in the formative period of Sufism, a particular Sufi might appear as a guide in one circle and as a disciple, a companion, or even an aspirant in another. Only from the eleventh century onward did Sufis emphasize the difference between master and disciple and increase the distance between them with regard to the position they occupied toward each other, their distinctive traits, and their precise duties.[126]

For all the fluidity of the mystical wayfarer's environment, however, by the end of classical Sufism small circles that were united by common devotions and methods of spiritual discipline were spreading throughout Islamic lands and far beyond. Collectively designated by the terms *jamāʿa* (community, group) or *ikhwān* (brethren), these circles consisted of *aṣḥāb* (committed companions or disciples and followers of a shaykh), *murīdūn* (aspirants, novices), and *aqrān* (colleagues, associates) of a great shaykh or, more often, a number of shaykhs in their time.[127] Clusters of wayfarers who saw themselves as intellectually and spiritually related companions of certain shaykhs would follow these shaykhs wherever they happened to sit to receive their guidance and blessing, or they would join them to pray, travel, or perform the pilgrimage to Mecca. The stories about Ibn al-Jallāʾ, his master Dhū l-Nūn, and his own circle of disciples come to mind. Despite the scarcity of information that they provide, references to such circles indicate the tendency of disciples to group around venerated Sufi shaykhs rather than to retain the individualistic character of many other spiritual wayfarers.

Utterances and tales in praise of service to and care for one's brethren in faith reveal early sentiments of fraternity among fellow wayfarers. "The 'true' Sufi *(al-faqīr al-ṣādiq)* is he who meddles in the affairs of this world for the sake of others rather than for his own benefit," asserts Ibn al-Jallā'.[128] His disciples seem to have carried forward and implemented his ideal of altruism. The rules of proper conduct of the aspirant *(murīd),* in Mumshād al-Dīnawarī's perception, consist of veneration of the shaykhs and also service to the brethren *(khidmat al-ikhwān).*[129] Whenever a group of his Sufi brethren intended to visit him, he would go to the market to collect bread for them beforehand.[130] Muḥammad al-Duqqī routinely spent on the Sufis whatever God had granted to him; while in Ramla, he gave all that he had—a half coin—to a group that called on him.[131]

References to early Sufis—loners though they were—who sought out the advice and counsel of their fellow wayfarers and cared for each other demonstrate that from the very beginning, companionship was considered essential for progress in the spiritual life. Accordingly, very soon the term *ṣuḥba* (companionship) was used not only in a limited sense to mean companionship of direction with a mystic or mystics mentors or among equals, guiding one another but also to mean companionship among Sufis in general. The value of companionship in its comprehensive sense was emphasized, and seclusion was not considered to be significant in the building up of a spiritual personality. Some notable mystics went even further in their high appreciation of companionship. Al-Nūrī remarked, "Beware of seclusion for it is connected with Satan, and cleave to companionship for therein is the satisfaction of the merciful God."[132]

Integrated by spirit and aim rather than by any formulized mutual commitments and focused on several shaykhs, the earlier Sufi circles were nonetheless loose and mobile associations. The more established the authority of the Sufi shaykh came to be and the more structured the master-disciple relationship, the more the bonds between them tightened, leading to a significant change in the character of Sufi associations. As early as the second half of the tenth century, a coherent, locally embedded congregation of spiritual mentors with their disciples—committed followers of his path *(ṭarīqa)*—began clustering around Sufi shaykhs who settled in Palestinian spiritual centers and their environs, gradually growing and extending its horizons in the course of the Islamic middle periods.

NOTES

1. For the construction of Bishr al-Ḥāfī's life as a spiritual heir to the Prophet in biographical literature and the interplay of actual events and figments of imagination in his presentation, see Michael Cooperson, *Classical Arabic Biography: The Heirs of the Prophet in the Age of al-Ma'amūn* (Cambridge: Cambridge University Press, 2000), chap. 5.
2. Mujīr al-Dīn al-ʿUlaymī, *al-Uns al-jalīl bi-ta'rīkh al-Quds wa-l-Khalīl,* 2nd ed. (Baghdad, 1995), 1:295.
3. The first to stress the importance of Jerusalem and the Holy Land for the Muslim mystics was S. D. Goitein, "The Sanctity of Jerusalem and Palestine in Early Islam," in *Studies in Islamic History and Institutions* (Leiden: Brill, 1966), 142–46. M. J. Kister was the first to draw attention to the important role of the earliest *zuhhād* in the development and dissemination of the "Traditions in Praise of Jerusalem" in his "A Comment on the Antiquity of Traditions Praising Jerusalem," *Jerusalem Cathedra* 1 (1981): 185–86. For more recent studies, see O. Livne-Kafri, *The Sanctity of Jerusalem in Islam* (Ph.D. thesis, Hebrew University, Jerusalem, 1985), 27 ff. (in Hebrew); Amikam Elad, *Medieval Jerusalem and Islamic Worship: Holy Places, Ceremonies, Pilgrimage* (Leiden: Brill, 1995), 66.
4. See Goitein, "The Sanctity of Jerusalem," 142 and the references there.
5. Ibn al-Murajjā, *Faḍā'il,* f. 272a, ff. 69 b. Cited by O. Livne-Kafri, "Early Muslim Ascetics and the World of Christian Monasticism," *Jerusalem Studies in Arabic and Islam* 20 (1996): 109.

6. Goitein, "The Sanctity of Jerusalem," 146; Livne-Kafri, "Early Muslim Ascetics," 109.
7. Cited by Goitein, "The Sanctity of Jerusalem," 145 and the primary sources on 142. See also Russell Jones, "Ibrāhīm b. Adham," *EI2*.
8. Shams al-Dīn al-Muqaddasī, *Aḥsan al-taqāsīm fī maʿrifat al-aqālīm*, 2nd ed., ed. M. J. de Goeje (Leiden: Brill, 1906), 172. Al-Muqaddasī was also the first to discuss the hosting practices that were developed in Hebron in the second half of the tenth century.
9. Mujīr al-Dīn, *al-Uns al-jalīl*, 1:203.
10. Elad, *Medieval Jerusalem*, 64.
11. J. Kister, "You Shall Only Set Out for Three Mosques: A Study of an Early Islamic Tradition," *Le Muséon* 82 (1969): 192.
12. Mujīr al-Dīn, *al-Uns al-jalīl*, 1:285.
13. Elad, *Medieval Jerusalem*, 66 and the examples in n. 76.
14. Amikam Elad, "The Coastal Cities of Palestine during the Early Middle Ages," *Jerusalem Cathedra* 2 (1982): 146–67 (in Hebrew).
15. On the unique form of asceticism that evolved on the Arab-Byzantine frontier, see especially Michael Bonner, *Aristocratic Violence and Holy War: Studies in the Jihad and the Arab Byzantine Frontier* (New Haven, CT: American Oriental Society, 1996), 107–34.
16. On early Muslim ascetics who, under the influence of their Christian counterparts, sought a hermitage in the mountains of Syria-Palestine, see Houari Touati, *Islam et Voyage au Moyen Âge* (Paris: Éditions du Seuil, 2000), 223–28.
17. For overviews of earlier regional expressions of asceticism and mysticism, see especially Margaret Smith, *Studies in Early Mysticism in the Near and Middle East* (London: Sheldon Press, 1931); Alexander Knysh, *Islamic Mysticism: A Short History* (Leiden: Brill, 2000), 39–115. There are several historically grounded studies on the evolution of specific regional trends in early Sufism, most notably Jacqueline Chabbi, "Remarques sur le développment historique de mouvements ascétiques et mystiques au Khurasan," *Studia Islamica* 46 (1977): 5–72; Jacqueline Chabbi, "Réflexions sur le soufisme iranien primitif," *Journal Asiatique* 266/1–2 (1978): 37–55.
18. Mujīr al-Dīn, *al-Uns al-jalīl*, 1:296. Al-Maqdisī, writing in the middle of the fourteenth century, mentions that people would

come to Abū Shuʿayb's grave to pray for rain. Aḥmad b. Muḥammad al-Maqdisī, *Muthir al-gharām bi-faḍā'il al-Quds wa-l-Shām,* ed. Aḥmad Ṣāliḥ al-Khālidī (Jaffa, 1946), 56.

19. For example, Reynold A. Nicholson in his classical work, *The Mystics of Islam,* 4th ed. (London: Arkana, 1989), 4.
20. For a recent comprehensive study of the interpretations and meanings of the *ḥajj* in premodern Sufi thought and practice, see Muhammad Khalid Masud, "Sufi Understanding of *Hajj* Rituals," in Alfonso Carmona, ed., *El Sufismo y las normas del Islam,* Trabajos del IV Congreso Internacional de Estudios Jurídicos Islámicos: Derecho y Sufismo (Murcia: Consejería de Educatión y Cultura, 2006), 271–90 (in English).
21. Mujīr al-Dīn, *al-Uns al-jalīl,* 1:287. For additional examples, see O. Livne-Kafri, "Khitām al-Qur'ān," *Maʿof ve-Maʿase* 3 (1997): 107–09 (in Hebrew).
22. Cited by Annemarie Schimmel, *Mystical Dimensions of Islam* (Chapel Hill: University of North Carolina Press, 1975), 107.
23. Muḥammad b. Saʿd, *Kitāb al-ṭabaqāt* (Leiden: Brill, 1905), 8(2):206; Abū l-Faraj b. al-Jawzī, *Ṣifat al-ṣafwa,* 4 vols. (Hyderabad: Da'irat al-Maʿārif al-ʿUthmāniyya, 1355–57 AH), 4:305; Ibn Ḥajar al-ʿAsqalānī, *Tahdhīb al-tahdhīb,* ed. M. Hārūn (Hyderabad, 1327 AH), 11:334.
24. Mujīr al-Dīn, *al-Uns al-jalīl,* 1:288.
25. See Goitein, "The Sanctity of Jerusalem," 144–48, for the traditions that shaped the image of al-Shām as the mine of the ascetics and holy men. The term *the Holy Land* was extended in Islamic literature to cover the whole of al-Shām, including Lebanon and Syria.
26. John Binns, *Ascetics and Ambassadors of Christ: The Monasteries of Palestine, 314–631* (New York: Oxford University Press, 1994), provides a comprehensive and lively picture of the monasteries of Palestine.
27. For studies that highlight the similarity between certain aspects of late antiquity and early medieval Eastern Christian monasticism and early Islamic asceticism, see Tor Andrae, "Zuhd and Mönchtum," *Le Monde Oriental* 25 (1931): 296–327; I. Goldziher, *Introduction to Islamic Theology and Law,* trans. A. Hamori and R. Hamori (Princeton, NJ: Princeton University Press, 1981), 116–66. A recent contribution to the study of the meeting

of the Syriac and Byzantine monastic heritage with the world of Islamic asceticism is Livne-Kafri, "Early Muslim Ascetics," 105–25. For a discussion of night vigil in prayer among Christian ascetics, see especially Smith, *Studies in Early Mysticism,* 139.

28. Mujīr al-Dīn, *al-Uns al-jalīl,* 1:289.
29. Ibid.
30. About the ideal of annihilation of all bodily needs and its impact on Syriac and Byzantine monasticism of late antiquity, see especially Arthur Vööbus, *A History of Asceticism in the Syrian Orient* (Louvain: Secretariat du Corpus SCO,1958–), 1:69 ff.; Sebastian P. Brock, *Syriac Perspectives of Late Antiquity* (London: Variorum Reprints, 1984), 1:6–8; C. Hall, "Asceticism," in *Encyclopedia of Religion and Ethics,* ed. James Hastings (New York: Clark, 1964), 2:67–69; Aline Rousselle, *Pomeia: de la maîtrise du corps à la privation sensorielle* (Paris: Presses Universitaires de France, 1983), trans. Felicia Pheasart as *Pomeia: On Desire and Body in Antiquity* (Cambridge: Blackwell, 1993). For a comprehensive study of this topic, see Peter Brown, *The Body and Society: Men, Women, and Sexual Renunciation in Early Christianity* (New York: Faber and Faber, 1988).
31. For examples of these exceptions, see Livne-Kafri, "Early Muslim Ascetics," 112.
32. See Binns, *Ascetics and Ambassadors,* for a detailed portrait of a monastic society of monastery cities that was fully integrated into the soils of the Judean Desert and the life of the Church and empire. The second part of the book describes the environment that the monasteries grew in and that led to their distinctive characteristics. On the character of monastic life in the Judean desert, see also D. J. Chitty, *The Desert a City* (Oxford: Oxford University Press, 1966); J. Patrich, *The Judean Desert Monasticism in the Byzantine Period: The Institutions of Sabas and His Disciples* (Jerusalem: Yad Izhaq Ben-Zvi, 1995) (in Hebrew).
33. The meaning of *zuhd* and the moderate and extreme forms of early Islamic asceticism have received considerable attention by Islamicists. Recent contributions include Leah Kihnberg, "What Is Meant by *Zuhd?,*" *Studia Islamica* 61 (1985): 27–44; Nimrod Hurvitz, "Biographies and Mild Asceticism: A Study of Islamic Moral Imagination," *Studia Islamica* 85 (1997): 41–65.
34. Mujir, *al-Uns al-jalīl,* 1:287.

35. Ibid., 1:288.
36. ʿAbd al-Raḥmān b. Rajab, *Dhayl ʿalā ṭabaqāt al-ḥanābila,* ed. H. Laoust and S. Dahhan (Damascus, 1951), 1:48, cited by George Makdisi, "The Sunni Revival," in D. S. Richards, ed., *Islamic Civilization, 950–1150* (Oxford: Cassirer, 1973), 166.
37. On the ideal of moderate asceticism in medieval Christian thought and practice, see especially Giles Constable, "Moderation and Restraint in Ascetic Practices in the Middle Ages," in Haijo J. Westra, ed., *From Athens to Chartres: Neoplatonism and Medieval Thought. Studies in the Honour of Edouard Jeauneau* (Leiden: Brill, 1992), 319 ff.
38. See the comments of Christopher Melchert in "The Piety of the Hadith Folk," *International Journal of Middle East Studies* 34:3 (2002): 429.
39. For the figure of Ibn al-Mubārak and his devotional attitude, see B. Reinert, *Die Lehre vom tawakkul in der klassischen Sufik* (Berlin: de Gruyter, 1968), 220, 309; A. Arberry, *Sufism: An Account of the Mystics of Islam,* 5th ed. (New York: Harper and Row, 1970), 40; J. Van Ess, *Theologie und Gesellschaft im 2. und 3. Jahrhundert Hidschra* (Berlin, 1992–1996), 2:552.
40. On the Malāmatī condemnation of extreme asceticism and ostensible spiritual attainments, see Sara Sviri, "Ḥakīm Tirmidhī and the Malāmatī Movement in Early Islam," in Leonard Lewisohn, ed., *Classical Persian Sufism: From Its Origins to Rumi* (London: Khaniqahi-Nimatullahi Publications, 1993), 583–602. See also F. De Jong and H. Algar, "Malāmatiyya," *EI2.*
41. On the rejection of Christian monastic life in early Islam, see Sara Sviri, "wa-rahbāniyatan ibtadaʿūhā," *Jerusalem Studies in Arabic and Islam* 13 (1990): 195–208.
42. On the Karrāmiyya in Khurasan, see especially C. E. Bosworth, "The Rise of the Karrāmiyya [sic] in Khurāsān," *Muslim World* (1960): 6–14; Richard W. Bulliet, *The Patricians of Nishapur: A Study in Medieval Islamic Social History* (Cambridge, MA: Harvard University Press, 1972), 62–64; Chabbi, "Remarques sur le développment historique," 30, 41, 48–49.
43. See L. Massignon, *Recueil de textes inédits concernant l'histoire de la mystique en pays de l'Islam* (Paris: Geuthner, 1929), 24.
44. Al-Muqaddasī, *Aḥsan al-taqāsīm,* 179, 182, 323, 365.
45. Bulliet, *The Patricians,* 42.

46. Max Weber, *The Sociology of Religion,* trans. Ephraim Fischoff, introduction by Tolcott Parsons (Boston: Beacon Press, 1963), 166. See also Nimrod Hurvitz, "From Scholarly Circles to Mass Movements," *American Historical Review* 108:4 (October 2003): 1001, for an eloquent discussion of this point.
47. Manuela Marín's study of the *zuhd* that was practiced in al-Andalus in the tenth century is probably the most important contribution to an understanding of the characteristic features and various nuances of medieval Islamic asceticism. Manuela Marín, "Zuhhād of al-Andalus (300/912–429/1029)," in M. Fierro and J. Samsó, eds., *The Formation of al-Andalus,* Part 2, *Language, Religion, Culture and the Sciences* (Aldershot: Ashgate, 1998), 103–31. See also Daphna Ephrat, "In Quest of an Ideal Type of Saint: Some Observations on the First Generation of Moroccan *Awliyā Allāh* in *Kitāb al-tashawwuf,*" *Studia Islamica* 94 (2002): 67–84, for a study of the various ways in which *zuhd* was understood and practiced by the friends of God of eleventh- and twelfth-century Morocco.
48. Roy P. Mottahedeh makes this observation with regard to the world of religious learning in the tenth century. Roy P. Mottahedeh, *Loyalty and Leadership in an Early Islamic Society* (Princeton, NJ: Princeton University Press, 1980), 140. See also Daphna Ephrat, *A Learned Society in a Period of Transition: The Sunni ʿUlamaʾ of Eleventh-Century Baghdad* (Albany: SUNY Press, 2000), for the inclusive class of the *ʿulamāʾ* of Baghdad during the period covered.
49. Ibn Ḥajar, *Tahdhīb,* 11:334.
50. See above note 23.
51. Ibn Ḥajar, *Tahdhīb,* 8:229–28.
52. For early traditions praising poverty and urging support for the poor, see Livne-Kafri, "Early Muslim Ascetics," 114–17.
53. Mujīr al-Dīn, *al-Uns al-jalīl,* 1:287.
54. Ibn Ḥajar, *Tahdhīb,* 12:465.
55. See Livne-Kafri, "Early Muslim Ascetics," 116 n. 127.
56. On the forerunners of Ḥanbalīsm and their understanding of asceticism, see Jacqueline Chabbi, "Fudayl b. ʿIyad: Un precurseur du Hanbalisme (d. 187/803)," *Bulletin d'études orientales* 30 (1978): 331–45; Gerard Lecomte, "Sufyān al-Thawrī: Quelques remarques sur le personnage et son oeuvre," *Bulletin d'études*

orientales 30 (1978): 51–60. For a study that highlights the combination of mild asceticism and social activism in Ḥanbaī ideology and operation in the public sphere during the ninth and tenth centuries, see Nimrod Hurvitz, *The Formation of Hanbalism: Piety into Power* (London: Curzon, 2002); Hurvitz, "From Scholarly Circles to Mass Movements."

57. Mottahedeh, *Loyalty and Leadership,* 147.
58. See Richard Bulliet's important observation that by the latter part of the ninth century, asceticism and pietism constituted a significant current of Islamic belief and practice. His quantity analysis shows that the rate of occurrence of the terms *ascetic* and *pietistic* in the Iranian cities of Nishapur and Isfahan doubled during this century when conversion from the non-Muslim regions and urbanization were at their peak. Bulliet, *Islam,* 91.
59. See, for example, George Makdisi's observation that in biographical literature of intellectuals, generally much is made of those *ʿulamāʾ* who led the life of an ascetic. Makdisi, "The Sunni Revival," 166.
60. See especially Schimmel, *Mystical Dimensions,* 228, following the examples in Tor Andrae, *Islamische Mystiker* (Stuttgart: Kohlhammer, 1960), 75 ff. (trans. from the Swedish).
61. Mojaddedi, *The Biographical Tradition,* 104. For a detailed discussion of the criteria of inclusion and strategies of presentations applied by al-Qushayrī to serve the prime intent of his *Risāla,* see ibid., 100–07; Jawid A. Mojaddedi, "Legitimizing Sufism in al-Qushayrī's *Risāla,*" *Studia Islamica* 90 (2000): 37–70.
62. Al-Sulamī originally wrote this treatise as an appendix to his famous *Ṭabaqāt al-ṣūfiyya.* Separated from the original work soon after its author's death, it was thought lost until 1991, when a unique manuscript of the work was found in Riyadh. The Riyadh manuscript was edited and translated with introduction and notes by Rkia E. Cornell in *Early Sufi Women* (Louisville, KY: Fons Vitae, 1999).
63. Cornell, *Early Sufi Women,* 82, 124 (biographical entries 2, 22).
64. For the importance of ascetic piety in the mystical journey and the contribution of ascetic ideals and actual practices to the mystic's self-transformation and spiritual ascent, see Sara Sviri, "Self and Its Transformation in Ṣūfism, with Special Reference to Early Literature," in David Shulman and Guy G. Stroumsa, eds., *Self and*

Self-Transformation in the History of Religions (Oxford: Oxford University Press, 2002), 197. For a different outlook that suggests a linear transition from the early, lesser stage of asceticism to mysticism and the existence of a clear borderline between ascetic and mystical piety, see Christopher Melchert, "The Transition from Asceticism to Mysticism at the Middle of the Ninth Century C.E.," *Studia Islamica* 83:1 (1996): 51–70.

65. See Binns, *Ascetics and Ambassadors,* 239–44, for the development of the concept of friends of God in this literature, primarily in the writings of Cyril of Scythopolis.

66. Scholarship on the Muslim friend of God is vast. See the article by John Renard in *Historical Dictionary of Sufism* (Oxford: Scarecrow Press, 2005), 90–91 and the references there. See also Michel Chodkiewicz's important comment that notwithstanding the existence of significant analogies between the Muslim *walī* and the Christian saint, the etimologies of the two words and some of the theories built around them are not identical. Michel Chodkiewicz, Review of Julian Baldick, *Mystical Islam,* in *Studia Islamica* 73 (1991): 167. See further below in chapter 3 on the status of the *walī.*

67. On Sarī al-Saqaṭī's perception of asceticism and actual manifestations of ascetic piety, see Reinert, *Die Lehre,* esp. 118, 123, 131. See also below on the influence of Ibn al-Jallā''s Sufi masters on their disciple's ascetic and mystical precepts.

68. This utterance appears first in Abū ʿAbd Allāh al-Raḥmān al-Sulamī, *Ṭabaqāt al-ṣūfiyya,* 2nd ed., ed. N. Shurība (Aleppo, 1986), 176.

69. For Ibn al-Jallā's life and teachings, see Abū Naṣr al-Sarrāj, *Kitāb al-lumaʿ fī l-taṣawwuf,* ed. M. ʿAbd al-Ḥalīm and S. al-Bāqī (Cairo: Dār al-Kutub al-Ḥadītha, 1960), index; Abū Bakr al-Kalābādhī, *The Doctrines of the Ṣūfīs,* trans. A. J. Arberry (Cambridge: Cambridge University Press, 1989), index; al-Sulamī, *Ṭabaqāt,* 176–79; Abū Nuʿaym al-Iṣfahānī, *Ḥilyat al-awilyā' wa-ṭabaqāt al-aṣfiyā',* 10 vols. (Beirut: Dār al-Kitāb al-ʿArabī, n.d.), 10:314–15; Abū l-Qāsim al-Qushayrī, *al-Risāla al-qushayriyya fī ʿilm al-taṣawwuf,* ed. M. Zuriq and ʿA. al-Balṭajī (Damascus, 1988), 403–04, partial translation by B. R. Von Schlegell, *Principles of Sufism by al-Qushayri* (Berkeley: Nizam Press, 1990); al-Hujwīrī, *Kashf al-*

maḥjūb, trans. R. A. Nicholson (London: Luzac, 1976), 37, 134–35; Abū Bakr al-Khaṭīb al-Baghdādī, *Ta'rīkh baghdād,* 14 vols. (Cairo: Maṭba'at al-Sa'ada, 1349 AH), 5:213–15; Ibn al-Jawzī, *al-Muntaẓam fī ta'rīkh al-muluk wa-l-umam,* 6 vols. = vols. 5–10 (Hyderabad: Da'irat al-Ma'ārif al-'Uthmāniyya, 1358–59 AH), 6:148–49; Ibn al-Jawzī, *Ṣifat al-ṣafwa,* 2:250; Ibn 'Asākir, *Ta'rīkh madinat dimashq,* ed. M. Abū Sa'īd and 'U. al-'Amrawī, 40 vols. (Beirut, 1995), 6:81–93; Abū l-Fidā' b. Kahīr, *al-Bidāya wa-l-nihāya,* 14 vols. (Cairo: Maṭba'at al-Ṣalāfiyya, AH 1351), 11:129; Ibn al-'Imād al-Ḥanbalī, *Shadharāt al-dhahab fī akhbār man dhahab,* 8 vols. (Beirut, n.d.), 2:248–49; Shams al-Dīn Muḥammad al-Dhahabī, *Siyar a'lām al-nubalā',* ed. S. al-Arna'ūṭ et al., 25 vols. (Beirut: Mu'assasat al-Risāla, 1981–1985), 14:251–52; 'Abd al-Wahhāb al-Sha'rānī, *al-Ṭabaqāt al-kubrā,* 2 vols. (Cairo, 1954), 1:152; Abū Ḥafṣ 'Umar b. Mulaqqin, *Ṭabaqāt al-awliyā',* ed. N. Sharība (Cairo: Maṭba'at Dār al-Ta'līf, 1973), 82; 'Abd al-Ra'ūf al-Munāwī, *al-Kawākib al-durriyya fī tarājim al-sāda al-ṣufiyya,* ed. M. H. Rabī', 2 vols. (Cairo, n.d.), 2:14–15; Ibn al-Athīr al-Jazarī, *al-Lubāb fī tahdhīb al-ansāb,* 3 vols. (Beirut: Dār Ṣādir, n.d.), 1:318; 'Abd al-Raḥmān al-Jāmī, *Nafaḥāt al-uns min ḥaḍarāt al-quds,* ed. M. A. al-Jādur, 2 vols. (Beirut: Dār al-Kutub al-'Ilmiyya, 2003), 1:166–67; Yūsuf Ismā'īl al-Nabhānī, *Jāmi' karāmāt al-awliyā',* 2nd ed., 2 vols. (Beirut, 1983), 1:484.

70. See P. Nwyia, *Exégèse coranique et language mystique* (Beirut, 1970), 213–16.
71. Quoted first by al-Sarrāj, *Kitāb al-luma',* 240.
72. Al-Iṣfahānī, *Ḥilyat al-awilyā',* 10:315. See also the biographical section of al-Qushayrī, *al-Risāla,* 403; Ibn al-Jawzī, *al-Muntaẓam,* 6:148; Ibn 'Asakir, *Ta'rīkh,* 6:83–84; Ibn Mulaqqin, *Ṭabaqāt,* 82.
73. Schimmel, *Mystical Dimensions,* 199 ff.; H. J. Kissling, "Abdāl," *EI2.*
74. Goitein, "The Sanctity of Jerusalem," 144.
75. Sviri offers this explanation in "Self and Its Transformation in Ṣūfīsm," 196.
76. Al-Qushayrī, *al-Risāla, al-taṣawwuf,* 283, and Von Schlegell, *Principles of Sufism by al-Qushayri,* 306 (transliteration is mine). Quoted first by al-Sarrāj, *Kitāb al-luma',* 46.
77. Al-Sulamī, *Ṭabaqāt,* 177.

78. Bernd Radtke, "Theologen und Mystiker in Hurāsān und Transoxanien," *Zeitschrift der Deutschen Morgenlandischen Gesellschaft* 136:1 (1986): 556–57.
79. On Ibrāhīm b. Muwallad, see al-Sulamī, *Ṭabaqāt,* 410–13; al-Iṣfahānī, *Ḥilyat al-awilyā',* 10:364; Ibn al-ʿImād, *Shadharāt al-dhahab,* 3:362; al-Shaʿrānī, *al-Ṭabaqāt,* 1:136; al-Jāmī, *Nafaḥāt al-uns,* 1:316–17.
80. Al-Sulamī, *Ṭabaqāt,* 411.
81. On al-Duqqī, see al-Sarrāj, *Kitāb al-lumaʿ,* index; al-Sulamī, *Ṭabaqāt,* 448–50; al-Qushayrī, *al-Risāla,* 412; Abū Saʿd al-Samʿānī, *al-Ansāb,* 5 vols. (Beirut, 1988), 2: 486; al-Khaṭīb al-Baghdādī, *Ta'rīkh,* 5:266; al-Shaʿrānī, *al-Ṭabaqāt,* 1:140; al-Jazarī, *al-Lubāb,* 1:422; Ibn Mulaqqin, *Ṭabaqāt,* 306–10; al-Munāwī, *al-Kawākib al-durriyya,* 2:44; al-Jāmī, *Nafaḥāt al-uns,* 1:279–80.
82. Quoted first by al-Qushayrī, *al-Risāla,* 279, and Von Schlegell, *Principles of Sufism,* 299.
83. Quoted by al-Shaʿrānī, *al-Ṭabaqāt,* 1:140.
84. Quoted first by al-Sulamī, *Ṭabaqāt,* 178.
85. Al-Sulamī, *Ṭabaqāt* (ed. J. Pedersen), 5.7–10, as cited by Mojaddedi, *The Biographical Tradition,* 106.
86. Al-Sulamī, *Ṭabaqāt,* 178.
87. Ibid., 179.
88. Ibid., 316. On Mumashād al-Dīnawarī, see ibid., 316–18; al-Sarrāj, *Kitāb al-lumaʿ,* index; al-Iṣfahānī, *Ḥilyat al-awliyā',* 10:353: al-Qushayrī, *al-Risāla,* 413; Ibn al-Jawzī, *Ṣifat al-ṣafwa,* 4:60; al-Shaʿrānī, *al-Ṭabaqāt,* 1:160; al-Munāwī, *al-Kawākib al-durriyya,* 1:269–70; Ibn Mulaqqin, *Ṭabaqāt,* 288–89; al-Nabhānī, *Jāmiʿ,* 2:268; al-Jāmī, *Nafaḥāt al-uns,* 1:141–43.
89. Al-Sulamī, *Ṭabaqāt,* 316.
90. Ibid., 449.
91. Ibn ʿAsākir, *Ta'rīkh,* 6:88; see also R. Gramlich, *Alte Vorbilder des Sufitums* (Wiesbaden: Steiner, 1995), 1:327.
92. Al-Iṣfahānī, *Ḥilyat al-awilyā',* 10:315.
93. Mojaddedi makes this point in his *The Biographical Tradition,* 106.
94. Al-Qushayrī, *al-Risāla,* 110, and Von Schlegell, *Principles of Sufism,* 33 (transliteration is mine).
95. Ibid., *al-Risāla,* 111, *Principles of Sufism,* 34 (transliteration is mine).

96. Ibid., *al-Risāla,* 116, *Principles of Sufism,* 42 (transliteration is mine).
97. Ibid., *al-Risāla,* 275, *Principles of Sufism,* 293 (transliteration is mine). See also al-Kalābādhī's slightly different version of the same saying as cited by Arberry: "This is poverty, that there should be nothing that is yours; and even there is something, that it should not be yours." Arberry, *Sufism,* 86.
98. Al-Qushayrī, *al-Risāla,* 278, and Von Schlegell, *Principles of Sufism,* 296 (transliteration is mine).
99. Al-Sulamī, *Ṭabaqāt,* 316.
100. Ibn Mulaqqin, *Ṭabaqāt,* 309.
101. Ibid., 310.
102. Abū ʿAbd Allāh al-Raḥmān al-Sulamī, *Manāhij al-ʿĀrifīn,* ed. E. Kohlberg (Jerusalem: Jerusalem Studies in Arabic and Islam, 1979), 25.
103. See Ignaz Goldzhier, "Arabische Synonymik der Askese," *Der Islam* 8 (1918): 204–13, a study of the technical terms of early Sufism. See also Sviri, "Self and Its Transformation in Ṣūfīsm," esp. 197.
104. Abū ʿAbd Allāh al-Raḥmān al-Sulamī, *Jawāmiʿ Ādāb al-ṣufiyya* and *ʿUyūb al-Nafs wa-Mudāwāthuhā,* ed. with an introduction by E. Kohlberg (Jerusalem: Institute of African and Asian Studies, Hebrew University, 1976), 66–68.
105. Quoted first by al-Sulamī, *Ṭabaqāt,* 177.
106. Fritz Meier, "Hurasan und das Ende der klassischen Sufik," in *Atti del Convengo internationale sul Tema: La Persia nel Medioevo* (Rome, 1971), 131–56; Fritz Meier, "Khurāsān and the End of Classical Sufism," in *Essays on Islamic Piety and Mysticism,* trans. John O'Kane with the editorial assistance of Bernd Radtke (Leiden: Brill, 1999), 190–92; Fritz Meier, "The Mystic Path," in Bernard Lewis, ed., *The World of Islam: Faith, People, Culture* (London: Thames and Hudson, 1992), 117–28. See also Margaret Malamud, "Sufi Organizations and Structures of Authority in Medieval Nishapur," *International Journal of Middle East Studies* 26 (1994): 432.
107. J. Paul makes this point in "Au début du genre hagiographhique dans le Khorasan," in D. Aigle, ed., *Saints orientaux* (Paris: Deboccard, 1995), 27–34.
108. Meier, "Khurāsān," 192, 195.

109. For a recent study that reassesses the commonly received view of the pattern of guidance in classical Sufism, see Laury Silvers-Alario, "The Teaching Relationship in Early Sufism: A Reassessment of Fritz Meier's Definition of the *shaykh al-tarbiyya* and the *shaykh al-taʿlīm*," *Muslim World* 93 (January 2003): 69–72. Her suggestions and ample examples have provided inspiration for what follows.
110. Told first by al-Khaṭīb al-Baghdādī, *Taʾrīkh*, 5:214.
111. Al-Iṣfahānī, *Ḥilyat al-awilyāʾ*, 10:294.
112. Ibn ʿAsākir, *Taʾrīkh*, 6:88.
113. Al-Qushayrī, *Risāla*, 275, and Von Schlegell, *Principles of Sufism*, 293 (transliteration is mine).
114. See chapters 2 and 3 below for examples of mosques as gathering places for Sufis in Palestine during the Islamic middle periods.
115. Ibn ʿAsākir, *Taʾrīkh*, 6:89.
116. Quoted first by al-Sulamī, *Ṭabaqāt*, 317.
117. Al-Sulamī, *Ṭabaqāt*, 502; ʿAbd Allāh-i Harawī al-Anṣārī, *Ṭabaqāt al-ṣufiyya*, ed. ʿAbd al-Hayy-i (Kabul, AH 1341), 249, sub. ʿAlī b. Bundār.
118. See Albrecht Hofheinz, *Internalizing Islam: Shaykh Muḥammad Majdhūb, Scriptural Islam and Local Context in the Early Nineteenth-Century Sudan*, doctoral thesis, University of Bergen, 1996, esp. 1:526–28, for an eloquent discussion of the psychological means used by the shaykh to establish a paternalistic relationship between himself and his followers.
119. Al-Khaṭīb al-Baghdādī, *Taʾrīkh*, 5:266.
120. Al-Sulamī, *Ṭabaqāt*, 448. Meier makes this observation in "Khurāsān," 195.
121. Al-Shaʿrānī, *al-Ṭabaqāt*, 1:140.
122. Ibid., 1:119.
123. Quoted first by al-Sulamī, *Ṭabaqāt*, 318.
124. Al-Shaʿrānī, *Ṭabaqāt*, 1:152.
125. Al-Dhahabī, *Siyar aʿlām al-nubalāʾ*, 252, sub. Ibn al-Jallāʾ.
126. For the change in master-disciple relationship, see especially Meier, "Khurāsān, 197.
127. See Silvers-Alario, "The Teaching Relationship," 77–80, 88, for the usage of these various terms in early Sufi texts. The term *murīd* usually refers during the early period to an aspirant of the path rather than a committed companion of the shaykh. The term

qarīn seems to denote companionship among contemporary shaykhs, as opposed to the term *ṣāḥib,* which was most often used to designate a relationship of direction between the shaykh and his subordinate companion.

128. Al-Sarrāj, *Kitāb al-luma',* 176.
129. Al-Sulamī, *Ṭabaqāt,* 318.
130. Al-Sarrāj, *Kitāb al-luma',* 254.
131. Ibn Mulaqqin, *Ṭabaqāt,* 308–09.
132. For the all-embracing meaning of the term *ṣuḥba* in early mystical parlance, see Khaliq Ahmad Nizami, "Ṣuḥbah," *The Encyclopedia of Religion,* ed. M. Eliade, 13:123–24 and the bibliographical references there; Silvers-Alario, "The Teaching Relationship," 88–90. See also chapter 2 below for the development of the ideal of companionship in Sufi thought and practice.

· TWO ·

Integration

Running along the north side of the Ḥaram area and between the two gateways just mentioned [Gate of the Tribes and Gate of Gates] is a colonnade supported by arches that rest on solid pillars, and adjacent to it is a dome supported by tall columns and adorned with lamps and lanterns. This is called the Dome of Jacob. . . . Further along the breadth (or northern wall) of the Ḥaram is [another] colonnade, in the wall of which is a gate that leads to two cloisters belonging to the Sufis, who have their place of prayer there and have built a fine prayer niche. There are always in residence a number of Sufis. They make this oratory the place of their daily devotions, except on Friday when they go into the Ḥaram itself to attend the prayer service there.

—*Nāṣir-ī Khusraw,* Diary of a Journey through Syria and Palestine *31–32, as translated by Guy Le Strange,* Palestine under the Muslims: A Description of Syria and the Holy Land from a.d. 650 to 1500 *(Boston: Riverside Press, 1890) 176–77 (my transliteration and slight stylistic alterations)*

Chapter 2 highlights the local manifestations of the religious and social evolution of Sufism that took place during the late tenth to mid-thirteenth centuries (referred to by Marshall Hodgson as the Islamic earlier middle period). It begins with a discussion of the emergence of a mainstream Sufi tradition that situates the history of Sufism in Palestine within this broader context. The central concern of this discussion is to scrutinize the doctrinal, social, and institutional dimensions in the development of Sufism, the consolidation of the Sufi main tradition as a legitimate version of the prophetic Sunna, and its early consolidation in the form of a fraternity. The subsequent sections of the chapter narrate the lives and activities of the Sufi traditionalists and jurists and the spiritual leaders in Palestinian cities who played a major role in building bridges between Sufis and legalists and between Sufis and the local communities. After considering the integration of Sufis and Sufism into the scholarly and social world of the established legal schools and the fabric of social and communal life, the final sections trace the development of modes of operation, associations, and institutions that were distinctive to the Sufis. These sections inquire into the birth and early growth of the locally embedded Sufi-inspired congregation around the Sufi guide and explore the advent and character of the first lodges that were established by and for the Sufis in this particular historical and physical setting.

BUILDING BRIDGES

Several renowned Sufi shaykhs lived in Tyre in the late tenth century. Among them was Aḥmad b. al-ʿAṭāʾ al-Rūdhbārī (of Rūdhbār, a village near Baghdad). After leaving Baghdad, he lived at first in the neighborhood of Acre and died in Tyre in 369/980.[1] As one of the eminent Sufis of his time, whose fame spread far beyond his final residing place, his biography is included in al-Sulamī's *Ṭabaqāt al-ṣūfiyya,* where he is classified as a member of the fifth and final generation:

> Among them is Shaykh Abū ʿAbd Allāh al-Rūdhbārī, and his name is Aḥmad b. ʿAṭāʾ [b. Aḥmad al-Rūdhbārī], the nephew of Abī ʿAlī al-Rūdhbārī and the shaykh of al-Shām in his lifetime. He gained distinction due to his mystical states *(aḥwāl)* and the mastery of various fields of the Islamic traditional sciences *(al-ʿulūm)* that he had attained. These included knowledge of the variant readings of the Koran *(ʿilm al-qirāʾāt),* knowledge of the divine law *(ʿilm al-sharīʿa),* and knowledge of the true reality *(ʿilm al-ḥaqīqa).* He is [also] distinguished for his morality *(akhlāq),* good qualities *(shamāʾil),* and glorification of poverty. His honor was

> upheld, and his rules of decorum *(ādāb)* were adhered to. He was beloved by the Sufis *(al-fuqarāʾ)*, favored them, and was courteous toward them.[2]

The shaykh thus represented and disseminated a sophisticated tradition that developed and matured in Baghdadi circles. He combined esoteric and exoteric sciences in his own education and his teaching of others and gained fame due to his comprehensive knowledge, personal qualities, and moral values.

During al-Rūdhbārī's lifetime, a new period in the history of Sufism ensued. The Baghdad school, to which he presumably belonged in his youth, survived the fateful episode of al-Ḥallāj and with time was able to extend its influence far beyond the confines of Iraq. Disciples and associates of al-Junayd (d. 298/910) conveyed his teaching of mystic sobriety and articulated what came to be termed "the science of Sufism" *(ʿilm al-taṣawwuf)*. Sufi textbooks began to appear that covered all major aspects of the "Sufi science" and gave Sufism its final shape. Beginning with *Kitāb al-lumaʿ fī l-taṣawwuf* (The Book of the Essentials of Sufism) by al-Sarrāj (d. 378/988), this literature grew rapidly over the course of the eleventh century. By the close of this century, the main Sufi tradition had been systematized, its science had matured, and its path was accepted as a legitimate version of the prophetic Sunna.

The Sufism described in the writings by such great mystics of the Muslim East as al-Qushayrī and al-Ghazzālī was then not their exclusive creation but rather an elaboration and articulation of the teachings of a number of late tenth-century Sufi religious scholars, many of them followers of al-Junayd in Khurasan and Iraq.[3] The purpose of their writings was twofold—to extol the Sufis as one of the Sharʿī-minded groups that were pursuing and disseminating the truth of Islam and to define the essential concepts and practices that those who considered themselves Sufis should adhere to and undertake to disseminate. Thus, a literature known as *ādāb al-murīdīn* set forth rules of proper conduct for the seekers of the path and reasserted the ideals and practices of guidance and discipleship. One of the most widely read of these Sufi handbooks was written by Abū l-Najīb al-Suhrawardī (d. 563/1168).

The insistence on unquestionable obedience to an accomplished guide, which runs like a thread through the *ādāb al-murīdīn* literature, was closely linked with the institutionalization of Sufism as a path to God. It set limits to the mystical experience that led to proximity with the divine and established ways of defining and controlling spiritual authority. Whatever the veils that separated the wayfarer from the beloved creator, every seeker of the path had to attach himself to an authoritative guide who should guard his steps and protect him from straying away either by experiencing ecstasy or by endeavoring to experience the last state of self-annihilation in God *(fanā')* and subsequent survival in him *(baqā')*. This guide must be part of a spiritual chain *(silsila)* that reaches back across the generations to the Prophet himself.

The belief that true knowledge must be imparted directly from the mouths of the great masters in an unbroken chain *(isnād)* of authoritative transmitters was deeply embedded in Islamic tradition and was adopted by the Sufis. By being acknowledged as part of a *silsila,* the shaykh acquired the authority that was necessary to transmit sacred knowledge and a particular spiritual way. By the late eleventh century, this method of legitimating the transmission of authority had become widespread in Sufi circles.[4]

On the doctrinal level, the essence of the consolidation of mainstream Sufism resided in its evolution into a moderate tradition that was intimately linked to the prophetic legacy. Centering on the model of the Prophet, this tradition embraced the religious outlook and behavioral patterns of the early innerworldly *zuhhād.* In other words, it represented a continuous, though more sophisticated, form of mild asceticism and sober spiritual experience of the divine that had its origins in nascent Sufism. Thus began a shift of emphasis from the mystical and ecstatic to the sober and ethical aspect of Sufi piety and a reconciliation between the normative exoteric religious dimension of Islam *(sharīʿa)* and the experimental, intuitive vision of its reality *(ḥaqīqa)*. What came eventually to be known as Sufism brought together normative, ethical community-oriented behavior and the attainment of spiritual experience through a devotional life as laid down by the Sunna and the Shariʿa. What is more, the formulation of the lines of moderate Sufism made the tradition accessible to Muslim believers who could never reach the heights of mystical experience. In the world of the Sufis under study here and presumably in other historical and geographical settings, this new stage in the history of Sufism began as early as the latter part of the tenth century.

The recognized spiritual genealogy, the *silsila,* while enhancing the spiritual and intellectual authority of the Sufi shaykh within his immediate circle of companions and associates (the *aṣḥāb* and *aqrān*), served to legitimize his role and position as a disseminator of righteous Islamic belief and conduct. From the late tenth century onward, Sufism gradually moved from the fringes of the Islamic intellectual world to the center, spreading its message far beyond the small circles of mystical wayfarers. Sufi shaykhs played a valuable role in disseminating and internalizing Islam within Muslim societies and in converting non-Muslims, beginning with the Turks of the steppes of Central Asia, far beyond the lands ruled by Muslims. Sufis did not act as the sole agents of Islamization, but they figured prominently as performers of the final act of conversion to Islam.[5]

The integration of Sufi thought and practice with other forms of Islamic belief and practice gained stimulus in the latter part of the eleventh century. This was a crucial period in Islamic history that is often called the *Sunni revival,* even though the dramatic notion of revival is somewhat misleading. Its origins can be traced back to the late tenth century, which witnessed severe internal turmoil—caused no less by bitter disputes between rival Sunni factions over proper Islamic beliefs and behavior than by fights between Sunnis and Shiʿis. Above all, the attacks waged by leaders of the "traditionalists" or the "people of *ḥadīth*" *(ahl al-*

ḥadīth) against leaders of the "rationalists" or the "masters of opinion" *(aṣḥāb al-raʾy)*. In their effort to end the religious ferment of the late classical period, leaders in Islamic learning and piety and others strove to maintain a unified Islamic community by bridging the differences among their various religious traditions and delimiting a commonly accepted form of Islam.[6] This process of homogenization of religious doctrine and practice must have involved the strengthening of what may be labeled the mainstream Sunni camp—Sharʿī-minded and inclusive of Ashʿarī theology, moderate Ḥanbalī theology, and moderate Sufism. Accordingly, Shiʿis, so-called *zindīq*s (heretics), radical Ḥanbalī theologians, philosophers, or freethinkers, ecstatic or antinomian Sufis, and popular preachers who drew inspiration from Sufi mysticism—all were doomed to marginalization and sometimes severe persecution. One of the most dramatic persecutions in late twelfth-century Syria was that of Shihāb al-Dīn Yaḥyā Suhrawardī, the great reviver of Hermetic Gnosticism in Islam and founder of the school of illumination. He was sentenced to death on charges of violating the Sharīʿa, holding heretical theological views, and following the path of the pagan philosophers and suffered a martyr's death.[7]

Beginning in the Muslim East, the process of forming the Sunna filtered into the Syrian-Palestinian milieu during the twelfth century. Representatives of mainstream Sufism at this time adhered to greater uniformity and conformity and participated actively with legal scholars in the Sunnization movement, which set out to define the contours and content of acceptable knowledge and to establish the methods for its transmission. In the texts studied for this book, they appear as arbiters of religious knowledge and practice *(al-ʿilm wa-l-ʿamal)* and of the central moral tenet of "commanding right and forbidding wrong" *(al-amr bi-l-maʿrūf wa-l-nahy ʿan al-munkar)*. Moreover, as jurists themselves, some must have adopted the legal approach of incessant concern with the regulating and shaping society in accordance with the ordinances and norms of the Sunna and the Sharīʿa.

The process of homogenization of religious doctrine and practice had an institutional dimension as well. Associations and frameworks were developed to teach the Islamic religious and legal sciences, apply religious law, and harness mainstream Sufism. By the close of the eleventh century, the main foundations of a new social order had been laid in the central Islamic regions. The four Sunni schools of legal interpretation (the *madhhab*s) were consolidated as scholarly establishments, the nuclei of the Sufi fraternities (the *ṭarīqa*s) were formed, and the law college *(madrasa)* and Sufi lodge *(khānqāh, ribāṭ)* were founded. These developments took place against the background of the ʿAbbasid caliphate's disintegration. In the politically divided, socially unstable, and unpredictable world that was created by the dissolution of the centralized caliphal empire and by the rise to power of the alien postimperial succession regimes, more institutionalized forms of organization were necessary to sustain the communities' Islamic character and secure the essential unity of their heritage.[8] During the twelfth century, the new social order flourished, excelling best in those fields that were most distinctive in it by the end of the earlier middle period.[9] Self-created associations of Islamic social, religious, and spiritual life crystallized and spread throughout the "abode of Islam" under leaders in religious learning and piety and took the form of scholarly communities and Sufi fraternities. With its emphasis on spirituality and morality modeled on the Prophet, mainstream Sufism came to be an immense success as the focus of associations.

Significantly, religious leadership and *ʿulamāʾ* and Sufi-led associations developed out of internal dynamics, were independent of the official sphere governed by the alien elite of the military lords, and were little affected by the policies of the Seljuks and their successors—even though the rulers must have contributed to or at least facilitated the process of forming the Sunna and consolidating its forms of organization. The role that they played in this process was clearly revealed in their patronage and sponsorship of *madrasa*s for the teaching of the law in accordance with one or other of the Sunni legal schools and of *khānqāhs* for the cultivation of a deeper spiritual life based on the Sunna and the Sharīʿa. By invoking the law of the *waqf*, the founders—Seljuk men of the regime and their Zangid and Ayyubid successors—ensured the perpetuity of these establishments and the permanent support of those who were considered representative of the broad mainstream of Islam and who taught, studied, or lodged in them. Housed in glorious buildings in the great cities of Islam, the *madrasas* and *khānqāhs* signified the dedication of the rulers to the revitalization of Sunni Islam in the face of enemies within (the Shiʿis) and without (the Crusaders). The foundation of *madrasas* and *khānqāhs* on substantial endowments was another major instrument that was employed by individual rulers and members of their entourage to strengthen the mainstream Sunni camp and help spread its message rather than to achieve control over the beneficiaries or to meddle in their affairs.[10]

Moreover, as in other cases of *waqf* foundations in the public sphere, the *madrasas* and *khānqāhs* symbolized the adherence of the endowing ruler to the norms of proper social order that were inherent in the ideology of the *waqf*. As such, endowments of religious establishments must have also helped to establish a bond of shared norms and values between the rulers and the beneficiaries and to generate a public opinion that approved of and even legitimized the rule of the endowing ruler in the territories he had conquered.[11] The decision of individual rulers to endow religious establishments must be seen against this background. The famous vizier Niẓām al-Mulk established a number of *madrasas* (most famously the Niẓāmiyya of Baghdad) and founded a string of *khānqāhs* throughout the lands that the Seljuks had conquered from the Sunni Ghaznavids and Shiʿi Buyids.[12] The Ayyubids replicated this form of support and patronage and introduced it in Palestine. Saladin, in 1189, about two years after the liberation of Jerusalem from the Crusader yoke, turned the convent adjacent to St. Anne's (the well-preserved Crusader church near the Sheep Pool) into a magnificent *madrasa* for

Shāfiʿī legal scholars and founded a *khānqāh* for the "virtuous Sufis" *(al-ṣulaḥāʾ l-ṣūfiyya)*. He named both "Ṣalāḥiyya" in his own honor and endowed them liberally.[13]

Muslim scholars who lived during the earlier middle period still debated a considerable number of issues relating righteous Islamic belief and practice, and variants and dissensions could exist even within the same school of law or thought. Most instructive in this regard is the reaction of the Ḥanbalīs toward those of their own allegiance who were sufficiently curious to listen to teachers of other intellectual traditions, which reached its dramatic apex in the persecution of Ibn ʿAqīl. Despite the efforts to build bridges between the mystical and juristic sides of Islam, some individuals with a deep commitment to text-based knowledge and the rigorous transmission of religious lore still felt aversion to some doctrines and practices of the Sufis.[14] But it was *within* Sufi Islam that diversity and fluidity were most illustriously revealed: sober Sufism existed alongside gnosis and the various old forms of moderate and extreme asceticism. While many perceived the *ʿilm* of the jurist and the *maʿrifa* of the mystic as complementary paths to true knowledge and devotion, others still oscillated between the exoteric and esoteric dimensions of Sufism and even overtly placed gnosis above traditional or rational knowledge. Some preferred a life of contemplation and renunciation to a life of learning and operating within society according to the rules and regulations laid down by the Sharīʿa. Many others adopted the community-oriented approach of the early ascetics. At the same time, new groups of extreme, antinomian Sufis, often known as *dervishes,* appeared everywhere from around the mid-twelfth century.[15] In Jerusalem, members of these groups affiliated primarily with the Qalandar dervish path, which represented a new form of religious renunciation manifested in total poverty, begging or alms taking, homeless wandering, and celibacy.[16]

Nevertheless, for all the diversity within the Sufi tradition as a whole and the vast differences among the various groupings and shaykhs within each stream, a relatively uniform class of Sufis consolidated that may be classifiable as learned or institutional. Though difficult to typify, it would be fair to suggest that their characteristics included meticulous obedience to the sacred law, mild asceticism, and interaction and intermingling with both the legal scholars of the established legal schools and the political rulers.[17]

The cosmopolitan character of the learned societies remained intact. The old manner of learning—wandering from one intellectual and spiritual center to another, seeking the teaching and training of many masters, and imparting knowledge in a variety of informal study circles—did not fade from the Muslim world of the earlier middle period. Although the Islamic domains were ruled by autocratic regimes, political boundaries were vague and porous. Indeed, one of the most beneficial effects of the breakdown of the monolithic ʿAbbasid state was greater freedom of social mobility and intellectual expression. Instead of a single court, many small courts arose throughout the Muslim world during the tenth and eleventh Muslim centuries, and they endeavored to develop their capitals into economic and cultural centers. The lack of formal and stable organizations comparable to the feudal manor and the European trade guild or corporation in medieval Islamic societies was also beneficial to newcomers. In an environment that offered abundant opportunities for patronage and recognition, people and ideas moved freely from one place to another. Thus, the intellectual and spiritual centers of Islam were incorporated in a thriving, widely dispersed world of Islamic learning and devotion where a perpetual confluence among various religious traditions took place.[18]

Sufis, in particular, were linked to this world. They traveled constantly far and wide in the hope of benefiting from the spiritual guidance of teachers who would initiate them into a mystical understanding of religion or in search of associates with whom they could share their spiritual world in an attempt to deepen their apprehension of reality. In effect, the mystical wayfarer, the *sālik,* considered journeying—the worldly projection of the Sufi way *(al-sulūk)*—to be a major spiritual discipline. In examining the medieval mystical treatises, the favor accorded to journeying is apparent and in fact largely shared by many great Sufi masters. The *siyaḥa* (or *safar*) was a form of journey in search of knowledge that was peculiar to the Sufis, and it aimed primarily at spiritualizing the Islamic space.[19] At the same time, the pain of separation from one's native land and family and the hardships that one encountered en route were regarded as principle instruments of repentance and self-purification. In the words of the Sihāb al-Dīn ʿUmar al-Suhrawardī (d. 632/1243), one of the most prominent Sufis of all time: "Doubtless, in subduing refractory lusts and in softening hard hearts, journeying *(safar)* profits much. . . . In subduing lusts, the effect of *safar* is no less than the effect of supererogatory acts of worship *(nawāfil)*, fasting and praying."[20] Through their travels and worldwide connections, the great mystics of Islam disseminated their ideas both within the lands ruled by Islam and far beyond and harnessed a thriving, far-reaching Sufi-inspired world of learning and devotion. The networks that they formed cut across political and geographical boundaries and blurred regional differentiation.[21] Hence, Sufis played an important role in ensuring the unity of the Islamic civilization when Islamic lands were no longer held together by a single political entity, and Muslims—following the rapid enlargement of the "abode of Islam" over the hemisphere—grew from being a minority Arab community to becoming a majority multiethnic community.

Palestinian cities constituted major stations in the Sufi's wanderings. Though politically marginalized and economically deteriorating under the Fatimids before the Crusades and the succession of Sunni dynasties that followed, their position as pilgrimage and spiritual centers remained intact. Sufis continued to be drawn to Palestinian cities—both the holy cities ruled by the Seljuks and the successor Ayyubid dynasty and the coastal towns that remained under Crusader rule. They came from regions of the Muslim world as far away as Spain and Afghanistan. Some made Palestinian cities and towns their homes; others merely included them in their never-ending journeys.

The example of early ascetics and mystics, who were fervent champions of the sanctity of Jerusalem and Palestine in general, was followed by later generations of Sufis, above all the great al-Ghazzālī, who—as he reveals most illuminatingly in his autobiography, *al-Munqidh min al-Ḍalāl* (The Deliverer from Error)—traveled long in search of God. His seclusion in the sanctuary of Jerusalem (in 1095 and 1096), described by him in "The Deliverer," was reported by several Muslim historians as a remarkable historical event. On his departure from Baghdad (following his relinquishment of the professorship in the prestigious Niẓāmiyya *madrasa*), he spent some time in Damascus and then went on to Jerusalem, sojourning there for about a year. In the words of Mujīr al-Dīn: "He was burning with the desire to commit himself to a life of devotion and to visit the tombs of the martyrs and the holy places of the holy city."[22] According to Mujīr al-Dīn and others, he was in Jerusalem when he wrote a part of his classic, *Iḥyā' 'ulūm al-dīn,* including the part called *al-Risāla al-qudsiyya* (The Epistle from Jerusalem)—the epitome of the Muslim creed. From Jerusalem, he proceeded to Hebron and from there to Medina and Mecca to take part in the pilgrimage.[23]

The incorporation of Jerusalem and other Palestinian spiritual and pilgrimage centers into the wide world of Sufism is revealed in accounts of the journeys of other great mystics of the time as well. Abū l-Najīb al-Suhrawardī, after spending many years of treading the mystical path and simultaneously teaching Islamic law at the Niẓāmiyya *madrasa* of Baghdad, left the caliphal city for Jerusalem but could not proceed beyond Damascus.[24] In his quest for spiritual tutors, the famous Muḥyī al-Dīn Ibn 'Arabī of Spain (d. 638/1240) directed his steps first to the Maghreb and then to the Muslim East, where he composed most of his famous works. While in the East, Ibn 'Arabī continued his search for renowned scholars and Sufis, and his quest brought him to the holy cities of the Hijaz, Palestine, Syria, Iraq, and Anatolia.[25]

Other spiritual wayfarers are reported to have traveled in quest of a particular shaykh. Al-Hujwīrī, writing in the late eleventh century, relates how he set from Damascus with two dervishes to visit Ibn al-Muʿallā, who was living near Ramla. Their goal was that this venerable Sufi master would tell them their most secret thoughts and solve their difficulties.[26] The story appears in a chapter on the rules of companionship that pertain to both residents *(muqīmān)* and travelers *(musāfirān)*. The shaykhs often regard "the travelers as superior to themselves because they go to and from in their own interest, while the resident dervishes have settled down in the service of God. [But] in the former is the sign of search, in the later is the token of attainment; hence those who have found and settled down are superior to those who are still seeking."[27]

Al-Hujwīrī's rules of conduct for the group of resident Sufis hints at a change in the world of the Sufis. In the earlier middle period, a fluid, free-floating environment was still in evidence, but a general trend toward more coherent religious associations around resident shaykhs became increasingly apparent. Gradually, the small and mobile grouping of the early wayfarers yielded its place to the particular Sufi congregation that centered on *one* shaykh. Some of these associations developed into the major Sufi *ṭarīqa*s—fraternities or *orders*, as they came to be known in Western literature—which branched out to the entire Muslim world. Others took a more modest form as small local congregations that were restricted to a particular locality and slowly extending beyond the innermost circles of ascetics and mystics. Such, as is shown below, were the early Sufi congregations formed in Palestinian cities—notably, Jerusalem, Ramla, and Tyre.

Focusing on the lives and teachings of prominent Sufi shaykhs who lived in Palestine during the earlier middle period, the next section looks into the process by which Sufism consolidated as an activist spiritual and ethical tradition that built bridges both between mystics and jurists and between Sufis and the community as a whole. My central aim here is to highlight the affinity between the dissemination of mainstream Sufism in this form and the emergence of coherent Sufi congregations that were integrated into the fabric of social and communal life and reached out to the local community of fellow believers. Special emphasis is placed on a changed concept regarding the ultimate goal of guidance and the practices of training in Sufism and transmitting of spiritual knowledge that developed around it.

PROFILES OF SUFI TRADITIONALISTS

In common with the majority of biographies in al-Sulamī's *Ṭabaqāt*, the brief introduction to the biography of the abovementioned Abū ʿAbd Allāh al-Rūdhbārī is followed immediately by an expounding of *ḥadīth* transmission. Stretching back from the time of the author to the time of the Prophet through generations of the "pious predecessors" (the *salaf*) and including the subject of the biography, the chain of authority *(isnād)* linked the Sufis and Sufism to the prophetic Sunna.[28] The chain of this particular *ḥadīth* links it up with the Prophet through the line of the first Shiʿi *imāms*. Like many other *ḥadīth*s presented in al-Sulamī's *Ṭabaqāt* and other compilations, this particular tradition is not related specifically to the Sufi tradition but represents a recurrent topic in *ḥadīth* literature. Its text provides information on the simple, basic nutrition of the prophets: "Meat in wheat is the broth of the prophets."[29] The message encoded is one of moderate self-discipline in dietary matters that is modeled on the last of the prophets and his predecessors.

The inclusion of *ḥadīth*s that were outside the Sufi tradition served the function of justification. It implied that prophetic traditions were a vital source of Sufism and asserted that exemplary Sufis shared with religious scholars an interest in collecting and transmitting them. Indeed, *ḥadīth,* accepted as sound by all, became a part of the Sufi literature that was composed by al-Sulamī and the other great formulators of the Sufi tradition of his epoch, who sought to demonstrate the resemblance between their doctrine and the Sunna.[30] Furthermore, given the highly edifying function of *ḥadīth,* the presentation of the Sufi as a *muḥaddīth* was proof of his inner-worldly outlook, showing him to be aware of the society around him and dedicated to the dissemination of the norms and values of the prophetic Sunna within the community of his fellow believers.

Utterances that are quoted by al-Sulamī in the main body of Abū ʿAbd Allāh al-Rūdhbārī's biography and attributed to him in a number of later biographical dictionaries and chronicles afford insights about the interplay of Sunni traditionalism and Sufism in his teaching. The following sayings illustrate his attempt to promote Sufism in the form of the moderate ethical tradition that was gaining dominance during his lifetime:

> And he [Abū ʿAlī Muḥammad b. Saʿīd] also told us that he had heard him [Aḥmad b. ʿAṭāʾ al-Rūdhbārī] saying: "The most repulsive person is the avaricious Sufi."[31]
>
> I heard Abū Naṣr saying that he heard Abū ʿAbd Allāh saying: "*al-taṣawwuf* removes avarice *(bukhl)* from the adherent, while the writing down of the *ḥadīth* removes ignorance from him. Hence, once brought together in one person, it is sufficient for [the attainment of the rank of] the exalted *(nubalāʾ)*."[32]

Another utterance reflects his desire both to defend the Sufis from objections to ecstasy that were raised by traditionalist scholars and to outline and elucidate the basic Sufi practices and doctrines for seekers of the path. To this end, true to the spirit of the Sufi discourse characteristic of his time, he makes a distinction between the advanced, "true" Sufis and the beginners or imitators.[33] An ecstatic state is permitted and justified only for the former since it springs up in their hearts and emerges from their spiritual experience of longing for God and drawing nearer to him:

> Muḥammad b. Saʿīd told us that he had heard Abū ʿAbd Allāh al-Rūdhbārī saying, "Direct tasting *(dhawq)* of true realities [unveiling, mystical intuition] is what first induces ecstatic trance *(wajd)*. When those who are absent [from true reality] drink [have a *dhawq* experience], they stray, while when those who are "present" [wholly occupied with true reality] drink, they [truly] live."[34]

Abū ʿAbd Allāh al-Rūdhbārī's image as an advocate of reconciliation between Sufism and Sunni traditionalism was further fostered by later Sufi and non-Sufi biographers alike. Probably under the influence of al-Sulamī's presentation, they designated the Sufi shaykh of Tyre as one of the outstanding shaykhs of his time, both in his righteous conduct and in his spiritual path *(aḥsan al-sīra wa-l-ṭarīqa)*. While occupying themselves constantly with the pursuit of the Sunna, such men of good qualities travel along the path of religious devotion. Abū ʿAbd Allāh al-Rūdhbārī's adherence to a mysticism of sobriety by bringing together major Sufi concepts, traditional knowledge, and normative practice *(al-ʿilm wa-l-ʿamal)* is clearly displayed in his utterance as quoted by Ibn ʿAsākir:

> Abū ʿAbd Allāh al-Rūdhbārī' was quoted by al-Khaṭīb [al-Baghdādī] as saying, "The traditional knowledge *(al-ʿilm)* is based on the outward act *(al-ʿamal)*, and the *ʿamal* is based on sincerity *(ikhlāṣ)* [a perfect lack of self-consciousness, the diametric opposite of hypocrisy], and sincerity in his worship bequeaths comprehension of almighty God [the meaning of his decrees].[35]

Abū ʿAbd Allłah al-Rūdhbārī's biographers do not mention the names of any Sufi shaykhs who might have initiated him into the path or the names of his companions or disciples. The only reference linking him to the Sufi tradition is that relating to his paternal uncle, Abū ʿAlī al-Rūdhbārī, one of the most famous disciples of al-Junayd in Baghdad (d. 323/934). There is no indication in the biographies of his teachers of the law or reference of his school of law or legal community. Neither is his name included in any of the biographical dictionaries that are devoted to one or other of the Sunni *madhhabs*. What his biographers do seem to have concerned themselves with were his activities and position in the field of *ḥadīth*.

Despite inserting him into a chain of reliable authorities, several biographers seem to have had doubts about Abū ʿAbd Allāh al-Rūdhbārī's trustworthiness as a *ḥadīth* transmitter. Al-

Khaṭīb al-Baghdādī, the eminent *ḥadīth* expert, theologian, and preacher of eleventh-century Baghdad, even accused him of transmitting outright fabricated, even "disgraceful" pious dicta.[36] This severe accusation, which appears in several of his biographies by later, non-Sufi authors as well,[37] implies the persistence of the old suspicion on the part of traditionalist scholars about a Sufi's reliability in the transmission of *ḥadīth,* especially if he was not associated with one or other of the established legal schools. But despite all the ongoing controversies between some traditionalist scholars and some Sufis over the identity and qualifications of disseminators of the prophetic legacy, an increasing number of Sufis came to be generally recognized as *ḥadīth* scholars.

This tendency is lucidly exemplified in the well-known figure of Abū l-Faḍl Muḥammad al-Maqdisī al-Shaybānī, known as al-Qaysarānī (son of a man of Caesarea, d. 507/1113). He was one of the most renowned Sufis of his generation and earned fame and recognition in the fields of Arabic language and poetry and, above all, *ḥadīth.* He was the author of numerous works, some of them substantial, concerned mostly with the technicalities of the transmission of traditions. Born in Jerusalem (in 448/1056), he studied in Baghdad and spent many years in the East, finally settling in Hamadhan (western Iran), continuing the long-standing connection between Jerusalem and the great intellectual and spiritual centers of Iran. On what proved to be his last pilgrimage, he went to Jerusalem to perform the sanctification *(iḥrām)* and died in Baghdad on his return journey.[38]

Muḥammad al-Qaysarānī's biographers depict him as an extremely zealous Sufi and ardent *ḥadīth* collector. Like other men of his generation, he was eager to hear as large a number of prophetic traditions handed down directly from as many qualified transmitters as possible, and he keenly pursued the custom of journeying in search of knowledge, the *riḥla.* Such travels persisted long after the compilation of the sixth genuine *ḥadīth* collections (in the late ninth century) that constituted an alternative to the old method of gathering and transmitting pious dicta.

This universal practice is attested in the recurring phrase in the biographies of *ḥadīth* transmitters living in the earlier middle period: "He was among those who wandered in the remotest parts of the earth *(wa-kāna min al-jawalin fi l-āfāq)*."

Muḥammad al-Qaysarānī is said to have generally traveled on foot and carried his books on his back—a description frequently encountered in the biographies of the keen seekers of *ḥadīth*, connoting their humility before God. He himself testified that he never ceased traveling in search of prophetic traditions, notwithstanding the hardships he experienced while en route:

> I bled twice in my search for *ḥadīth*, once in Baghdad and the other time in Mecca. I was walking barefoot, enduring the heat, and suffered much from this. Yet never have I ridden an animal while in search of *ḥadīth*. . . . Nor have I asked anyone for anything while seeking. I have lived on whatever [God] has provided me."[39]

In his quest for accuracy and proficiency in recording prophetic traditions, he is quoted as saying that he copied the canonical sixth *ḥadīth* compilations several times.[40]

Authors of standard biographies of religious scholars who were known for their role as collectors and recorders of prophetic traditions seem to be unanimous in their high regard of Muḥammad al-Qaysarānī's diligence and authenticity. The fourteenth-century historian Shams al-Dīn al-Dhahabī, who included him in his biographical dictionary of the celebrated *ḥadīth* transmitters *(Kitāb tadhkirat al-ḥuffāẓ)* and in several of his other compilations, quotes a number of great *ḥadīth* authorities who praise him for his trustworthiness as well as his personal integrity.[41]

While earning him an entry into the ranks of the most celebrated collectors and transmitters, Muḥammad al-Qaysarānī's proficiency in *ḥadīth* study also enabled him to defend Sufi practices based on prophetic traditions. In his *Ṣafwa al-taṣawwuf* (The Best of Sufism), "He opened gates for the seekers of the way with regard to the Sunna." Among other accusations, the

Sufis were often rebuked for saying, "When food is served, it is a time of prayer." He based his justification of this practice on a tradition ascribed to a pious forebear who testified that during a journey the Prophet ordered his muezzin to summon the accompanying companions for prayer and eating.[42]

Despite Muḥammad al-Qaysarānī's apologetic efforts, however, several traditionalist scholars—most clearly the Ḥanbalī scholars ʿImād al-Dīn and Ibn Rajab—denied or at least doubted his orthodox inclinations. Above all, they criticized him for regarding as permitted "listening to music" and "dancing" (the *samāʿ*) to invoke mystical ecstasy. On the theoretical plane, *samāʿ* implies more than the simple hearing of music accompanied by dance or other bodily movements. It is described by Sufi authors as unveiling of the secrets of Sufism and as an instrument for attaining higher spiritual states. According to many Sufis, *samāʿ* can induce intense emotional transports *(tawājud)*, states of grace *(aḥwāl)*, and direct encounters with the divine reality *(wajd, wujud)*, which may be accompanied by ecstatic behaviors and visions. This view of the meaning of *samāʿ* and its effect on the participant most probably circulated within Sufi circles of Muḥammad al-Qaysarānī's time. They are eloquently described in Sufi discourse on the devotional practice, beginning with al-Junayd in the early tenth century.[43]

Condemnations for permitting the *samāʿ* indicate the spread of the practice in its diverse forms. Initially appearing in the mid-ninth century among Baghdad Sufis, the practice of the *samāʿ* subsequently made its way to other parts of the Muslim world and was enthusiastically accepted among Sufis of different origins and traditions. Traditionalist authors of the tenth and eleventh centuries devoted long chapters to a denunciation of listening to music and whirling as being a deviation from the precepts of primeval Islam. Their attacks gave rise to the first writings on *samāʿ* by eminent Sufi theoreticians. Prominent among them were Sulamī, Qushayrī, and Ghazzālī, who set out to defend the practice on the basis of prophetic traditions and statements ascribed to the early great mystics. They argued that the *samāʿ* was but a means to attain purity, serenity, and nearness to the divine beloved for those whose inner self is attached to nothing else but him. At the same time, moderate Sufi theoreticians themselves warned of the dangers inherent in *samāʿ*. Their warnings were addressed both to beginners who were incapable of the complete self-control of their masters and to imitators from among the common believers who sought in the *samāʿ* a means of quickly inducing a state of trance, neglecting the spiritual and pedagogical dimensions that had been formulated by earlier Sufi masters.[44] Thus Muḥammad al-Qaysarānī was condemned not only for permitting the *samāʿ* as a means to achieve mystical experience but also for approving the "gazing at beardless youths"[45] by the participants who sought to contemplate glimpses of divine beauty in the human form, a practice that both traditionalist scholars and moderate Sufis found immoral and alarming.

Sufi discourse on the *samāʿ* reveals another important aspect of the consolidation and systematization of the main Sufi tradition, particularly the contribution made by moderate Sufi theoreticians in cleansing Sufism of its ecstatic and uncontrollable elements. Similarly important was the legacy of many other mystics who were considered models of righteous conduct. These moderate Sufis combined immersion in the quest for religious knowledge with the practice of self-control and self-discipline to overcome human passions and drives. An example is Abū ʿAbd Allāh al-Ṭāliqānī, a central Sufi figure, scholar, and poet who lived in Tyre in the latter part of the eleventh century (d. 466/1073). His biographer relates:

> Abū ʿAbd Allāh al-Ṭāliqānī al-Sufi set out on journeys to many countries and heard numerous traditions. . . . He imparted *ḥadīth* on the authority of Abū ʿAbd Allāh al-Sulamī [in a chain extending back to] Abū l-Ḥusayn al-Thawrī through Muḥammad b. ʿAbd Allāh al-Rāzī. He told: "While in Baghdad, I happened to encounter a handsome young man and stopped to gaze at him. The youths were tap dancing in the city's streets. The young man

> turned to me and said, 'You should better embellish yourself with knowledge *(ʿilm)*.'"[46]

As moderate, sober, and ethical Sufism became consolidated, the old animosities between Sufis and traditionalists gave way to controversies within Sufism itself over the characteristic qualities of the "true" Sufi. As Ahmet Karamustafa eloquently recounts in *God's Unruly Friends,* from around the late twelfth century vigorous dissension between "extreme" Sufis (the so-called dervishes) and moderates colored the history of Sufism. Prominent representatives of moderate Sufism harshly condemned the irreligious practices of the mendicant antinomian dervishes.[47] Consistently featured in Sufi manuals of the later middle period was the clear distinction drawn between mainstream Sufism and its margins, with warnings being addressed to frivolous imitators or pseudo-Sufis not to act in ways that might bring into question the legitimacy of the Sufis. This distinction had social meanings as well. A social category of "true" Sufis was emerging. They derived their authority and standing in society from the *silsila* of the mystic and the *isnād* of the jurist and set themselves apart from the extreme groups.

THE SUFI JURIST

The inclusion of a considerable number of Sufis of the earlier middle period in the ranks of the most outstanding *ḥadīth* scholars reflected the integration of Sufism into the mainstream of Islam, blurring in turn the distinctions between Sufi shaykhs and traditionalist *ʿulamāʾ*. Moreover, some Sufis who were living during this period gained recognition and fame as legal experts *(fuqahāʾ)*—the elite of the *ʿulamāʾ* class—as attested in the recurrent compound label "Sufi, jurist *(faqih)*" in biographical compendiums. Some are characterized as learned mystics *(al-ʿulamāʾ al-ʿārifīn);* they were those who combined knowledge of the divine law with knowledge of the true reality. Yet others are depicted in their biographies as moderate ascetics and as pious and virtuous worshipers *(ʿubbād, ṣāliḥūn),* models of proper conduct to be followed rather than Gnostics. Indeed, while surveying Mujīr al-Dīn's accounts of the most virtuous legal scholars and Sufi shaykhs of medieval Jerusalem and Hebron one of the most noticeable points is his inclusion of many persons who were not particularly mystics. The term *Sufi* is used to cover a broad category of persons known for their righteous conduct rather than for the mystical knowledge or general wisdom they attained.

Conversely, biographical compendiums are replete with descriptions of legal scholars bearing the appellations *zāhid* and *ʿābid,* which are often associated with the Sufis. These men were known for their self-control and self-discipline and shared with the Sufis their opposition to materialism and worldliness. The kind of Sufism that they ventured confined itself to moderate asceticism. Significantly, biographers speak as much about the piety and virtue of these figures as about their scholarly achievements.[48]

A noteworthy example of an ascetic jurist in late eleventh-century Jerusalem is Abū l-Qāsim ʿAbd al-Jabbār al-Rāzī (a man of Rayy, today a Teheran neighborhood), who moved to the city from Baghdad and was killed in a massacre that was carried out by the Crusaders during their conquest. An outstanding figure among the Muslim intellectuals of his generation, he is praised by his biographers for his ascetic mode of life and his profound legal learning (he adhered to the Shāfiʿī school of legal interpretation).[49] Another telling example is Abū Muḥammad Hiyāj al-Ḥusayn of Hittin, who moved to Mecca and was killed there during a confrontation between the Sunnis and Shiʿis in the early eleventh century. He heard prophetic traditions from many authorities and devoted himself to the study of jurisprudence in accordance with the Shāfiʿī rite until he became the *faqih* of the Ḥaram and its mufti. He was a *zāhid,* a god-fearing man *(wariʿ),* and was totally immersed in worshiping *(ʿibāda),* praying, and fasting. He used to perform the "minor *ḥajj,*" the *ʿumra,* three times daily on foot and the pilgrimage to the Prophet's tomb barefoot, thereby embodying the highest expression of humility before God. When traveling, he would take the opportunity to impart lessons to his accompanying disciples *(aṣḥāb)*. He never accumulated any belongings and possessed only a single garment.[50]

The occurrence of overlapping designations and characterizations in the biographical literature should not appear surprising once the supposedly unbridgeable barriers between strict legalism and Sufism are reasserted. Indeed, this supposed dichotomy conceals an ongoing blurring of the lines that were so characteristic of Islamic religiosity during the Sunni revival and the earlier middle period as a whole. As a path that was embraced by many men of religious learning, moderate asceticism and pietism—both as a perception of proper conduct and in practice—transcended the lines drawn between legalists and Sufis. As best illustrated by the teaching careers of al-Ghazzalī and his disciple Abū Najīb al-Suhrawardī, prominent legal experts and Sufis studied together in the same scholarly circles, grouping themselves around a common shaykh who combined the role of jurist with that of a Sufi guide.

Sufis searching for a middle ground between legalism and Sufism were generally attracted to the more traditionalist versions of the Sunnization movement. They were inclined to the legal and theological schools that rigorously relied on the prophetic traditions as guidelines of righteous belief and conduct and as a source of the law. Some therefore assimilated into the Shāfiʿī school of legal interpretation and cultivated Ashʿarī theological tendencies, while others found their home in antinationalist Ḥanbalīsm.[51] The "orthodox"-moderate form of asceticism and pietism practiced by these Sufis must have been most closely in harmony with that of the followers of Ibn Ḥanbal.

The Sufis' contribution to the legacy of the legal schools led to the inclusion of their names in biographical dictionaries devoted to the celebrated scholars of the *madhhab*s, primarily the Shāfiʿī. The many examples in al-Tāj al-Dīn al-Subki's *Ṭabaqāt al-shāfiʿiyya al-kubrā* come to mind. In fact, it was al-Sulamī who launched the particular strain of Shāfiʿī-oriented works in his *Ṭabaqāt al-ṣūfiyya* that was followed by the likes of al-Subkī and al-Yafiʿī, the latter himself a Sufi master.[52] Since many biographies are claimed by both the Sufis and the Shāfiʿīs or Ḥanbalīs, who selected the material and accommodated it to their own school traditions, it is sometimes difficult to pin down whether the legal school was the principal element in the personality of particular Sufis. Was it an earlier element in their upbringing or of secondary importance? Were the biographees above all Sufis rather than Shafiʿīs or Ḥanbalīs? For all this vagueness, the scholarly activities and web of connections of Sufi legalists do testify to their association with the legal schools, primarily the Shāfiʿī.

The close association of Sufism with Shāfiʿīsm, clearly revealed in the figures of such leading Sufis from the East as al-Sulamī, al-Qushayrī, and al-Ghazzalī, is confirmed by biographical accounts of contemporary Sufi-Shāfiʿīs of Palestine. ʿAṭāʾ al-Maqdisī of late eleventh-century Jerusalem (d. unknown) was most prominent among the latter. By his time, Palestinian cities, above all Jerusalem, had become important centers of the Shāfiʿī school. Here, the mainstream of Shāfiʿī scholarship was continuously augmented by the worldwide ties between native-born scholars and those who had moved to Palestinian cities from elsewhere, primarily from the East.[53] In Jerusalem, the Shāfiʿī study circles *(ḥalaqāt)*, as with those of other legal communities, were often convened in the teachers' private homes and in the city's teaching mosques, notably al-Aqṣā. In the late twelfth century, a new framework of legal learning appeared in Jerusalem. This was Madrasa al-Ṣalāḥiyya—the most prestigious educational institution of its kind in Ayyubid and Mamluk Jerusalem.[54]

Jerusalem-born ʿAṭāʾ al-Maqdisī, having acquired renown, established his position in both Sufi and Shāfiʿi circles. He is described in the travel journal of Abū Bakr b. al-Arabī, the Andalusian writer who stayed in the city from 1093 until 1095, as "the eldest shaykh of the Shāfiʿīs and the Sufi wayfarers *(shaykh al-ṣūfiyya bi-l-ṭarīqa)* of Jerusalem" and in another compilation as "the learned shaykh of Jerusalem and its most devout Sufi" and "the eldest shaykh of the *fuqahā'* and the Sufis *(fuqarā')* in al-Aqṣā mosque." Ibn al-ʿArabī also relates that ʿAṭā' had shared with him his Sufi precept that the only justified causes for weeping are the loss of a loved one and being afflicted by a calamity. And since God is the ultimate beloved and "there is no greater affliction than that of His fury, nothing justifies weeping but the quest for intimacy with him and fearing him."[55]

Neither Ibn al-ʿArabī nor any later authors specify the content of ʿAṭā' al-Maqdisī's teachings. Did he concentrate his efforts on transmitting his spiritual method? Or if the education that he imparted to his disciples and other followers focused on the essentials of the law, was the law common to all schools, or was it confined to the legal doctrine of the Shāfiʿī school with which he was affiliated? His designation as the teaching shaykh of both the Shāfiʿīs and the Sufis in al-Aqṣā mosque indicates the integration of Sufis and Sufism into the city's scholarly life, which was dominated during his lifetime by the established legal schools. Thus began the phenomenon of spiritual wayfarers and seekers of legal learning studying under the same roof and of Sufi shaykhs combining the role of the shaykh of the *fuqarā'* with that of shaykh of the *fuqahā'*.

ʿAṭā' al-Maqdisī seems to have been the disciple of another Jerusalemite, Naṣr al-Maqdisī al-Nābulusī (d. 490/1096), who more than any other contemporary Shāfiʿī-Sufi connected with the history of legal learning in the Palestinian intellectual and spiritual centers that embodied the combination of legal scholarship with the attributes and mode of life associated with the Sufis, particularly *zuhd*.[56] Like other scholars of religion and mainstream Sufis of his time, he was a sharp opponent of Ibn Karrām, of whom there were evidently still many disciples in Jerusalem at the time. Born in Nablus, Naṣr al-Maqdisī studied in Tyre and from there moved to Jerusalem. He later returned to Tyre, where he taught for some ten years. Goitein notes that al-Maqdisī's leaving Jerusalem for Tyre (in 1078) was connected with the Seljuk occupation (1071–1098), and the same applies to the transfer of the Jewish yeshiva.[57] From Tyre, he moved to

Damascus, where he spent the latter part of his life and where his position as a mufti and as one of the leading masters of his legal school was established. There he also met al-Ghazzālī, who sought his instruction in legal matters. He was the author of many books on the law (among them *al-Ishāra,* a commentary on the legal compendium of his mentor in Tyre, the great Shāfiʿī Sulymān b. Ayūb al-Rāzī) and had many disciples, one of the most celebrated being Idrīs b. Ḥamza of Ramla. Ibn al-ʿArabī, who met Naṣr al-Maqdisī in Damascus shortly before his death, describes him as an outstanding legal and *ḥadīth* scholar and as unequaled among his generation in his asceticism and praiseworthy conduct *(al-sira al-ḥamīda).*[58]

However, notwithstanding the blurring of lines between prominent representatives of legalism and mainstream Sufism, there were still important differences. Under the Seljuks and their Ayyubid successors, who offered abundant career opportunities to the *ʿulamāʾ* of the established legal schools, the career of an *ʿālim* (a member of one or other of the *madhhab*s) came to be more definable than that of his counterpart learned Sufis. Authors of biographical dictionaries use the term *ʿālim* to designate a man from this period who was fully occupied in the instruction and application of the law. As opposed to the typical learned Sufis of his generation, the typical, full-time scholar of religion would often be a religious or civil official (or both) and, as such, incorporated into the state bureaucracy and closely associated with the official sphere.[59] This distinction is well attested in Mujīr al-Dīn's collection of biographies of the Shāfiʿī and Ḥanafī *fuqahāʾ* and the Sufi shaykhs of late Ayyubid and Mamluk Jerusalem and Hebron.[60]

Moreover, to define the learned Sufi whose name appears in biographical collections written by *ʿulamāʾ* about other *ʿulamāʾ* as "orthodox"-ascetic or Sharʿī-mystic would play down another important dimension. Above all, his persona was that of an authoritative spiritual and moral guide, and he was the focus of veneration by the disciples and followers who orbited round him. Similarly, overemphasis on such a person's operation within the large camp of mainstream Sunnism might overshadow his peculiar modes of operation within society. From the late tenth century onward, as Sufism was integrated into the mainstream of Islam and the scholarly world of the legal schools, the Sufi shaykh and his grouping constructed their own inner life and organizational forms and devised their own ways of integrating into the fabric of social and communal life.

THE MORAL GUIDE AND THE BIRTH OF THE LOCAL CONGREGATION

Learned Sufis, disseminators of "true" knowledge and proper Islamic conduct, are praised primarily for their mild ascetic habits and moral posture rather than for the spiritual stations and mastery of gnosis they attained. Moreover, as we have already seen, their biographies show them to be virtuous ascetic worshipers rather than mystics. The stories about Naṣr al-Maqdisī serve as a good example. Settling finally in Damascus, he pursued his ascetic mode of life, refusing to eat anything beyond what was necessary for his mere subsistence. A small loaf of bread was baked from the harvest of a plot he had in his hometown of Nablus and sent to him in Damascus every night. His *fatwa*s decreed the pursuit of one way *(ṭarīqa)* only—asceticism in this world and purity from base qualities or habits.[61]

Sufi and non-Sufi Muslim authors have long distinguished between the mystical and ethical dimensions of Sufism—*al-taṣawwuf alladhī li-l-takhalluq* as opposed to *al-taṣawwuf alladhī li-l-taḥaqquq*. Some even defined Sufism as etiquette, thereby stressing the importance of the ethical over the mystical dimension. Abū l-Najīb al-Suhrawardī in his famous manual, *ādāb al-murīdīn* (composed in the late twelfth century), quotes earlier Sufis of great renown:

> The noblest characteristics of the Sufis are their moral qualities. . . . A saying of Abū Bakr al-Kattānī: "Sufism is ethical disposition, so whoever is better than you in his ethics is greater than you in Sufism." . . . When Sahl b. ʿAbd Allāh was asked about

> good ethical behavior, he said that its minimal requirements were to suffer evil with forbearance, to abstain from retribution and to have compassion for him who wrongs you. It is these qualities which are characteristic of the Sufis.[62]

Elsewhere in his compilation, al-Suhrawardī makes a clear distinction between the ethical and mystical dimensions, which corresponds to the division between its visible-outward and hidden-inward dimensions: "This school [Sufism] has external and internal aspects (*ẓāhir* and *bāṭin*). The external aspect is to observe the rule of ethical behavior in relation to mankind, and the inner aspect is to launch into states and stations (*aḥwāl* and *maqāmāt*) in relation to the real one *(al-ḥaqq)*."[63] About two hundred years later, the fourteenth-century Andalusian scholar Lisān al-Dīn b. al-Khaṭīb designates classical Sufism as "mysticism of ethical behavior" *(al-taṣawwuf al-khuluqī)*.[64]

Indeed, the emphasis placed on Sufism as etiquette comes out clearly in Sufi manuals that were composed from the late tenth century onward, all subsumed under the term *adab* or *ādāb* (ethics and manners). Al-Sulamī in *Jawāmiʿ ādāb al-ṣūfiyya* (A Collection of Sufi Rules of Conduct), apparently the first single work entirely devoted to describing many disparate *ādāb,* placed unprecedented emphasis on correct behavior. The acquisition of *adab* is described as more important and praiseworthy than the accumulation of knowledge *(ʿilm)* or prolonged engagement in ascetic practices; any disrespect for *adab* might lead to the loss of faith in God.[65] In his *Manāhij al-ʿārifīn* (The Manners of the Gnostics), al-Sulamī traces the various stages through which the novice has to pass. First one learns *adab* from his shaykh, which leads to the second station, morals *(akhlāq)*. On this basis, he advances to the final station, mystical states *(aḥwāl)*.[66] The perception that acquiring ethics and manners is the first and foremost objective of training in Sufism and a precondition for advancement along the spiritual path is nowhere more clearly expressed than in al-Suhrawardī's manual. Sufism in its entirety is viewed in *ādāb al-murīdīn* from the standpoint of *adab*. For "each moment [of mystical experience *(waqt)*], each state *(ḥāl)* and each station *(maqām)* has its *adab*."[67]

The great importance that authors of Sufi manuals ascribed to moral guidance was manifested in practice as well. An early testimony concerns Abū ʿAbd Allāh al-Rūdhbārī, the great mystic of Tyre. Qushayrī depicted him as *shaykh al-tarbiyya* and as closely monitoring the behavior of his disciples. The shaykh, who was deeply concerned with safeguarding the reputation of members of his grouping as righteous people among the community of their fellow believers, disseminated his norms and values within society:

> It is related that one day Abū ʿAbd Allāh al-Rūdhbārī was following the *fuqarāʾ*. It was his habit to follow them. They directed their steps to a private house for the performance of the supplication prayer *(daʿwa)*. Someone was heard to remark: "These people take things unlawfully," and added, "One of them did not pay me back one hundred silver coins *(dirhem)* he borrowed from me, and I know not where I should find him." The house where they gathered belonged to a "lover" *(muḥibb)* of this group *(ṭāʾifa)*, and when they entered it, Abū ʿAbd Allāh al-Rūdhbārī said to the house owner, "If you care about my peace of mind, give me one hundred *dirhem*." The request was immediately granted. He then ordered one of his close companions *(aṣḥāb)*: "Take the money to the greengrocer with the following explanation: Here is the money that one from among our group borrowed from you. He now returns the loan in the hope of your forgiveness for the belated repayment." And the disciple did so. On their way back from the *daʿwa*, they all stopped at the shop of the greengrocer, who, on seeing them, started to praise them, exclaiming: "These are righteous and trustworthy worshipers, may God bless them."

Al-Rūdhbārī concludes the episode with the words: "The most repulsive [man] is the stingy Sufi."[68] This last statement is also attributed to him in *Bāb al-taṣawwuf* (the chapter on the Sufi doctrines) of al-Qushayrī's *Risāla*."[69]

Later authors cast further light on the shaykh's role and reputation as a moral guide. Ibn ʿAsākir recounts:

> It is related that Abū ʿAbd Allāh al-Rūdhbārī used to invite his disciples to follow him to the houses of the common people *(sūqa),* who were not Sufis, where they would assemble for the supplication prayer. Before entering the houses, however, he would supply them with a meal so that they would not help themselves to the host's food, thereby marring their reputation as people of virtue.[70]

As his moral virtues were publicly manifested, the belief that he was endowed with divine grace spread among the people.[71] At the same time, he gained renown in scholarly circles due to his mastery of all the Islamic sciences.

During al-Rūdhbārī' lifetime, ideas circulated regarding the attributes of the accomplished Sufi guide. Abū l-Najīb summarizes a series of qualities. His description indicates that by the time he composed his work, calling on an accomplished shaykh for advancement on the path had become habitual. Much significance is accorded to the moral virtues—such as humility, generosity, and altruism—that the genuine guide should possess:

> The following were among their rules of conduct: When they meet, they choose one of themselves to be their head, so that they may turn to him and rely on him. He should be the most excellent in his wisdom as well as in his [religious] zeal and [mystical] state, the most learned in the school tradition *(madhhab),* and the eldest. . . . He should be the best in his character *(khulk)* and the first to emigrate [retreat] and perfect in his manners *(adab).* . . . He who will serve them should be the most sincere in his intention, compassion, and forgiveness, [the one] whose heart is the strongest, and the [one] most distinguished in his piety, faith, and modesty. He should also be [the] one who less than anyone else is concerned with his own soul and own self.[72]

The accomplished Sufi master embodies the behavior patterns and ethical positions of the Prophet, which were imparted to him through successive generations of outstandingly pious and virtuous figures. Hence, it is through him that the prophetic Sunna is revitalized. This perception, which had its origins in the writings of al-Sulamī, was elaborated on by later Sufi authors of *adab* literature. It was lucidly expressed by Shihāb al-Dīn ʿUmar al-Suhrawardī: "The characters *(akhlāq)* of the masters have been polished through their perfection in molding themselves after the Messenger of God, peace and blessing be upon him. They are the most successful of people in revitalizing the Sunna, in all that he commanded and commissioned, censured and enjoined."[73]

The shaykh's central role—indeed, the very essence of his guidance—is to serve those who call on him, and the prime goal of this service is to pass on to them his virtues *(manāqib)* and morals *(akhlāq)*, even the divine blessing *(baraka)* with which he was endowed. All these attributes make him indispensable. This ultimate goal of transmitting religious lore was not peculiar to the Sufis but was shared by the religious elite generally. Still, education under the Sufi guide acquired a special significance. Molding behavior is often described in terms of a total transformation of a disciple's entire mode of life, even a transformation of his self. Al-Ghazzālī presented the authoritative guide as a healer of souls. In his words, addressed to the seeker of the spiritual path, "Know that whoever treads this path *(ṭarīqa)*, should attach himself to a shaykh, a guide and educator through whose guidance his bad qualities will be rooted out."[74] Shihāb al-Dīn al-Suhrawardī, following this line, stated, "The shaykh's purpose is to cleanse the *murīd*'s heart from the rust and lust of nature, so that in it, by attraction and inclination, may be reflected the rays of the unity's beauty and the glory of eternity."[75] Accordingly, the disciple must enter a life dominated by his shaykh's guidance or, in the language of the great Sufi thinkers, of constant service *(khidma)*, which dictates that he owes total obedience to his shaykh, just as every man owes obedience to God. Abū l-Najīb put it this way:

> The *murīd* (novice) should not leave his shaykh before the eye of his heart opens. Rather, during the period of service *(khidma)*, he should forbear whatever his educator commands and forbids. One of the shaykhs said: "He who was not educated by the

shaykhs' words and ordinances would not be educated by the Koran and the Sunna."[76]

Sayings by Sufi authors living in the earlier middle period are a clear indication of the change from the fluidity of the mystical wayfarer's environment to a much more structured, authoritarian, master-disciple relationship. By attaching himself to the prophetic model through a recognized spiritual lineage and revivifying the Sunna, both in his own conduct and in his teaching of others, the accomplished Sufi shaykh succeeded in embodying the authority that resides in the Prophet, the central symbol of authority and most perfect of humans. The shaykh is thus presented as the living heir of the Prophet, and the relationship between a shaykh and his disciples is parallel to that between the companions and the Prophet.[77] In the words of Shihāb al-Dīn al-Suhrawardī: "The shaykh in the midst of his *murīd*s is as Muḥammad in the midst of his *aṣḥāb*."[78]

As the shaykh-disciple relationship became more hierarchical and structured, the bond between them became more intensely personal. Sufi authors frequently use the word *ṣuḥba*—companionship or discipleship—to describe the intimate all-encompassing, albeit no less hierarchical relationship forged between them. Originally associated with the companions of the Prophet (the *ṣaḥāba*), who internalized his message and carried on his teaching after him, *ṣuḥba* came to be applied principally in the fields of *ḥadīth,* jurisprudence, and, above all, Sufism.[79] The set of linkages between a Sufi guide and those who submitted themselves to intense training under his tutelage are described in Sufi literature as surpassing all other linkages in terms of attachment and reciprocal obligations.

The Sufi shaykh's unquestionable authority as a spiritual and moral guide and the new and deeper bonds uniting guides and disciples were the basis of more lasting loyalties. Previously, members of the Sufi circles had sought instruction and guidance from as many shaykhs as possible. From around the late tenth century, however, they tended to attach themselves to one shaykh whose spiritual method *(ṭarīqa)* they would follow and transmit to future generations. The shaykh was fully committed to the service of his disciples. Imparting to them his norms and values and closely monitoring their conduct, he combined the roles of educator, psychologist, and caring spiritual father.[80] Thus, even without formal patterns of initiation and advancement along the path or any formal hierarchy of mentors and disciples, such as those that developed in medieval Western monasticism, the stage was set for the transition from loose and mobile circles into coherent local congregations. Beginning in the late tenth century, the phenomenon of an authoritative guide living among his disciples, committed followers of his spiritual method, came to be increasingly common in the course of the earlier middle period.

The stories about al-Rūdhbārī related above reflect the early phase in the formation of a local Sufi congregation around the shaykh. The shaykh and members of his *ṭā'ifa* clung to each other, performed their rituals together, and interacted as a coherent group with other members of the local community. The term *ṭā'ifa* (faction), which appears first in the Koran to denote a group or party in general and which in a later period denoted a Sufi order or branch, is used here to cover a specific category of people with shared identity and leadership.[81] Another example is a group *(jamā'a)* orbiting around Naṣr al-Maqdisī during his days in Jerusalem that was called Naṣriyya after him and that continued to operate long after his departure for Damascus.[82] Though little is known about the identity of members of the early Sufi congregation (the *ṭā'ifa* or *jamā'a*) and its forms of operation, the notion conveyed is that of a spiritual family united by shared loyalties and commitments to a particular Sufi guide.

Deeply entrenched in the Sufi tradition, the maxim of service to others led to fraternal love, which became a prime aspect among the Sufis of a specific group. Caring for one's companions, preferring them to oneself, and giving up prestige for the sake of one's fellows was one of the main rules for the Sufi, and it was applicable throughout his lifetime. "Whoever excuses himself from service to his brethren, God will give him a humiliation from which he cannot be rescued," asserts one tradition, and "If you cannot serve properly your human companion, how could you serve God?" demands another. To do good for his brethren, the Sufi should even disregard his religious principles. He should interrupt his fasting if he sees a member of his community who needs or wants food, since the joy of a brethren's heart is more valuable than the reward of fasting.[83] Similarly, "To render service to the brethren is more valuable than to be engaged in supererogatory prayers."[84] Sufi authors from the earlier middle period neatly consolidated all the information that was available in earlier works about companionship *(ṣuḥba)* and service to others *(khidma)* and developed elaborate rules of residence and discipline. Al-Hujwīrī considered companionship to be the ninth among the eleventh veils that have to be lifted before gnosis can be attained. Meticulous care in the performance of duties pertaining to *ṣuḥba* could lift this veil and make gnosis available.[85] The practical application of fraternal love is the obligation of the authoritative guide. In the chapter in *al-Kashf* that is devoted to the rules of *ṣuḥba,* the renowned Sufi thinker states:

> The Sufi shaykh demand from each other the fulfillment of the duties of companionship and enjoin their disciples to require the same, so that among them companionship has become a religious obligation. . . . The most important thing for the novice is companionship. The fulfillment of its obligations is necessarily incumbent on him.[86]

Living within a Sufi congregation had an edifying function. It obligated the disciple to the values of companionship and service to others through imitation of his master's moral conduct and compliance with his requirements. Inducement of these values and supervision of their implementation must have been considered essential for constituting one's disciples and companions as a cohesive social unit. Due to the enhancement of his authority, the shaykh was capable of instilling his understanding of *ṣuḥba* and supervising its practical application. This is how Abū ʿAbd Allāh al-Rūdhbārī, acting as *shaykh al-tarbiyya*, induced in his disciples the Sufi rule of bountifulness and generosity *(al-jūd wa-l-sakhāʾ)* toward one's companions:

> I [al-Qushayrī] heard shaykh Abū ʿAbd al-Raḥmān al-Sulamī (may God grant him mercy) relate, "Abū ʿAbd Allāh al-Rūdhbārī went to the home of one of his companions. No one was at home, and the door of the house was locked. He stated, 'This man is a Sufi, and he locks his door? Break open the lock.' They complied with the order. He then ordered them to take all the goods found on the grounds and in the house, carry them to the market, sell them, and take wages for the work from the money received. Then he and his companions waited in the house. When the owner came in, he was speechless. His wife came in afterward, wearing an outer garment. She threw off her cloak, declaring, 'O companions, this is also part of our worldly property, so sell it, too.' Her husband asked her, 'Why do you choose to suffer like this?' She replied, 'Keep quiet! How can you grudge anything from one such as this shaykh, who honors us with such familiarity and disposes of our affairs?'"[87]

The early Sufi congregation seemingly remained a cohesive social unit only until the death of the master, after which it disbanded. But though often unable to perpetuate itself, during the early stage of its development the infrastructure was created for the evolution of Sufism from loosely knit circles into fraternal associations. This evolution must be seen as an integral part of the larger and widespread transformation of Islamic societies during the earlier middle period. Networks of personal ties defined by family, ethnic origins, or sectarian or professional homogeneity evolved, laying the basis for the creation of coherent local associations. However informal and unstructured these associations of people with a common identification and shared loyalty might appear to the modern historian, by taking over the place of formal and stable institution they constituted the nucleus of the social and sometimes even the political order in the post-ʿAbbasid era.[88]

Disciples and intimates who constructed their loyalties and identities around a certain shaykh—clinging to him for a long period, complying with his devotional and ethical requirements, and entering the *silsila* through him—probably formed the nucleus of the local Sufi congregation. Around them, another circle of lay believers began to emerge. This universal development is clearly attested in Abū l-Najīb al-Suhrawardī's famous manual. A careful distinction is made here between two categories of membership of a Sufi congregation. The "fully committed members" are obliged to undertake the rigors and self-imposed deprivations implicit in its rules of conduct, and others can partake of its spiritual life without forsaking their material possessions and social connections.[89] By applying the traditional concept of *rukhṣa* (a dispensation from some of the severer Sufi requirements for believers who were unable to observe them to the maximum),[90] Abū l-Najīb responded to the phenomenon of attachment to Sufism of lay members of the public, called *muḥibbūn* ("lovers" and supporters of the Sufis).[91]

In return for sharing in the spirituality of the local Sufi congregation and the charisma of the fully committed members, the *muḥibbūn* were expected to render services to that congregation—in particular, to support its local members through charitable donations and provide hospitality for itinerant fellow Sufis. The *muḥibb* of al-Rūdhbārī's *ṭā'ifa* hosted the local brethren and lent them money.[92] Abū Turāb al-Ramlī (d. unknown), while making his way back from the *ḥajj,* directed the disciples who accompanied him to an easier route to save them the hardship of traversing the desert. When they arrive in his hometown of Ramla, he instructed, they should dwell in the house of a certain *muḥibb.* And so they did. The "lover" of this *ṭā'ifa* provided them with shelter and food aplenty (pot roast and chicken) throughout their stay until their shaykh's return.[93]

Thus, at the heart of the transition from an itinerant, marginal elite of wayfaring mystics to locally embedded Sufi-inspired communities resided the dissemination of Sufism as a way of moral behavior, or ethical Sufism, as opposed to a mystical doctrine. In the case of the Sufis who were connected with medieval Palestine and perhaps also those of other Islamic historical times and settings, this transition began as early as the end of classical Sufism. Embodying the authority of the Prophet and replicating the prophetic pattern of discipleship and companionship, the Sufi moral guide constituted his circle as a spiritual family. Still, only through his operation *within* society could the scope of his influence be enlarged and the horizons of Sufism be extended beyond the core circles of seekers of the path. Certainly, the adoption of the legalist, community-oriented approach—incessant concern with the regularization and shaping of public norms and customs—helped establish the learned Sufi shaykh's position as a moral guide within his community. More important, however, were the actual manifestation and dissemination of the virtues and morals that were usually associated with the Sufis.

Indeed, representatives of activist ethical Sufism in Palestine during the earlier middle period did not act simply as arbiters of religious knowledge and practice with the scholars of the established legal schools within which they integrated. Rather than isolating themselves in the hope for spiritual perfection, they practiced their virtues within society, disseminating Sufi norms and values throughout the local community and integrating Sufism into the fabric of social and communal life. This is how the stage was set for the transformation of Sufism into a generalized religious pattern that was accessible to every believer and that led beyond the confines of exclusive affiliations and enforced loyalties.

THE ROLE OF THE MOSQUE

Interaction and intermingling with other segments of society probably took place in a private home or in a mosque, the *masjid* or the *jāmiʿ* (congregational mosque). By the twelfth century, a dense net of mosques had spread throughout Syria-Palestine. From the ninth century on, an increasing number of mosques was erected in Palestinian cities and towns and in the surrounding villages. The numerous examples provided by al-Muqaddasī in his description of al-Shām (composed in the late tenth century) are a clear, eyewitness testimony.[94] By now, the mosque had become the main center of devotion and learning for all. Members of the public routinely gathered there. Besides the daily and Friday prayers and the public ceremonies on feast days and special occasions, public sessions for the recital of and instruction in the Koran and the *ḥadīth* were regularly convened in mosques.[95]

The mosques of medieval Palestine, like those of other Muslim lands, also housed permanent scholarly circles of the *ʿulamāʾ* of the established legal schools. According to al-Muqaddasī's account of scholarly life in the mosques of Jerusalem, Ḥanafī legal scholars convened a permanent assembly for study and *dhikr* in al-Aqṣā mosque,[96] legal scholars of all schools lingered habitually in the mosque between daily prayers, and Koran readers convened their assemblies in the great congregational mosques.[97]

With the possible exception of vocal *dhikr* practices that were accompanied by ritual music or long periods of seclusion *(khalwa)*, mosques could house all of the other religious activities of the Sufis.[98] Sufi shaykhs, as has been shown, had from earliest times congregated in mosques with their exclusive circles of disciples and companions, while later shaykhs acted both as teachers of the law and as Sufi guides in the same teaching mosque. Extremely zealous ascetics and mystics found in the mosque a place of temporary retreat for meditation and pious exercises—constant prayer by day and night, fasting, and *dhikr.* A study by Daniella Talmon-Heller provides a lively example: Shaykh Salāma of Jamaʿīl (a village in the Nablus region) is typically portrayed sitting in a mosque, reciting the Koran with someone, and weeping each time that verse 17:21 ("Verily, the hereafter will be greater in degree and greater in preferment") is read aloud.[99]

Nothing better illustrates the role of al-Aqṣā mosque as a public space that was available to bring together individuals and groups that pursued various religious traditions and emphasized different forms of worship than the account of the celebration that took place in it immediately after the recapture of Jerusalem by Saladin. Spiritual guides and ascetics participated enthusiastically in the celebration along with all other members of society. While praying with the entire crowd, they performed their own rituals. ʿImād al-Dīn al-Iṣfahānī, secretary to Nūr al-Dīn and Saladin, describes the public celebration in great detail in his history of the conquest of Syria-Palestine:

> The Koran readers arrived, the official prayers were read, the ascetic and pious men congregated, with the great saints and 'pillars.' . . . They joined in groups to pray and prostrate themselves, humbling themselves and beating their breasts, dignitaries and ascetics, judges and witnesses, zealots and combatants in the Holy War, standing and sitting, keeping vigil and committed by night prayer, visitors and ambassadors. . . . The traditionalists recited, the holy orators comforted men's souls, the scholars disputed, the lawyers discussed, the narrators narrated, the traditionalists transmitted canonic traditions. The spiritual guides performed pious exercises, the pious ascetics acted as guides, the worshipers adored God with devotion, the sincere devotees lifted their prayers to heaven.[100]

The epigraph to this chapter provides another graphic illustration of Sufis as they participated in the devotional life of the local community of Jerusalem in the city's great mosques and holy sites. The Persian traveler Nāṣir-ī-Khusraw, in his account of his visit to the Ḥaram al-Sharīf (written in 1047), noted that a group of Sufis would enter it as a matter of routine for the observance of the Friday public prayer. At the same time, he observed that the group had developed its own communal center. Two cloisters by the northern wall belonged exclusively to this group, and they lodged and performed their daily prayers and rituals there.

THE ADVENT OF THE SUFI ESTABLISHMENT

While asceticism and mysticism originally flourished in informal and occasional gatherings or in mosques with other gatherings and teaching circles held nearby, from the end of the tenth century, establishments variously called *khānqāh*s or *ribāṭ*s or *zāwiya*s appeared that were associated with Sufi groups and served them as lodges or meetinghouses. After an early period of evolution, which is still obscure, these establishments became a characteristic feature of the Near Eastern urban scene, along with mosques and *madrasa*s.[101]

Several historians ascribe an important role to the advent of the Sufi lodge in the transition of Sufism from dispersed, mobile groups of spiritual wanderers to coherent associations. The foundation of a vast network of *khānqāh*s on bountiful religious endowments by the Seljuks and their successors for Sufi devotees, where they were lodged and fed and performed their rituals, is believed to be a major phase in the evolution of the Sufi *ṭarīqa* as an organization (as opposed to a mystical path). Thus, parallel to the foundation of *khānqāh*s, the loose Sufi associations yielded their place to organized systems of affiliation, instruction, and ritual. Each developed a hierarchy of spiritual guides who derived their authority from a kind of apostolic succession bestowed on them by the founder.[102] In this way, the *khānqāh* resembled the parallel institution of the *madrasa,* which according to the commonly accepted narrative, played a crucial role in the crystallization of the legal schools as scholarly and communal organizations.[103]

Institutions can play an important role in generating social change. However, they can assume this role only after the process of institutionalization is culminated—that is, after the organization, which forms the institution's core, becomes infused with commonly accepted values, comes to symbolize the community's aspirations and its sense of identity, and develops its own distinctive characteristics.[104] The *madrasa* and *khānqāh* are good examples of this institutionalization process. Only gradually did they grow into centers of activities and develop their distinctive tradition. Moreover, the importance ascribed to the institutional framework in the dynamic of social change overshadows the cultural and social practices beyond it. Given the personal character of training in Sufism and transmission of spiritual knowledge, it was around persons—the Sufi shaykhs—rather than places that aspirants and companions forged their social relationships and constructed their identities. Spencer Trimingham persuasively argues: "It was not through such an establishment [the *khānqāh*] that the next development of Sufi institutionalization took place but through a single master, sometimes settled in a retreat far from the distractions of *khānqāh* life, sometimes in his *zāwiya* home in the big city, frequently a wanderer traveling around with his circle of disciples."[105]

Indeed, biographical accounts of the Sufi shaykhs under study here demonstrate that long after the advent of the bountifully endowed *khānqāh,* training in Sufism, prayer, and *dhikr* or spiritual retreat took place wherever a shaykh happened to sit, just as sessions for legal instruction continued to be held in a variety of forums other than the endowed *madrasa.* Legal scholars and Sufis therefore constructed their identities and forged their relations independently of any institutional frameworks. The evolution of the infrastructure of their communities was more important than the development of the physical environment in which they congregated.

The varied terms used to describe particular cultural establishments and changes over time in their designations are themselves reflective of the flexible, personal character of the dissemination of Islamic learning and devotion. Historians and chroniclers accorded much more importance to accurately recording with whom a person had studied than to specifying and defining the building or institution where he acquired his education or training.[106] An examination of their accounts exposes the image and character of the early Sufi lodge and brings to light the differences among various types of establishments in various regions.

The main source for the development of Sufi establishments in medieval Palestine is Mujīr al-Dīn's history of Jerusalem and Hebron, which includes an extensive list of the establishments that were founded in the two sacred cities and their environs during the Ayyubid and Mamluk periods and that were based on the great number of deeds of endowment (*waqfiyya*s) he had before him. Added to this valuable primary source are endowment charters in the name of the founder and dedication inscriptions posted on the buildings themselves that have survived to this day.[107]

Several Sufi lodges that served the needs of either unorganized individuals or groups devoted to a particular master were founded in Palestine before Mamluk times, during which they witnessed their huge spread. Extracts from the endowment charters of the lodges, as recorded by Mujīr al-Dīn, contain valuable information about their founding, their building, their administration, and the functions they were expected to perform. Overall, however, there is no direct evidence of the actual activities that took place in these early Sufi establishments. Who were the Sufis who took up residence in them? Did they comply with the terms of the endowment that were stipulated in the charters? Were there any rules regulating life in these lodges? These are some of the hidden issues.

The first Sufi lodge that is mentioned in this historical setting is a *ribāṭ* in Ramla. It was founded in the eighth century by an ascetic who came to the capital of Umayyad Palestine from his hometown of Kufa.[108] Some stipulated that the early urban *ribāṭ*s, like that of Ramla or Baghdad, were modeled after the frontier *ribāṭ*s that served the pious warriors of the holy war as fortified abodes and meetinghouses. However, any historical connection between the *ribāṭ* of the frontier and medieval urban establishments associated with groups of Sufis is obscure. There is no mention of any Sufis dedicated to the holy war or immersed in inner *jihād* in accounts of the early *ribāṭ*s.[109] Whatever the character of the *ribāṭ* of Ramla and the operation of its dwellers, in common with other contemporary *ribāṭ*s—such as

ʿAbbadan Island (on the Persian Gulf) and Damascus—that were not supported by endowments for their maintenance and upkeep, this *ribāṭ* did not develop into a permanent center and broke up after its master's death or migration.

The term *khānqāh* appeared in the late ninth century and came to be widely used for Sufi residences in Khurasan and Transoxania. The emergence *khānqāh*s marked an important stage in the development of Sufi organizations in these regions. Sufis in Khurasan adopted the *khānqāh,* which was originally linked with the Karrāmiyya, and adapted it to their own purposes. Often a private benefactor or well-to-do Sufi would found a *khānqāh* and grant it to a Sufi shaykh and his family. By the eleventh century, the *khānqāh*s in Nishapur and other parts of Khurasan had already consolidated into an organized Sufi establishment. Rules for ethical behavior and companionship *(ṣuḥba)* were set to regulate the devotional and communal life of the residents, beginning with Abū Saʿīd b. Abī al-Khayr (d. 441/1049).[110] Such a self-created and well-organized Sufi establishment, which spread into the countryside of the Muslim East, did not develop in Palestine.

Not until the Ayyubid period did the first *khānqāh*—the prestigious Ṣalāḥiyya of Jerusalem (named after its famous founder)—make its appearance in Palestine (figure 2.1). Arab historians, in seeking to promote Saladin's image as the defender of Sunni Islam, closely link its foundation (in 1189) to his efforts to restore the city's Islamic character and revive its sacred position. ʿImād al-Dīn al-Iṣfahānī describes the beginnings of this *khānqāh* (called a *ribāṭ* in this account) thus:

> Al-Malik al-ʿĀdil had encamped in the Church of Zion; his troops were at the church's gates. The sultan's household, pious scholars and men of virtue, spoke to him of establishing a law school *(madrasa)* for the Shafiʿī lawyers and a convent *(ribāṭ)* for the Sufis.[111]
>
> He [Saladin] asked the Sufis about their conditions and set aside for them the use of the Patriarch's house near the Church of Res-

urrection, which he endowed for them as a convent. He stipulated a daily meal for its residents, added endowments, and ordered that all expenses be provided to them liberally.[112]

Figure 2.1. The Ṣalāḥiyya *khānqāh* in Jerusalem

The regulations regarding use of the endowment made clear that the establishment was designed by its founder both to safeguard mainstream Sufism and to promote his image as its supporter:

> Members of the above-mentioned group [i.e., the beneficiaries] should all congregate in this place every day after the afternoon prayer for the recital of the Koran and for *dhikr,* which should be followed by prayers for this *waqf* donor and for the Muslims in general. . . . They should [also] gather with their shaykh every Friday after sunrise, either in this place or in al-Aqṣā mosque, where they will be reciting the Holy Book as much as possible, then pray for the donor and the Muslims and read aloud in the presence of their shaykh the words of the leading Sufi shaykhs, may God make them beneficial.[113]

The following clause stipulates that the Ṣalāḥiyya is exclusively reserved for virtuous, "true" Sufis:

> If someone belonging to this group of beneficiaries has not yet been "educated," he should be expelled from this place and will not be entitled to return before journeying to the Hijaz al-Sharīf or to another place, where he will purify himself and repent to almighty God.[114]

The first director of the establishment and the trustee *(nāẓir)* of its pious endowments was Shaykh Ghānim al-Anṣārī al-Khazrajī, an inhabitant of Jerusalem at the time (he was born in a village in the Nablus region and died in Damascus in 632/1234) and known for his excellent qualities and virtuous deeds.[115] The founder, who created the office of the shaykh of the establishment and made the appointment, entitled him to pass it on either to his descendants or to anyone else of his choice.[116] Nonetheless, the deed of the endowment does not indicate that the Ṣalāḥiyya Khānqāh was founded and bountifully endowed for the benefit of a particular shaykh and his group of close disciples and followers. Rather, the best available information suggests that the establishment was granted to Sufi devotees in general, whether indigenous or, more probably, foreign. The *khānqāh,* in other words, was an official establishment that did not center on the shaykh and his circle.

The foundation of the Ṣalāḥiyya and the other great *khānqāh*s that fall into the same category is a clear indication of the process by which Sufism moved from the margins of intellectual and social life to become part of the social order and the fabric of Muslim devotion. These magnificent buildings are physical evidence of the growing recognition of Sufis as one of the groups that were disseminating the truth of Islam and shaping the communities' spiritual and social life. However, the formal institutional structure of the *khānqāh* could hardly contain the activities and energy of the growing numbers of medieval Muslim men and women who identified themselves in some way as Sufis.[117] No less important, it seems, was the wish of Sufis who were pursuing an ascetic mode of life to avoid the patronage of the ruling elite and distance themselves from an establishment that was founded by the powerful and closely associated with the official sphere. It is no wonder, then, that informal groups of Sufis with their shaykhs continued to gather in mosques and private homes. Alternatively, they would gather in the much more modest and less institutionalized Sufi establishment known as a *zāwiya*. Apparently, this was the tendency in medieval Palestine beginning in the Ayyubid period.

The term *zāwiya* could signify a particular corner or space in a large mosque, but it often referred to a small mosque or independent building that provided lodgings and a forum for the performance of Sufi worship and rituals. A glance at Mujīr al-Dīn's description of the Sufi establishments that were founded in Ayyubid and Mamluk Jerusalem indicates flexibility in the use of the term and exposes a number of patterns. The different terms that he uses to describe particular Sufi establishments are in themselves an indication that at least during the early phase of its development the *zāwiya* did not conform to a single pattern.[118] The term *shaykh* meant Sufi master as well as teacher of the Islamic religious and legal sciences, and the shaykhs of the *zāwiya*s listed by Mujīr al-Dīn in *al-Uns* sometimes taught *ḥadīth*, jurisprudence, and other subjects in those very institutions or in *madrasa*s.

Among the *zāwiya*s that were included in Mujīr al-Dīn's list is al-Naṣriyya. This seemingly very small Sufi lodge was named after the famous learned Sufi of Jerusalem, Shaykh Naṣr al-Maqdisī. Its description yields a complex picture: over time, changes took place in the character of the establishment and in the functions that it was designed to serve. According to Mujīr al-Dīn, Naṣr lived in Jerusalem in his *zāwiya* located atop the Gate (Gates) of Mercy (Bāb [Abwāb] al-Raḥma). Shortly afterward, however, the *zāwiya* was renamed al-Ghazzāliyya in honor of al-Ghazzālī, who had taken up residence there during his sojourn in the city (1095–1096). But when Ibn al-ʿArabī, who visited Jerusalem at the time, speaks in his travel journal of the Shāfiʿī *madrasa* near the Gate (Gates) of the Tribes (Bāb [Abwāb] al-Aṣbāt), he may be referring to the same institution. Later, according to Mujīr al-Dīn, the Ayyubid prince al-Malik al-Muʿaẓẓam ʿĪsaʾ refurbished the establishment (labeled a *madrasa* in this account) for use as a *zāwiya.* He designed it for the study of the Koran and syntax and donated many books as *waqf,* including *Thinking of Straight* by Abū Yūsuf Yaʿqūb al-Sikkir, for this purpose. Mujīr al-Dīn adds that in his day the *zāwiya* has fallen into ruin: it is no longer occupied and has been abandoned.[119]

Another establishment that Mujīr al-Dīn lists and describes is al-Naḥwiyya. This establishment—sometimes called a *zāwiya,* other times a *madrasa*—was the first to officially combine Sufism and the law on the institutional level. Its endowment charter stipulated that it should house under the same roof the *fuqarāʾ* and the *fuqahāʾ* and should offer lessons in jurisprudence and related sciences. Also founded by al-Malik al-Muʿaẓẓam ʿĪsaʾ (in 604/1207), it provided for a supervisor of prayer *(imām)* and twenty-five students and their shaykh, with the stipulation that the students receive instruction in grammar and affiliate with the Ḥanafī school of law.[120]

Whatever the various types and changing functions of the *zāwiya,* a fundamental distinction existed from the outset between this and other Sufi establishments of learning and devotion. In contrast with the royal establishments—the *madrasa* and the *khānqāh*—the *zāwiya,* as delineated by later historians and chronicles, was the home and realm of its first shaykh and his successors. Usually (although not invariably), it was founded on the private initiative of a shayk who presided over it. Moreover, even when members of the ruling elite built *zāwiyas* and endowed them liberally, their financing came from private sources for the benefit of a *particular* shaykh, his followers, and his successors.[121]

The individual pattern for establishing and endowing the *zāwiya,* which became increasingly apparent in Mamluk times, is revealed in a description by al-Ḥanthaniyya. Originally a prayer chamber, it is the first Sufi establishment in Ayyubid Jerusalem that is specifically and consistently called a *zāwiya,* as Mujīr al-Dīn relates:

> As for the *madrasas* and *zāwiyas* [in and] around the mosque [of al-Aqṣā]: the earliest is *al-Zāwiya* al-Ḥanthaniyya, inside the mosque behind the *minabr.* Al-Malik Ṣalāḥ al-Dīn, may God protect him with his grace, bequeathed it as *waqf* for one of the people of virtue. This is the honorable, ascetic, and pious man, Shaykh Muḥammad b. Aḥmad b. Muḥammad Jalāl al-Dīn al-Shāshī, an inhabitant of Bayt al-Muqqadas and, after him, for whoever would follow him. A group of the distinguished shaykhs has presided over it ever since.[122]

Symbolizing the presence and authority of its first shaykh and his successors, the *zāwiya* developed into the prime establishment for the dissemination of his knowledge and guidance and as the center for his circles of disciples and admires. As such, the proliferation of *zāwiyas* in Palestinian cities, towns, and villages in the later middle period made a significant contribution to the growth of local followings around pious and charismatic leaders who lived in their lodges among their fellow believers. This extension of the Sufi shaykh's realm and ambiance was closely related to the affinity between Sufism and sanctity.

NOTES

1. For the biography of Abū ʿAbd Allāh al-Rūdhbārī, see al-Qushayrī, *al-Risāla,* 414f; al-Iṣfahānī, *Ḥilyat al-awliyāʾ,* 10:383; Ibn al-Jawzī, *al-Muntaẓam,* 7:101; Ibn al-Athīr, *al-Kāmil fī l-taʾrīkh,* 12 vols. (Beirut, 1966), 8:710; Ibn Kathīr, *al-Bidāya wa-l-nihāya,* 11:296; Khalīl b. Aybak al-Ṣafadī, *al-Wāfī bi-l-wafayāt,* ed. H. Ritter, S. Dedering, et al., 22 vols. (Istanbul: Deutsche Morgenländische Gesellschaft, 1931–), 7:184; Ibn ʿAsākir, *Taʾrīkh,* 5:16–23; al-Khaṭib al-Baghdādī, *Taʾrīkh baghdād,* 4:336–37; al-Dhahabī, *Siyar aʿlām al-nubalāʾ,* 16:227; ʿAbd Allāh al-Yafiʿī, *Mirʾāt al-jinān wa-ʿibrat al-yaqzān fī maʿrifat ḥawādith al-zamān,* 2nd ed., 4 vols. (Beirut, 1970), 2:49; Ibn al-ʿImād, *Shadharāt al-dhahab,* 3:68; al-Shaʿrānī, *Ṭabaqāt,* 1:145; al-Munāwī, *al-*

Kawākib al-durriyya, 2:15; al-Jāmī, *Nafahāt al-uns,* 1:383–85. See also F. Sezgin, *Geschichte des arabischen Schrifttums,* 9 vols. (Leiden: Brill, 1967–), 1:663, for further references and details there on several of his treatises that have been preserved in manuscript.

2. Al-Sulamī, *Ṭabaqāt,* 497.
3. For a critique of the common narrative ascribing a pivotal role to Ghazzālī in reconciling between Sufism and the law, see George Makdisi, "Hanbalite Islam," in M. L. Swartz, ed., *Studies on Islam* (New York: Oxford University Press, 1981), 242–46. For key studies that discern the beginning of the consolidation of mainstream Sufism in late tenth-century Khurasan, see Chabbi, "Remarques"; Fritz Meier, *Abū Saʿīd-i Abū al-Ḥayr (357–490/967–1049): Wirklichkeit und Legende* (Leiden: Brill, 1976). Their observations have been eloquently elaborated on in Malamud, "Sufi Organizations."
4. See Malamud's comments on the increasing emphasis on the *silsila* beginning in the eleventh century in "Sufi Organizations," 433.
5. For brief discussions of the late tenth to eleventh centuries as a seminal period in the history of Sufism, see Hourani, *A History,* 154–55; Ira M. Lapidus, *A History of Islamic Societies* (New York: Cambridge University Press, 1988), 169–71. For the instrumental role played by Sufi shaykhs in converting non-Christians to Islam in the Islamic middle periods, see especially Claude Cahen, "The Turkish Invasion: The Selchükids," in K. Setton, ed., *A History of the Crusades,* 2nd ed. (Madison: University of Wisconsin Press, 1969), vol. 1; Mehmed Fuad Köprülu, *Islam in Anatolia after the Turkish Invasion,* trans. and ed. G. Leiser (Salt Lake City: University of Utah Press, 1993), esp. 5, 11 ff.; Speros Vryonis, *The Decline of Hellenism in Asia Minor and the Process of Islamization from the Eleventh through the Fifteenth Centuries* (Berkeley: University of Carlifornia Press, 1971; rpt. 1986), esp. 351–402. For inner Asia, see Devin Deweese, *Islamization and Native Religion in the Golden Horde: Baba Tükles and Conversion to Islam in Historical and Epic Traditions* (Pennsylvania: Pennsylvania State University Press, 1994), which is the most substantial study of Islamization in this region. See especially 135–42, where Deweese raises and addresses important questions regarding the

actual emergence of Sufis as bearers of Islam to the infidel courts of the Mongol Khans in the thirteenth and fourteenth centuries.

6. For studies that interpret the Sunni revival as an outcome of developments within Sunni Islam itself (namely, the triumph of traditionalism), see especially George Makdisi, *Ibn ʿAqīl et la resurgence de l'Islam traditionaliste au xi*[e] *siècle* (v[e] *siècle de l'Hégire*) (Damascus: Institut Français, 1963); Makdisi, "The Sunni Revival," 155–68. Bulliet, *Islam,* has proposed that the notion of Sunni recasting is a more accurate description of the process than the terms *revival* or *renaissance.* Traditionalism, in his view, was one aspect of a broader process of homogenizing Sunni religious life during this period. Most recently, this interpretation has been elaborated on by Jonathan Berkey in *The Formation of Islam,* 189–202. See also Ephrat, *A Learned Society,* 1–6, for Baghdad as a major scene of the Sunnization movement.
7. For some of the dramatic persecutions in Syria during Ayyubid times, see Daniella Talmon-Heller, "Religion in the Public Sphere: Rulers, Scholars, and Commoners in Syria under Zangid and Ayyubid Rule (1150–1260)," in M. Hoexter, S. N. Eisenstadt, and N. Levtzion, eds., *The Public Sphere in Muslim Societies* (Albany: SUNY Press and Van Leer Jerusalem Institute, 2003), 51–52. See also the many examples in Jonathan P. Berkey, *Popular Preaching and Religious Authority in the Medieval Islamic Near East* (Seattle: University of Washington Press, 2001), a pioneering and pathbreaking study about the struggle waged by traditionalist scholars against popular preachers and storytellers and a defense of them.
8. Several historians of medieval Muslim societies undertook to study the period 950 to 1150 and the transformation of Islamic civilization at the close of the twelfth century. For their interpretation, see D. S. Richards ed., *Islamic Civilization* 950–1150 (Oxford: Cassirer, 1973). See also Bulliet, *Islam,* for a social historian who abandons the view of Islamic history "from the center," focusing instead on changes in the social structure of the vast majority of Muslims who lived on the periphery, primarily eastern Iran. The literature on the origins and development of the *madrasa* is vast. See especially George Makdisi, "Muslim Institutions of Learning in Eleventh-Century Baghdad," *Bulletin of the School of Oriental and African Studies* 24 (1961): 1–58; George Makdisi, *The Rise of*

Colleges: Institutions of Learning in Islam and the West (Edinburgh: Edinburgh University Press, 1981), esp. 29–30. On the development of the *khānqāh,* see the final section in this chapter.

9. For panoramic studies of the evolution of the new social order in the course of the earlier middle period, see Hodgson, *The Venture of Islam,* 2:1–62; Lapidus, *A History,* 164–74.
10. For an extensive exposition of this argument with regard to the endowed and patronized *madrasas* of Seljuk Baghdad, see Ephrat, *A Learned Society,* 126–36; Daphna Ephrat, "Religious Leadership and Associations in the Public Sphere of Seljuk Baghdad," in Hoexter, Eisenstadt, and Levtzion, *The Public Sphere,* 32–37. See also in the same volume the well-documented and well-argued discussion by Daniella Talmon-Heller about the commitment of Nūr al-Dīn, Saladin and their successors to defending Sunni Islam against anything opposed to it and strengthen its mainstream camp. Talmon-Heller, "Religion in the Public Sphere," 49–63.
11. On the contribution of the *waqf* to the shaping of the urban public space and the molding of relations between the rulers, the religious scholars, and the community, see Miriam Hoexter, "The Waqf and the Public Sphere," in Hoexter, Eisenstadt, and Levtzion, *The Public Sphere,* 119–38. Following Hodgson in *The Venture of Islam,* 2:119, Hoexter describes the *waqf* as a major tool through which the Islamic idea of social order proper to the *umma* was implemented.
12. See A. Bausani, "Religion in the Seljuk Period," in J. A. Boyle, ed. *The Cambridge History of Iran: The Seljuk and Mongol Periods* (Cambridge: Cambridge University Press, 1968), 5:300.
13. See Y. Frenkel, "The Endowment of al-Madrasa al-Ṣalāḥiyya in Jerusalem by Saladin," in J. Drory, ed., *Palestine during the Mamluk Period* (Jerusalem: Yad Ben-Zvi, 1993), 64–85 (in Hebrew), and see below on the *khānqāh.*
14. See Berkey, *The Formation of Islam,* 231–34, for a detailed exposition of this objection and suspicion.
15. For a model study of the characteristics and dispersal of these groups, see Ahmet Karamustafa, *God's Unruly Friends: Dervish Groups in the Islamic Later Middle Period, 1200–1500* (Salt Lake City: University of Utah Press, 1994).
16. For the Jerusalem Qalandariyya, see ibid., 53–54, 100 n. 22;

Geoffroy, *Le Soufisme,* 236. See also below on the Qalandarī *zāwiya* in Jerusalem.

17. See, for example, the comments of Karamustafa in *God's Unruly Friends,* 88–89.
18. On the free and broad cultural dialogue of the earlier middle period, see Hodgson, *The Venture of Islam,* 2:152–200. On the thriving cosmopolitan world of Islamic religious learning and devotion of the late tenth to early twelfth centuries, see Sam I. Gellens, "The Search for Knowledge in Medieval Muslim Societies: A Comparative Approach," in Dale F. Eickelman and James Piscatori, eds., *Muslim Travellers: Pilgrimage, Migration, and the Religious Imagination* (Berkeley: University of California Press, 1990), 55–63. For particular manifestations, see Joan E. Gilbert, "Institutionalization of Muslim Scholarship and Professionalization of the ʿUlamāʾ in Medieval Damascus," *Studia Islamica* 32 (1980): 107–108; Ephrat, *A Learned Society,* chap. 2.
19. On the idea and practice of journeying in medieval Sufism, see Touati, *Islam et Voyage,* 187–207.
20. Shihāb al-Dīn ʿUmar al-Suhrawardī, *The ʿAwārifu-l- Maʿārif,* trans. H. Wilberforce Clarke (New York: Weiser, 1970), 26.
21. For the worldwide links of noted Sufis of eleventh-century Baghdad, see Ephrat, *A Learned Society,* 54–55 and figs. 2.4–2.5.
22. Mujīr al-Dīn, *al-Uns al-jalīl,* 1:299.
23. Ibid. See also Ibn al-Athīr, *al-Kāmil fī l-taʾrīkh,* 10:172; al-Yafiʿī, *Mirʾāt al-jinān,* 3:146; Ibn Kathīr, *al-Bidāya wa-l-nihāya,* 12:149.
24. Arberry, *Sufism,* 68.
25. On the travels of Ibn ʿArabī, see Knysh, *Islamic Mysticism,* 164–65 and the references there.
26. Al-Hujwīrī, *Kashf al-maḥjūb,* 343–44.
27. Ibid., 340.
28. See Mojaddedi, *The Biographical Tradition,* 20–21, for the structure of the biographical unit in al-Sulami's *Ṭabaqāt* and its functions.
29. Al-Sulamī, *Ṭabaqāt,* 498.
30. Mojaddedi, *The Biographical Tradition,* 21. See also the remarks of M. J. Kister in his introduction to Abū ʿAbd Allāh al-Raḥmām al-Sulamī, *Kitāb ādāb aṣ-ṣuḥba,* ed. M. J. Kister (Jerusalem: Israel Oriental Society, 1954), 6–8.

31. Al-Sulamī, *Ṭabaqāt,* 498.
32. Ibid., 500.
33. On Sufi discourse on ecstasy, see Schimmel, *Mystical Dimensions,* 178–79; William C. Chittick, *Sufism: A Short History* (Oxford: Oneworld, 2000), 80. See also the discussion below on *samāʿ.*
34. Al-Sulamī, *Ṭabaqāt,* 498.
35. Ibn ʿAsākir, *Taʾrīkh,* 5:18.
36. Al-Khatib al-Baghdādī, *Taʾrīkh baghðad,* 4:336.
37. For example, al-Ṣafadī, *al-Wāfī,* 7:178.
38. On Muḥammad al-Qaysarānī and his treatises, see ʿUmar Riḍā Kaḥḥāla, *Muʿjam al-muʾallifīn* (Damascus: Maṭbaʿat al-Taraqī, 1960), 10:98–99; J. Schacht "Ibn al-Qaysarānī," *EI2.*
39. Al-Dhahabī, *Siyar aʿlām al-nubalāʾ,* 19:363.
40. Ibid.
41. Ibid. See also Shams al-Dīn Muḥammad al-Dhahabī, *Kitāb tadhkirat al-ḥuffāẓ,* 4 vols. (Hyderabad: Dāʾirat al-Maʿārif al-ʿUthmāniyya, 1968–1970), 4:1242–45.
42. Ibn Mulaqqin, *Ṭabaqāt,* 316–17. On his proficiency in *ʿim al-taṣawwuf,* see especially Ibn Khallikān, *Wafayāt al-aʿyān wa-abnāʾ al-zamān,* ed. I. ʿAbbās, 8 vols. (Beirut: Dār Ṣādir , 1971), 4:287.
43. See Schimmel, *Mystical Dimensions,* 181, on al-Junayd's reaction to the effect the *samāʿ* had on his disciple, the enthusiastic Nurī.
44. Scholarship abounds on the origins and spread of the *samāʿ* and the reactions of Muslim scholars to the various practices that were involved in it. For a general treatment of the practice in the Muslim medieval period, see Schimmel, *Mystical Dimensions,* 178–93.
45. Ibn al-ʿImād, *Shadharāt,* 3:18.
46. Al-Ṣafadī, *al-Wāfī,* 18:273.
47. See the examples in Karamustafa, *God's Unruly Friends,* esp. 5–6.
48. For the many examples of Sufi legal scholars in eleventh-century Baghdad, see Ephrat, *A Learned Society,* esp. 89–90, 144, and figs. 2.4–2.7.
49. Tāj al-Dīn al-Subkī, *Ṭabaqāt al-shāfiʿiyya al-kubrā,* ed. ʿA. F. M. al-Ḥilw and M. M. al-Tanāḥī, 10 vols. (Cairo: Maṭbaʿat ʿIsā al-Bābī al-Ḥalbī, 1964–1976), 5:98. See also Mujīr, *al-Uns al-jalīl,* 1:299.
50. Ibn al-Jawzī, *al-Muntaẓam,* 8:326.
51. On the historical links between Sufism and Shāfiʿīsm, see especially

Muhammad b. E. Monawwar, "Le soufisme et les shafiʿisme," *Les étapes mystiques du shaykh Abu Saʿid,* trans. and annotated by M. Achena (Paris: Sindbad, 1974). For the close association between them in medieval Nishapur, see Bulliet, *The Patricians,* 41–43. See also Margaret Malamud's argument that the spread of Sufism in Nishapur from the late tenth century was linked to its connection with the Shāfiʿī *madhhab* as Sufis in Nīshāpūr were exclusively Shāfiʿīs. Malamud, "Sufi Organizations," 429. On the linkage between medieval Ḥanbalīsm and Sufism, see especially George Makdisi, "The Hanbalite School and Sufism," *Humaniora Islamica* 2 (1974): 61–72; Makdisi, "Hanbalite Islam," 247–50.

52. See Terry Graham, Review of Mojaddedi, *The Biographical Tradition, Journal of Islamic Studies* 13:3 (2002): 339.
53. For examples, see Moshe Gil, *A History of Palestine, 634–1099,* trans. Ethel Broido (Cambridge: Cambridge University Press, 1992), 425–28.
54. Mujīr al-Dīn, *al-Uns al-jalīl,* 2:41. For the dedication inscription, see M. Van Brechem, *Matériaux pour un Corpus Inscriptionum ʿArabicarum, deuxième partie. Syrie du sud, Jérusalem, Ville* (Cairo, 1922), 35.
55. Joseph Drory, *Ibn al-ʿArabī of Seville: Journey to Eretz Israel (1092–1095)* (Ramat Gan: Bar Ilan University Press, 1993), 81–82 (in Hebrew).
56. For the biography of Naṣr al-Maqdisī, see al-Subkī, *Ṭabaqāt,* 5:351ff.; Ibn al-Athīr, *al-Kāmil,* 10:484; Al-Ṣafadī, *al-Wāfī,* 4:376ff.; Mujīr al-Dīn, *al-Uns al-jalīl,* 1:297–98; Al-Yāfiʿī, *Mirʾat al-jinān,* 3:152; Shams al-Dīn Muḥammad al-Dhahabī, *al-ʿibār fī khabar man ghabar,* ed. Ṣ. al-Dīn Munājid and F. Sayyid, 4 vols. (Kuwait, 1961–1966), 3:329; Ibn al-ʿImād al-Ḥanbalī, *Shadharāt al-dhahab,* 3:395–96.
57. S. D. Goitein, *A Mediterranean Society: The Jewish Communities in the Arab World as Portrayed in the Documents of the Cairo Geniza,* 5 vols. (Berkeley: University of California Press, 1967–1988), 2:201, 562 n. 14.
58. Drory, *Ibn al-ʿArabī,* 66–67.
59. For examples in eleventh-century Baghdad, see Ephrat, *A Learned Society,* 126–36. See also Gilbert, "Institutionalization of Muslim Scholarship," 105–34.

60. Mujīr al-Dīn, *al-Uns al-jalīl,* 2:143 ff.
61. See note 59 above.
62. Abū al-Najīb al-Suhrawardī, *A Sufi Rule for Novices,* trans. and abridged by Menahem Milson (Cambridge, MA: Harvard University Press, 1975), 37.
63. Ibid., 36 (translations of words in parentheses are mine).
64. See Meier, "The Mystic Path," 118. On the distinction between the mystical and moral dimensions of Sufism, see also Louis Brenner, "Separate Realities: A Review of Literature on Sufism," *International Journal of African Historical Studies* 5 (1972): 645. On Sufism as an ethical practice, see Carl W. Ernst, *Teachings of Sufism* (Boston: Shambhala, 1999), 118–20.
65. Al-Sulamī, *Jawāmiʿ ādāb al-Ṣūfiyya* and *ʿUyūb al-Nafs wa-Mudāwāthuhā,* 11 (summary of paragraph 7).
66. Al-Sulamī, *Manāhij al-ʿārifīn,* 31, 38.
67. Al-Suhrawardī, *A Sufi Rule for Novices,* 36 (additions in parentheses and square brackets are mine).
68. Al-Qushayrī, *al-Risāla,* 415–16.
69. Ibid., 281.
70. Ibn ʿAsākir, *Taʾrīkh,* 5:20.
71. Ibid.
72. Abū l-Najīb al-Suhrawardī, *Kitāb ādāb al-murīdīn,* ed. and with an introduction by M. Milson (Jerusalem: Studies in Arabic and Islam, 1978), 44–45.
73. Cited by Malamud, "Sufi Organizations," 440 n. 37.
74. Al-Ghazzālī, *Ayyuha al-walad* (Beirut, 1959), 37.
75. Al-Suhrawardī, *The ʿAwārifu-l-maʿārif,* 14
76. Al-Suhrawardī, *Kitāb ādāb,* 31.
77. See the comments by Kohlberg in his introduction to al-Sulamī, *Jawāmiʿ,* 11 and n. 28. For examples of the change in the relationship between the shaykh and his disciples in eleventh-century Khurasan, see Malamud, "Sufi Organizations," 432–35; Arthur F. Buehler, *Sufi Heirs of the Prophet: The Indian Naqshbandiyya and the Rise of the Mediating Sufi Shaykhs* (Columbia: University of South Carolina Press, 1998), 29–44 (based on Meier, "Hurasan.")
78. Al-Suhrawardī, *The ʿAwārifu-l- maʿārif,* 19.
79. On the meaning and significance of *ṣuḥba* in the world of the reli-

giously learned, see especially Makdisi, "Ṣuḥba et riyāsa dans l'enseignement médiéval," in *Recherches d'islamologie: Recueil d'articles offerts à Georges Anawati et Louis Gardet par leurs collègues et amis* (Louvain: Editions Peeters, 1978), 207–21.

80. Trimingham, *The Sufi Orders,* 13–15; Lapidus, *A History,* 169.
81. On the term *ṭā'ifa* and its applications in early Islamic societies, see Mottahedeh, *Loyalty and Leadership,* 107, 149, 159. For its usage and sense in Sufi mysticism, see Schimmel, *Mystical Dimensions,* 24; Éric Geoffroy, "Ṭā'ifa," *EI2*.
82. See the references in Drory, *Ibn al-'Arabī,* 66–67.
83. Schimmel, *Mystical Dimensions,* 229.
84. Al-Suhrawardī, *A Sufi Rule,* 43.
85. Al-Hujwīrī, *Kashf al-maḥjūb,* 123.
86. Ibid., 338.
87. Al-Qushayrī, *al-Risāla,* 250, and Von Schlegell, *Principles of Sufism: Bountifulness and Generosity,* 252 (transliterations of terms and proper names are mine).
88. See Lapidus, *A History,* 176–77. The most comprehensive study of the social bonds that created the social structure in the Byuid and Seljuk periods is Mottahedeh's *Loyalty and Leadership.*
89. Al-Suhrawardī, *A Sufi Rule,* 19, 53, 66; Knysh, *Islamic Mysticism,* 194–95.
90. I. Netton, "The Breath of Felicity: *Adab, Aḥwāl, Maqāmāmt* and Abū Najīb al-Suhrawardī," in Lewisohn, *Classical Persian Sufism,* 461.
91. J. Baldick, *Mystical Islam: Introduction to Sufism* (London: Tauris, 1989), 72.
92. See note 68 above.
93. Al-Iṣfahānī, *Ḥilyat al-awliyā',* 10:64; al-Jāmī, *Nafaḥat al-uns,* 1:78.
94. Al-Muqaddasī, *Aḥsan al-taqāsīm,* esp. 162, 164, 172, 174. For the dispersion of mosques throughout medieval Syria-Palestine, see Daniella Talmon-Heller, *Islamic Piety in Medieval Syria: Mosques, Cemeteries, Shrines,* (Leiden: Brill, 2007), 31–38. B. Johansen, "The All-Embracing Town and Its Mosques. Al-Miṣr al-Ǧāmī," *Revue de l'Occident musulman et de la Mediteranée* 32 (1981–1982), 176, notes that by the tenth century, many mosques had already been erected in the villages of Palestine.

95. For more about the popular and variegated crowds that attended sessions in the mosques of Damascus to recite and study the *ḥadīth,* see S. Leder, "Charismatic Scripturalism: The Ḥanbalī Maqdisis of Damascus," *Der Islam* 74 (1997): 279–304. See also Talmon-Heller, *Islamic Piety,* 67–72, for examples of the transmission of the Koran and the *ḥadīth* to the masses in the mosques of Ayyubid Syria-Palestine.
96. Al-Muqaddasī, *Aḥsan al-taqāsīm,* 182.
97. Ibid.
98. On the various Sufi religious practices that were performed in the mosques of the Muslim East, see Buehler, *Sufi Heirs,* 44–45. For examples in the mosques of Ayyubid Syria, see Talmon-Heller, *Islamic Piety,* 78–85.
99. Daniella Talmon-Heller, "The Shaykh and the Community: Popular Hanbalite Islam in 12th–13th Century Jabal Nablus and Jabal Qāsyūn," *Studia Islamica* 79 (1994): 118.
100. Translation by Francesco Gabrielli in *Arab Historians of the Crusades: Selected and Translated from the Arabic Sources,* 3rd ed. (London: Routledge and Kegan Paul, 1984), 164–65.
101. On the early history of Sufi establishments, see Jacqueline Chabbi, "K͟hānkāh," and "Ribāṭ," *EI2*. For a comprehensive history of the endowed Sufi lodge, see Muḥsin Kiyānī, *Tārīkh-i-khānaqāh dar Irān* (Teheran: Kitābkhānayi Ṣahūrī, 1990).
102. See especially P. M. Holt, *The Age of the Crusades: The Near East from the Eleventh Century to 1517* (London: Longman, 1986), 80.
103. See the comments by Lapidus in *A History,* 165–66.
104. See Philip Selznick, *Leadership in Administration* (New York: Row, Peterson, 1957); Leonard Broom, Philip Selznick, and Dorothy Broom, *Essentials in Sociology,* 3rd ed. (Itasca, ILL: Peacock Press, 1985), chap. 5; P. L. Berger and T. Luckmann, *The Social Construction of Reality: A Treatise in the Sociology of Knowledge* (London: Lane, Penguin Press, 1969), chap. 2.
105. Trimingham, *The Sufi Orders,* 10.
106. This is in line with Jonathan Berkey, who, while focusing on medieval Cairo, has made an invaluable contribution to the study of educational institutions and the world of religious learning in medieval Islam as a whole. Jonathan Berkey, *The Transmission of*

Knowledge in Medieval Cairo: A Social History of Islamic Education (Princeton, NJ: Princeton University Press, 1992), esp. 49.

107. For legal documents pertaining to Sufi establishments, see especially the works by Kamāl al-Dīn al-ʿAsalī (notes 113 and 120 below). For a detailed list of these establishments in Jerusalem and Hebron, see table 3.1 in Chapter 3 below.
108. L. Massigon, *Essai sur les origines du lexique technique de la mystique musulmane* (Paris: Geuthner, 1922), 234.
109. Jacqueline Chabbi makes this point in "La fonction du ribāṭ à Baghdad du Ve siècle au début du VIIe siècle," *Revue des études islamiques* 42 (1974): esp. 102.
110. Chabbi, "Kh̲ānkāh," *EI2*, based primarily on R. Frye, *The Histories of Nishapur* (Cambridge, MA: Harvard University Press, 1965).
111. ʿImād al-Dīn al-Iṣfahānī, *al-Fatḥ al-qussī fi'l-fatḥ al-qudsī* (Leiden, 1888), 69, cited in Gabrielli, *Arab Historians,* 174 (transliteration is mine).
112. Ibid., 442.
113. Kamāl al-Dīn al-ʿAsalī, *Wathāʾiq maqdisiyya taʾrīkhiyya* (Amman, 1983–1989), 94.
114. Ibid.
115. Mujīr al-Dīn, *al-Uns al-jalīl,* 2:146.
116. Al-ʿAsalī, *Wathāʾiq,* 94.
117. Jonathan Berkey makes this point in *The Transmission,* 58.
118. On the basis of al-Maqrīzī's description of the *zāwiya*s of Cairo in the early fifteenth century, Jonathan Berkey shows that even in the Mamluk period the *zāwiya* did not conform to a single pattern. Berkey, *The Transmission,* 58.
119. Mujīr al-Dīn, *al-Uns al-jalīl,* 1:34.
120. Ibid., 2:64. See also Kamāl al-Dīn al-ʿAsalī, *Maʿāhid al-ʿilm fī bayt al-maqdis* (Amman, 1981), 104.
121. Éric Geoffroy makes this observation about the *zāwiya*s that were founded in Syria and Egypt in the late Mamluk period. Geoffroy, *Le soufisme,* 168. See also Leonor E. Fernandes, *The Evolution of the Sufi Institution in Mamluk Egypt: The Khanqah* (Berlin: Klaus Schwarz Verlag, 1988), 16–32, for the fundamental difference between the *zāwiya* and the *khānqāh* as developed in Mamluk Egypt. For the individual character of establishing

and endowing Sufi lodges and educational institutions that considered particular local governors rather than the political endeavors of the Mamluk state, see Berkey, *The Transmission,* 12, 58, 62, 129–30, 132.

122. Mujīr al-Dīn, *al-Uns al-jalīl,* 1:34, 2:144 (in his biography of al-Shāshī).

· THREE ·

Expansion

Al-Shaykh ʿAlī al-Bakkāʾ ("the Weeper"), the pious and ascetic worshiper and friend of God (al-zāhid, al-ʿābid, walī Allāh), dwelt in al-Khalīl and was an object of visitation (ziyāra). *He bestowed his blessing on many. Al-Malik Qalāwūn praised him and related that while still a governor, he confided in him some of his experiences. He died in Jumādā al-Ākhira of 670 when almost one hundred years old and was interred in his famous* zāwiya *located in a quarter separated from al-Khalil to the north of the city. His grave there is a well-known site of* ziyāra.

—*Ibn Mulaqqin,* Ṭabaqāt al-awliyāʾ, *461–62*

Al-Shaykh ʿAlī al-Bakkāʾ, master of the zāwiya in Hebron (ṣāḥib al-zāwiya bi-madīnat sayyidinā al-Khalīl) . . . gained fame for his righteousness and piety and for eating only what passers-by and pilgrims left behind for him. . . . In 668, during the reign of al-Malik al-Ẓāhir Baybars, the provincial military governor (amīr) *ʿIzz al-Din Aydamar constructed the zāwiya, its sitting area and main room. Later in that year, Ḥusām al-Din Ṭaṭīṭāri, the authorized agent* (nāʾib) *of al-Malik al-Manṣūr Qalāwūn in al-Quds al-Sharif, erected a dome* (qubba) *over the grave. Finally, in Ramaḍān of 720, the amīr Saif al-Dīn, the* nāʾib *of al-Malik al-Nāṣir b. Qalāwūn in Egypt and Syria, added an entrance gate and a minaret to the building.*

—*Mujīr al-Dīn,* al-Uns al-jalīl, *2:149–50*

Who ever invokes God's name while standing between the graves of Ibn Arslān and al-Qurashī [in Māmilā cemetery], God will grant all his wishes.

—*Mujīr al-Dīn,* al-Uns al-jalīl, *2:175*

The final chapter of this book explores the concrete manifestations of the universal diffusion of Sufism and the extension of its social horizons in the so-called Islamic later middle period. Drawing largely on the biographies of charismatic Sufi shaykhs who lived in Palestine during the late Ayyubid and Mamluk periods (early twelfth to late fifteenth centuries), the analysis here looks at the universal and particular features of the Sufi *walī* and the growth of a local following around him. This examination focuses on the frameworks and modes of operation through which the Sufi "friend of God" in this spatial and temporal framework disseminated his teachings, established and routinized his charismatic authority, and enlarged his following. Examining complementary source materials—endowment deeds, inscriptions, and physical remnants—the final section chronicles the transformation of the charismatic Sufi shaykh's lodge-tomb complex into a public space, a center of communal devotion. The influence of the spread of Sufi lodges and saintly tombs on the growth of the local Sufi-inspired community and its effect on the Islamization of the landscape form an important part of this discussion. Close attention is also paid to the role played by the political rulers in this process of expansion.

DIFFUSING THE TRADITION

The institutionalization of Sufism and its prominence in the entire Sunni culture and social order of the Islamic later middle period (1250 to 1500) have received considerable attention in current scholarship. During the later middle period, the Sufi experience became more structured as particular groups of mystics and their disciples identified themselves by the spiritual path *(ṭarīqa)* that they followed, Sufi establishments proliferated throughout the Islamic Near East to become an integral part of the urban and rural scene, and devotional Sufism became the focus of religious and communal life. By the end of the later middle period, the Sufi movement as a whole had been transformed into a mass religion. Many Muslims who had not undergone a full initiatory experience might nonetheless embrace Sufi modes of piety and be brought into the orbit of Sufism.[1]

Among the religious and social practices that were associated with Sufism, those evolving around worship of the friends of God (the *awliyāʾ Allāh*) came to be the most central and widespread and contributed greatly to the growing popularity of devotional Sufism. During the thirteenth century, worship of the *awliyāʾ Allāh*, especially after their death, gained popularity among Muslims of different religious traditions and social standing. Visitation *(ziyāra)* at a shaykh's lodge and tomb to receive his blessing *(baraka)* became commonplace. The tomb of a famous shaykh became a center of local and even international pilgrimage that no Muslim failed to visit respectfully when in its vicinity. The term *mawlid* was applied generally to all the birthday celebrations of a *walī*, and the lavish public celebrations that were held at some revered shaykh's tomb to honor him became widespread, especially from the thirteenth century. The very popular character of these celebrations appealed to and invited the participation of large numbers of people who in other respects lived their life with little attention to Sufi precepts.[2]

In Palestine, the *mawlid* took the form of annual festivals (*mawsims*, a term widely used in Morocco). Mujīr al-Dīn describes the public gathering at the tomb of ʿAlī b. ʿAlīm (d. 474/1082) south of Arsuf-Apollonia (the site that is commonly known as Mashhad Sīdnā ʿAlī and is still the object of pilgrimage today): "Every year, in the summer, there is a season *(mawsim)* in which pilgrimages are made to the tomb from places far and near. Such a large number of people gather there that only Allāh can count them. They spend a great deal of money and gather beside the tomb to read the story of the birth of the Prophet Muḥammad."[3]

Islamicists tend to see the emergence of the major spiritual paths in the twelfth and thirteenth centuries as playing a major role in the popularization and geographical spread of Sufi affiliations and in the transformation of devotional Sufism into a mass religion. On the one hand, the *ṭarīqa* ascribed religious authority to particular persons through their initiation into a "spiritual genealogy" and their adoption of the practices and rituals that together constituted a kind of spiritual method. On the other hand, the shaykhs of the *ṭarīqa*s worked to diffuse such authority, practices, and rituals more broadly among different segments of society.[4] Normally, a *ṭarīqa,* which embraced and affirmed the exoteric traditions of juristic Islam and the usual forms of Muslim worship, attracted to its ranks a number of *ʿulamāʾ* who were not necessarily trained in the secrets of Sufism. The Shādhiliyya is a good example of this. Sufi affiliation became such a requirement among the *ʿulamāʾ* that prominent Ḥanbalī who were known for their hostility to Sufi ideals and practices—most notably, Ibn al-Jawzī—were themselves initiated into one or several *ṭarīqa* chains of authority. There were *ṭarīqas,* for example, that associated with Aḥmad al-Badawī (d. 659/1260) and that reached deeply into the rural scene, bringing under the umbrella of Sufism men and women who were only tangentially tied to a course of mystic discipline. Each *ṭarīqa* developed and established a method of spiritual worship, and the emphasis that its leading shaykhs placed on experience and above all *dhikr* recitation (as opposed to doctrine and discipline) provided an opportunity for a wider variety of lay believers to participate in Sufi rites, even if they had no mystical tendencies. In short, marked by its organization into *ṭarīqa*s and its concentration on devotional practices, the "new Sufism" has been often described as a form of "institutionalized mass religion."[5]

Details about the formative period in the history of the major Sufi *ṭarīqa*s are nonetheless rather sketchy. Was the *ṭarīqa,* at least in its early phase during the twelfth and thirteenth Muslim centuries, essentially a chain of spiritual authority *(silsila)* that stretched back to its putative founder rather than a constituted "brotherhood"? Did the eponymous masters of the *ṭarīqa*s intend to found an "order" or a social organization or even to form a body of rules, teachings, and practices to guide seekers of the path? What were the modes of affiliation with the early *ṭarīqa,* and what did commitment to the schools of mysticism mean? These are some of the major questions that still remain obscure.

In any event, the evolution of the "new Sufism" of the masses was not monolithic.[6] In Palestine, the process by which individual Sufis and Sufi modes of piety gained prominence often took place outside the framework of an established and widespread *ṭarīqa.* Greater Syria did not constitute the cradle of the major *ṭarīqa*s that evolved in the course of the Islamic later middle period. The overwhelming majority of the *ṭarīqa*s that appeared on its soil during this period (most famously, the Bisṭāmiyya and the Qādiriyya) were branches of mystical paths and spiritual chains that originated in other parts of the Muslim world—notably Iraq, eastern Iran, and Central Asia.

Originating in eastern Iran, the Bisṭāmiyya coalesced in Bilād al-Shām around the personalities of leading shaykhs and implanted itself first in Jerusalem. Shaykh ʿAlī al-Ṣafī al-Bisṭāmī (d. 761/1359) is mentioned as being the first famous master of the *ṭarīqa* in the city.[7] The Jerusalem branch of the Bisṭāmiyya had a recognized shaykh, designated by Mujīr al-Dīn and others as *shaykh al-bisṭāmiyya* or *ṣāḥib al-zāwiya al-bisṭāmiyya.* The first shaykh of this *zāwiya* was ʿAbd Allāh al-Asadābādī al-Bisṭāmī (d. 794/1391), successor of al-ʿAli al-Ṣafī, who studied the Islamic sciences in Baghdad before settling in Jerusalem.[8] Thereafter, this local branch of the *ṭarīqa* perpetuated itself through a nonhereditary succession of shaykhs. Its members, mentioned in *al-Uns,* came to Jerusalem from places around Syria. Several Sufi *fuqahāʾ* combined the roles of Sufi guide and teacher of the law in the Ṣalāḥiyya Madrasa. One of the shaykhs of the Jerusalem branch of the Bisṭāmiyya was a disciple of Kamāl al-Dīn, the leading shaykh *(imām)* of the Kamāliyya and master of al-Suyūṭī before he became the shaykh of the *zāwiya* in Jerusalem.[9]

As for the Qādiriyya, its appearance in Syria is often ascribed to the great thirteenth-century Ḥanbali families of Ibn Qudāma and Yunīnī, but it was only in the latter part of the subsequent century that the *ṭariqa* spread extensively and rapidly in the entire Syrian area. Although the expansion of the Qādiriyya was closely linked with the rise of the Ḥanbalī *madhahb* in Syria, certain of its shaykhs followed the Shafiʿī rite. Indeed, many of the great Shāfiʿī *fuqahāʾ* of Palestine affiliated with the Qādiriyya. The most reputable representative of the *ṭarīqa* in Palestine was Aḥmad b. Arslān of Ramla (d. 844/1440), who was born in Ramla and later moved to Jerusalem. A Sufi and Shāfiʿī *faqih* who claimed to be a descendant of the alleged founder ʿAbd al-Qādir al-Jīlānī, he is credited with making Jerusalem into another great hearth of the Qādiriyya in Bilād al-Shām (the other being in Hama). His disciple and successor, Shams al-Dīn Muḥammad Abū l-ʿAwn al-Jaljūlī (d. 910/1504), was born in Ghaza, settled first in Jaljuliyya, and finally moved to Ramla. He eventually was proclaimed to be "the Qādirī of his epoch." Although the later Qādirī shaykhs in Jerusalem and Ramla bore the appellation *shaykh al-shuyūkh al-qādiriyya,* their fame does not seem to have extended beyond their cities' limits. Thus, the Palestinian branch of the Qādiriyya remained a local association centering on its shaykh, his *zāwiya,* and his tomb.[10]

Moreover, during the later middle period, there were few strictly local spiritual paths in the cities and towns of Greater Syria as a whole,[11] and many of those designated as Sufis in Palestinian spiritual centers and their environs do not appear as fully and exclusively affiliated with one particular spiritual path or another. Thus, the term *ṭarīqa* in the texts normally denotes a method of spiritual guidance that is practiced by a particular Sufi master rather than by an institutionalized Sufi brotherhood or even a well-established spiritual route in terms of doctrine, rules, and rituals. Similarly, the expression "people of the way" (*ahl al-ṭarīqa,* or *ahl al-ṭarīq*) denotes the flock that gathered around a charismatic shaykh rather than members of a *ṭarīqa* as a social organization. Moreover, the earlier Sufis in the Syrian-Palestinian milieu and the entire Near East were far from being spiritually and socially homogeneous associations. Affiliation with several *ṭarīqa*s was not uncommon, and spiritual and social differences existed even within the same *ṭarīqa.*[12]

In spite of its highly heterogeneous character and seemingly unstructured pattern of evolution, the Sufism that was spreading in Palestine in the Islamic later middle period made its presence and modes of piety increasingly prominent. Under the Mamluk regime (1250–1517), Sufi masters and disciples were a widespread phenomenon in the Palestinian urban scene and its surroundings, and the number of Sufi establishments proliferated.[13] Jerusalem and Hebron, in particular, housed pious and charismatic figures. Collectively designated as *mashāyikh al-ṣūfiyya* by Mujīr al-Dīn, a considerable number of these people of virtue bear the appellation *walī Allāh.*

Most probably, the endeavor to be in the immediate vicinity or under the aegis of the sanctuary intensified in the wake of the Crusades. Many of the Sufi friends of God whose names appear in the pages of *al-Uns al-jalīl* were immigrants or merely transients who were drawn to Jerusalem and Hebron by the sanctified allure of those cities. Many were from distant lands such as Spain, where Muslims were driven out before the Spanish Christian reconquest, and from Afghanistan and India in the East. Often they were lodged in the various types of establishments that were put up in increasing numbers at Mamluk expense.[14]

The piety and traditional generosity of the Mamluks toward the institutions of Sunni Islam across their domains is well known. Ibn Khaldūn marveled at the effect of the *waqf* endowments on the cultural and intellectual life of Cairo under the Mamluks and the Ayyubids before them. What he said about Cairo was true of Mamluk Jerusalem as well.[15] Though only of slight political, economic, or strategic importance, Jerusalem in the eyes of the Mamluk ruling elite was a city holier than the administrative and commercial centers of either Cairo or Damascus and so had greater claim on the money that they gave to support pious works. In addition to the elaborate *khānqāh*s which were lavishly endowed for the benefit of groups of local and foreign Sufis and the *zāwiya*s for particular shaykhs, Mamluk Sultans, officials, and other wealthy individuals built hostels (*ribāṭ*s) and soup kitchens in Jerusalem for the needy among the *fuqarā'* to supply their basic needs. For example, Ribāṭ al-Baṣīr was constructed (in 681/1266) near Bāb al-Nāẓir (Gate of the Overseer) by the supervisor of the Ḥaram finances,[16] and facing it, another hostel, al-Ribāṭ al-Manṣūrī, was built on the private initiative of Sultan al-Manṣūr Qalāwūn.[17]

The gradual institutional rapprochement between mystical and juristic Islam reached its peak in the cities ruled by the Mamluks. There it became common for *madrasa*s to house Sufis and their rituals and for the endowment of Sufi establishments, especially the magnificent *khānqāh*s, to make provisions for the support of lessons in jurisprudence according to one or more of the *madhhab*s. The fusion of educational and devotional activities in the royal institutions that were founded in the great cities was so complete that by the end of the Mamluk period it became increasingly difficult to distinguish between the institutions that supported the activities of the jurists and those that supported the mystics. Similarly, the terms *madrasa* and *khānqāh* (and, at times, *mosque*) were often used interchangeably.[18]

The full social and intellectual integration of Sufism into the mainstream of Muslim intellectual life—the blending of legalism and Sufism in the same institutions and the recognition of Sufis as arbiters of "true" knowledge and proper conduct—revealed itself in one of its brightest forms in Jerusalem during the late Mamluk period. One noteworthy example is the Ashrafiyya Madrasa (facing the Ḥaram between the Gate of the Chain and the Gate of the Cotton Merchants) (figure 3.1). Perhaps the most splendid and innovative of the law colleges that were built and endowed by the Mamluks in the city, it is described by Mujīr al-Dīn as the third jewel of the Ḥaram:

> The architects drew themselves into work. . . . They covered its roof in the same manner as that of al-Aqṣā mosque with solid sheets of lead. But what constituted its greatest attraction was its

position on this noble terrain of which it has become the third jewel. These three jewels are the Dome of the Rock, the mosque of al-Aqṣā, and this *madrasa*.[19]

Figure 3.1. The Ashrafiyya *madrasa* in Jerusalem

After completing the construction of the final version of his law college in 877/1472–1473, Sultan al-Malik al-Ashraf Qayt Bāy lavishly endowed the college from properties he possessed. He also arranged for it to have a resident shaykh or spiritual director with stipends for sixty Sufis and lawyers and an unspecified number of professors and students of law. Thus, Sufis and lawyers shared the same quarters and facilities, and the functions associated with each went on the under the same roof—instruction in the law in the *iwān*s on the second floor and Sufi séances in the various *dargha*s throughout the building.[20] Similar purposes of the endowment are contained in an inscription dating from 695/1295 and affixed to the wall of the Dawādāriyya *khānqāh* on the street on the northern side of the Ḥaram:

> In the name of God, the Merciful the Compassionate: the devoted servant of Almighty God, Ibn ʿAbd al-Rabbihī b. al-Bārī Sanjar al-Dawādārī al-Ṣālīḥī, ordered the creation of this blessed *khānqāh* called the House of the Pious. He made it a pious foundation for the sake of Almighty God and for the benefit of thirty members of the Sufi community *(al-ṭāʾifa al-ṣūfiyya)* and their disciples, both Arabs and Persians, of whom twenty are celibate and ten married. They are to reside here and not depart either in summer or winter spring or fall, except in urgent cases and to extend hospitality to those Sufis and disciples who desire it for a period of ten days. He made its endowment [the income of] the village of Bir Nabla [of the territory of] blessed Jerusalem and of the village of Ḥajla of [the territory of] Jericho, as well as [the income of] a bakery and a mill and what is above these two enterprises in Jerusalem. These include a soap factory, six shops, and a paper factory in Nablus; of three gardens, three shops, and three mills in Baysan. This is all endowment for the benefit of this *khānqāh* and for the instruction of in the Shāfiʿī rite; for a professor of prophetic traditions and a reader to recite the same. For ten persons who will audit traditions and ten who will recite the Book of God in its entirety each day; also for a eulogist who will glorify the Prophet. All this [latter] is to be done in the Aqṣā mosque.[21]

The rich information that is available about endowed Sufi establishments constructed in Mamluk Palestine sheds light on the significance of the institutional dimension in the expansion of Sufism.[22] I propose that while the evolution of devotional Sufism as a focus of communal life took place around persons rather than institutional frameworks, the proliferation of institutions designed to support the Sufis and their rituals helped structure the Sufi experience and extend its horizons. Similarly, the Sufi-inspired and led association (the *ahl al-ṭarīqa*) under study here grew around the charismatic shaykh who lived apart from the sphere that was dominated by the Mamluk rulers—even though the ruling elite, by patronizing and sponsoring the Sufis in their lodges, must have played a significant role in this process. The endowed Sufi lodge, especially when it centered on a particular shaykh and developed into a complex containing the shaykh's "blessing-laden" tomb, was central to the expansion of Sufism.

At the close of the Mamluk period, Sufism was no longer confined to circles of mystical mentors, their committed disciples and other associates, or the "lovers" and supporters of the Sufi congregation. Moving to the public sphere, it attracted an ever-growing number of followers—the educated and uneducated, rulers and commoners, city dwellers and villagers alike. Companions and lay devotees who felt themselves attached in one way or another to charismatic shaykhs orbited around them during their lifetime or, more often, around their tombs. By that time, the *zāwiya*—the home and realm of the Sufi shaykh as well as his burial place—had transformed into an Islamic public space, a focus of religious and communal life that was common to Muslims of all social segments who sought to receive the shaykh's blessing and to partake of his community, each group and individual in its own way. In this way, the space that developed around the charismatic Sufi shaykhs helped to shape the Sufi experience and collective identity, extend the horizons of Sufism, and intensify its importance as one of the currents that was imprinting Islam on the human and physical environment. It is to a detailed account of the lives and activities of these figures that we now turn.

THE CHARISMATIC SHAYKH

No hagiographic or biographical compilations are devoted to a specific *walī* or group of *awliyā'* living in Palestine during the Islamic middle period. The stories of their lives and extraordinary virtues and deeds (*manāqib* and *karāmāt*) are incorporated in general biographical and hagiographic dictionaries and in the obituaries *(wafayāt)* that conclude the accounts of major events in chronicles. Among the chronicles, *al-Uns al-jalīl* by Mujīr al-Dīn is the most important source for Sufism and sanctity in Jerusalem and Hebron. The abundant information about the *awliyā*'s lives and the examples given of their *baraka* shed light on their emergence as charismatic figures in the Mamluk period.

In *al-Uns* and other compilations, the *awliyā'* are commonly described as virtuous worshipers *(ṣāliḥūn)* and ascetics *(zuhhād)* who are endowed with divine grace and hence with exceptional spiritual power. A close examination of their biographies, however, reveals a rich variety of saintly figures. This variety refers both to the religious traditions that the *awliyā'* represented and to the avenues that they pursued. Consequently, it is difficult to identify an individual *walī* or group of *awliyā'* as belonging exclusively to one or another locally embedded spiritual and intellectual current.

To begin with, many *awliyā'* in Mamluk Jerusalem and Hebron whose biographies are contained in the pages of *al-Uns* were immigrants who were drawn to the cities from regions of the Muslim world as far apart as Spain and India and who represented the varied religious traditions with which they had associated themselves in their places of origin and travel. Many among them had traveled widely, visiting or taking up residence in several places. Often these immigrants acquired fame long before settling in the cities, where they arrived at an advanced age. Consider, for example, Burhān al-Dīn Abū Isḥāq Ibrāhīm, a member of the famous Banū Jamā'a family of Shāfi'īs, some of whom are said to have embraced the Qādiriyya method of spiritual guidance.[23] Born in Hama (in 596/1200), he traveled to Damascus, where he studied jurisprudence *(fiqh)* and acquired mastery in the science pertaining to the mystical path *('ilm al-ṭarīq)* at the same time. He made a modest career for himself as a teacher of the prophetic traditions in a number of places, although Hama remained his permanent home. Having made several pilgrimages to Mecca, he directed his steps finally to Jerusalem. He bade his fellow townsmen farewell, carried his shroud with him, and died in the city soon after his arrival there (in 675/1277).[24] 'Alā' al-Dīn 'Alī al-Ardabīlī al-'Ajamī (d. 832/1428–1429), whose *manāqib* and *karāmāt* were, according to Mujīr al-Dīn, "too numerous to depict," is another example of a *walī* who settled in Jerusalem toward the end of his life. Son of a renowned mystic and miracle worker who had gained fame due to his own merits, he succeeded his father as leader of the Sufis *(shaykh al-ṣūfiyya)* in his home town of Ardabil. He then passed through Damascus on his way to Mecca, accompanied by his many disciples and followers. After dwelling in Mecca for a while, he proceeded to Jerusalem, died in the city, and was buried in the Bāb al-Raḥma cemetery (east to al-Ḥaram al-Sharīf) in the presence of a large crowd. His domed shrine *(qubba)*, erected by his closest disciples, came to be a famous pilgrimage site.[25]

Most famous and widely known of the immigrants to Jerusalem was undoubtedly Abū 'Abd Allāh Muḥammad al-Qurashī. He was born and raised in al-Jazirat al-Khadra' (on the Andalusian southern shore) and studied with many. According to his own testimony, the number of his masters or those who benefited him amounted to 600. His principal masters seem to have been Andalusian, and Yūsuf al-Shaṭṭanufī (d. 731/1314), in his treatise on the history and doctrine of Sufism, *Bahjat al-asrār,* considers him to be one of the disciples of Abū Madyan. He moved to Fustat, took up residence there for a long time, and departed for Jerusalem when he foresaw the terrible famine that was about to hit Egypt at the end of the twelfth century. While still in Fustat, he gained fame and recognition as a learned guide of exceptional spiritual power *(ṣāḥib al-karāmāt)*. Many stories circulated about his miraculous recovery from blindness and leprosy before his wife's eyes, his refusal to be cured by the mythic al-Khaḍir, his foresight, and his use of the *baraka* with which he was endowed for the benefit of his disciples and the people of Egypt in general. When he died in Jerusalem in 590/1194, he was interred in Māmilā cemetery (west to the city wall of our day). It was by the side of his tomb—a pilgrim site that was restored and enlarged—that the famous Ibn Arslān was interred about two and a half centuries later.[26]

Finding its precedents in works that constitute the main tradition of Sufi historiography,[27] the figure of the learned Sufi *walī* appears to be the most prominent of all. This is not surprising considering that the sacred biographies that were examined for this study were written by *ʿulamāʾ* for *ʿulamāʾ*. In an attempt to impose a normative homogeneity on the definition of the Muslim holy man, authors of these texts placed the figure of the *walī* within a universally recognized cultural model by highlighting the legalist element of his persona and including him in the pages of their compilations. Equally, the inclusion of men who were known primarily for their religious learning in the ranks of the *awliyāʾ* could serve the jurists. In light of the growing quest in Islamic societies for a new type of authority, one that had to do more with charisma than with *ʿilm,* jurists too could be accepted as channels to God. Accordingly, many *awliyāʾ* are presented as *al-ʿulamāʾ al-ʿārifīn,* blending together the *ʿilm* of the jurist and the *maʿrifa* of the mystic in their own education and practice and in their teaching of others. Some were peerless *(afrād)* in their generation due to the spiritual stations *(maqāmāt)* and mastery of gnosis they attained, while others apparently did not gain importance as mystics. Some were spiritual masters (*murshid*s, *musālik*s) who guided the aspirants who orbited around them, while others stressed individual salvation. Many are described as moderate ascetics, while a few appear as extreme worshipers who controlled their natural inclinations. Often, however, the Sufi *walī* appears as a multifaceted figure who represented a variety of religious traditions and pursued several avenues, either separately or simultaneously.

This characterization of the *walī* emerges when attention is shifted from the often-refuted dialectical model of popular versus elitist religion or the Sufi saint versus doctor paradigm, suggested by Ernest Gellner,[28] to the diversities and nuances *within* Sufism both as a mystical path and as a code of behavior.[29] At the same time, departure from the notions of popular religion in which the phenomenon of Muslim sainthood has been often submerged may expose the various dimensions of Sufism during the middle period.

The long biographical entries devoted to the *awliyāʾ* who combined esoteric knowledge with mastery of the legal sciences reasserted and nourished the rapprochement between legalism and Sufism and helped construct the figure of the Sufi *walī* as an arbiter of true knowledge and proper Islamic conduct. Consider, for example, Abū Bakr ʿAbd Allāh al-Shaybānī al-Shāfiʿī (d. 797/1394–1395), who was one of the greatest *awliyāʾ* and *ʿulamāʾ al-ṣūfiyya.* He had acquired qualification in *ʿilm* and advanced on the path *(salaka ṭarīq al-ṣūfiyya)* in his hometown of Mosul and in Damascus before settling in Jerusalem. Blending knowledge of the divine law with a knowledge of true reality *(jamaʿa bayna ʿilm al-sharīʿa wa-l-ḥaqīqa),* he became an undisputed authority in *al-ʿilm wa-l-amr.* People from all over al-Shām visited him frequently (in his house located north of the wall of al-Aqṣā) and followed his instructions.[30]

On the most general level, the jurists *(ahl al-sharīʿa)* did not intermingle with the mystics *(ahl al-ḥaqīqa)*. The *ʿulamāʾ* class as a whole at the end of the Mamluk period functioned materially and intellectually according to its peculiar characteristics even more than previously.[31] Indeed, in *al-Uns* the *ʿulamāʾ* who lived in Mamluk Jerusalem and Hebron appear as an identifiable professional category that was divided into subcategories. They were typically members of one or another legal school and holders of paid positions as qadis, witness-notaries, and official preachers in the religious establishment and as professors in the many *madrasa*s erected in Jerusalem for the teaching of the law. The typical mystic, on the other hand, was a spiritual guide who trained disciples and validated the *taṣawwuf* that was practiced by the founding masters of the path he followed. He was a charismatic figure whose influence extended far beyond his immediate circle of disciples. Still, by the end of the Mamluk period the rapprochement between the *fuqahāʾ* and the Sufi shaykhs had reached its culminating point. The rift between them, if it ever existed, was now undoubtedly bridged.

The testimonies of the relations that were forged between the great *ʿulamāʾ* and the Sufi masters indicate complementary social and spiritual functions—even a shared world vision. By the Mamluk period, mainstream Sufi masters and *fuqahāʾ* had long shared a commitment to disseminate religious learning and practice based on the Sunna and the Shariʿa. *Fuqahāʾ* shared with the Sufis ethical positions, a mode of life, and, above all, mild asceticism. Moreover, there were *fuqahāʾ*—including renowned Ḥanbalī such as Ibn Qayyim al-Jawziya and Ibn Rajab—who adopted such ideas as patience *(ṣabr)*, love of God *(maḥabba)*, and the existence of *karāmāt*, ideas that were perceived as representing the world vision of the mystics.[32] "Orthodox" Sufi masters who lived in the Mamluk period mingled with the *ʿulamāʾ* in scholarly circles, studying and teaching the same texts. Many adopted the legalist approach of being constantly concerned about the shaping of public norms, and some also adopted the attitude of puritan *ʿulamāʾ* who sought to enforce rigid Sunni orthodoxy on the Muslim population of Syria by criticizing and condemning pretenders, charlatans, and innovators of disgraceful deviations from the Shariʿa and thus from the proper public order. In their battle against those considered pseudo-Sufis, Sufi writers employed the tool of the *adab al-muridīn* treatises. While presenting a great deal of conformity and adherence to the roles of the disciple guide genre, the authors of Sufi guidebooks composed in the Mamluk period attempted to purify the Sufi-led community of components that could be judged as antinomian and reserved considerable space for such matters as diet, family life, donations, and material support by the rulers.[33]

Similar to previous generations of Sufis in Palestine who had combined the legal and mystical avenues to religious virtuosity, the overwhelming majority of the Sufis who attained mastery in the legal sciences adhered to the Shāfiʿī rite of jurisprudence, the dominant Sunni rite in the Mamluk sultanate. Several among them simultaneously held the position of *mudarris* (teacher of the legal and Islamic sciences) in a teaching mosque or a *madrasa* and of *shaykh al-ṣūfiyya* in the Sufi establishment (the *khānqāh*). Reflecting the social and intellectual assimilation of Sufis and Sufism into the mainstream of Muslim intellectual life, this combination was nowhere more clearly revealed than in the state-sponsored Salāḥiyya Shāfiʿī *madrasa* and *khānqāh,* the most prestigious educational institutions of their kind in Ayyubid and Mamluk Jerusalem. Thus, Shihāb al-Dīn Aḥmad al-Bisṭāmī al-Shāfiʿī (d. 881/1476), whom his biographer describes as a humble Sufi blessed with divine grace, was one of the *fuqahāʾ* of the Salāḥiyya Madrasa and the shaykh of the Sufis in their *khānqāh* before assuming the *mashayikha* of the Bisṭāmīyya *zāwiya* in Jerusalem, a position that he held for the rest of his life.[34] Another example is Shams al-Dīn Muḥammad al-Qazzāzī al-Shāfiʿī (d. 894/1488). He served as a *naqīb* (witness-notary) of Qadi Burhān al-Dīn b. Jamāʿa and studied the Koran with another member of the Banū Jamāʿa family and *ḥadīth* with several authorities, eventually becoming a teacher in both the Salāḥiyya Madrasa and *khānqāh.*[35]

Notwithstanding the growing combination of legalist and mystical learning, many among those designated as *awliyāʾ* seem still to have oscillated between the two streams, seeking an alternative to religious attainment and devotion in the Sufi way. Viewing the *madrasa* as the representative of formal knowledge, book learning, and worldliness, normally at an advanced age they refrained from teaching or studying in the royal institution or resigned their paid teaching positions. One of the most famous examples is the above-mentioned Ibn Arslān, the revered Qādirī mystic wayfarer *(sālik)* and Shāfiʿī legal expert who is known mostly for his treatise on *fiqh, Matn al-zubad.* A reputable *faqih* and "the leader of the Sufis attaching themselves to the strict practice of the law" *(raʾs al-ṣūfiyya al-mutasharriʿa fī waqtihi),* he trained a number of important *fuqahāʾ* who benefited from him, adhered to him, and were affected by his teaching. Relinquishing the positions of *mudarris* in al-Khāṣakiyya *mad-*

rasa and mufti that he had held for a long period and leaving his hometown of Ramla for Jerusalem, he settled in al-Ḥanthaniyya Zāwiya (behind the prayer nich of al-Aqṣā mosque) and devoted himself thereafter to advancing on the stages of the path, training others to approach God more directly and intimately at the same time. Thus, he came to merit the highly dignified appellations of *shaykh al-Islam, al-quṭb* (a spiritual pole or a Sufi leader of the highest level) and *amīn al-dīn* (guardian of religion).[36] Al-Sakhāwī describes his pious and moral conduct:

> He not only excelled in mastery of the religious sciences but surpassed any other man in the entire Bilād al-Shām and in Egypt in his asceticism, pious practices, and moral conduct. No year passed without him dwelling by the sea (of Jaffa) spending days and nights in constant prayer, both secretly and openly, preferring obscurity and passionate love of God to ostentation and refusing any worldly benefits or paid positions offered to him. He never cursed or abused anyone, never harbored feelings of hatred against anyone, and treated with gentleness anyone who tried to dispute with him.[37]

Other *awliyā'* are praised primarily for their inner struggle for personal perfection through constant *mujāhada,* the struggle against the passions and drives of the lower soul. One such was ʿUmar b. al-Ḥātim al-ʿAjlūnī, the famous *walī* of Hebron who was designated in the introductory formula of his biography as *ṣāḥib al-mukāshafāt* (unveiling, direct witnessing of God), *mujāhadāt,* and *karāmāt.* Until he knew the entire Koran by heart, he did not cut his hair or his fingernails and did not wash his body or his clothes. At the same time, he was an advocate of sober, mainstream, or "orthodox" Sufism. Moving to Halab, where he stayed for a while, he dedicated himself to *al-amr bi-l-maʿrūf wa-l-nahy ʿan al-munkar.* He studied the *Iḥyā', Qūt al-qulūb, Risāla al-qushayriyya,* and *ʿAwārif al-maʿārif*—classical Sufi textbooks that gave Sufism its orthodox tone—and insisted that no one can become a Sufi until he masters these four books.[38] Shaykh al-Ṣāliḥ Muḥammad, his contemporary in Jerusalem, was another *walī* known for his mortification of the flesh *(taqashshuf)* as well as his extreme purity in dietary matters *(al-ḥalāl al-mahd),* a prime characteristic of the extremely devout ascetic in medieval Islam.[39] He ate snakes and dung beetles, imagining the snakes as cucumbers and the dung beetles as grapes. Notables and commoners alike venerated him because *karāmāt* and *mukāshafāt* were revealed in him. He had even been seen among the pilgrims on ʿArafāt mountain and in al-Quds al-Sharīf on the morning following *ʿīd al-aḍḥā.*[40]

What distinguished the Sufi *awliyāʾ* from other virtuous figures known for their religious learning and piety were his constant striving for spiritual perfection and the public enactment of his heroic virtues. More than their *maʿrifa,* what made them *ṣūfiyya mubāraka* and placed them above all other believers was the extraordinary extent to which they practiced their outstanding asceticism, scrupulousness, self-control, and the other virtues of the purity of the heart *(ṣafāʾ al-qalb)*—humility, honesty, generosity, and altruism—with which they were imbued. Thus, through the actual manifestation of the spiritual and ethical qualities *(manāqib)* that were usually ascribed to mainstream Sufis, men and occasionally women acquired the qualifications to be deemed close to sacred reality.

The following two stories convey the glorified image of the *walī* as constructed retrospectively by the hagiographer and shed light on the identification of a genuine *walī Allāh* by the local community of believers. The first story concerns Shihāb al-Dīn Abū l-ʿAbbās Aḥmad. Mujīr al-Dīn describes him as pious warrior. He attended the conquest of Jerusalem (by the Ayyubids, most probably in 1187), astride his ox:

> The ascetic worshiper, al-Shaykh Shihāb al-Dīn . . . *al-zāhid, al-ṣāliḥ,* was known by the surname of Abū Thawr. This is because he arrived in al-Bayt al-Muqaddas while riding his ox. On the 25th of Rajab of the year 594, al-Malik al-ʿAzīz Abū l-Fatḥ ʿUthmān b. al-Malik Ṣalāḥ al-Dīn instituted as *waqf* for him a village in the vicinity of the Gate of Hebron (Bāb al-Khalīl, one of the nine gates of Jerusalem and today known as Jaffa Gate). This

> is a small village, and in it is a cloister built during the Byzantine (al-Rūm) period. Previously called Dayr Mārqūs, it is known now as Dayr Abū Thawr. . . . When he died, he was buried in this village, and his burial place *(turba)* there is a well-known pilgrimage site. His descendants have lived there to this day.
>
> It is related that whenever he needed food, he used to write down his specific need and then place the paper around the ox's neck and send the ox to al-Quds. Roaming the city's streets, the ox would finally reach a seller who would provide the food requested. And this is one of his many *karāmāt*.[41]

The second story is contained in the biography of al-Shaykh Ibrāhīm al-Hudma (d. 730/1328–1329), of Kurdish origin, who came to be one of the most revered *awliyā'* of Hebron:

> Coming to al-Shām from the east, he chose some land between al-Quds and al-Khalīl to settle in, toiling and cultivating it. He became the object of *ziyāra* [as] *karāmāt* were revealed in him. Toward the end of his life (he reached one hundred years), he married and was blessed with children who all came to be known as virtuous worshipers. It is related that ten loaves of bread were bought for him daily in the market of Sayyidinā al-Khalīl. . . . Preserved from the beginning of each week to its end, crumbled and seasoned, on the last day the bread was put in vessels and brought to his dwelling. He used to eat all of it at once, abstaining from any nourishment during the rest of the week.[42]

The dramatic, epic terms in which the *walī's* way of life and mode of conduct are presented yield an ideal figure—a model of virtue who is placed above all other believers. This presentation implies a certain contradiction. To earn the idealization that validates his closeness to God, the *walī,* like any other holy man, must be an elevated "other." On the other hand, to become both the believers' example of conduct to be followed and their intercessor before God, he cannot be an isolated ascetic who is totally separated from his natural and social environment. In common with the Christian holy man, his austerity has to do more with his own body and spirit than with separating himself from others.[43] Furthermore, the *walī* is a *ṣāliḥ,* a virtuous worshiper who is constantly enacting his spiritual and moral qualities for the welfare *(maṣlaḥa)* of mankind.[44] In similar vein, the incredible stories about the *walī*'s miracles, while attesting his closeness to God, are proof of his attention to the needs of his fellow believers. His miraculous deeds are entrenched in the natural and social environment as he manipulates divine power to fulfill his disciples' spiritual and material needs. Thus did compilers of sacred biographies justify the *walī*'s supernatural powers and fostered an ideal-type Muslim friend of God.[45]

On the more concrete historical plane, the universal human quest for a charismatic benefactor—a channel to God—must have acquired particular significance in the Islamic middle periods following the breakdown of the ʿAbbasid state and the rise to power of alien regimes of military overlords (Seljuks, Ayyubids, Mamluks, and Mongols). In the absence of stable institutions that were capable of providing protection, social identity, and coherence, and with legal scholars of the *madhhab*s at courts and *madrasa*s who were increasingly involved in the official sphere, Muslims of all social categories turned to those whom they recognized as *awliyā'* for spiritual guidance or to plead their case before God. Apparently, many believers who lived in the later middle period experienced encounters with the figure of the *walī Allāh* (whether living or dead), his heroic virtues, and his charisma and acknowledged his spiritual authority over his companions and followers. The *walī* would transmit guidance and knowledge, foster piety, cure diseases, distribute charity, and avert calamities, thereby assuming a variety of religious and social roles.[46] His prominence in the society was due to his roles both as a beneficial patron and as a ground-level negotiator of a working compromise (that was tinted with Sufi pietism) between normative religious beliefs and practices and the widespread veneration of saintly figures who were able to act as intercessors before God.

It is also important to remember that the *walī* was more than a prototype, a model of virtue, or one in a spiritual chain *(silsila)* of charismatic figures. The accounts of his ascetic habits and the actual practices of his heroic virtues provide a sense of his personality and reveal the various dimensions in which he acted. Being orthodox, he might have held the traditional public offices of an *ʿālim* such as mufti or a teacher of the Islamic sciences (the example of Ibn Arslān comes to mind); being a Sufi, he was known for his self-control, austerity, and altruism; and being charismatic, he was venerated for his supernatural powers.

The maxim of service to others, even at the expense of his own self *(īthār),* was thus extended beyond the Sufi guide's small group of close disciples and other intimates to include a wider circle of local followers. The virtuous and charismatic benefactor is exemplified in Abū l-ʿAwn Muḥammad al-Jaljūlī, the close disciple of Ibn Arslān and his successor as leader of the Palestinian Qādirī branch (figure 3.2). Al-Ghazzī, author of *al-Kawākib al-sāʾira*—a biographical compilation with a strong emphasis on the manifestations of sanctity and the spiritual virtues of the biographees (composed in the seventeenth-century)[47]—designates al-Jaljūlī as *al-imām al-ʿālim, al-ʿāmil, al-khāshiʿ* (humble), *al-nāsik* (ascetic) *walī Allāh* who "knows" God. Moreover, he was deserving of the appellation of *al-quṭb al-rabānī* (the supreme pole) and *al-ghauth al-faradānī* (unique "help"—that is, the highest spiritual guide of the faithful), his *aḥwāl* having been manifested and his numerous *karāmāt* made visible. It was related that God made him visible in the dark century and that his splendorous appearance (as a *walī*) was due to his many sound mystical revelations *(kashf)* as well as to his training *(tarbiyya)* of the Sufis *(fuqarāʾ)* and his benefiting the people in general *(al-nās).* The biographer moves on to describe the role of al-Jaljūlī as a charismatic benefactor: he bestowed gracious benefits on those seeking to be near to him and was hospitable to all fellow believers who approached him to receive his blessing and intercession *(shafāʿa)* on their behalf. People flocked to his doorstep with gifts to make oaths and receive his blessing. He was the intercessor of the oppressed before kings and the princes, and he dispensed as charity all the gifts he received from royalty, never taking or even wishing to take anything for himself.[48]

Figure 3.2. A portion of the tombstone of Abū l-ʿAwn Muḥammad al-Jaljūlī in Ramla. The inscription, dating from 1504, tells of the Muslim scholar Abū l-ʿAwn, "the head of the Qādiriyya on the borders of Palestine and the Muslim kingdom." (Source: Mayer L.A. Finkerfeld and J. Hirschberg, *Some Religious Buildings in the State of Israel.* [Jerusalem, 1950, p. 25]).

By the end of the Mamluk period, a gallery of charismatic figures had emerged in Palestinian cities and their environs who corresponded to the spiritual needs and social concerns of different audiences and thereby became the focus of their veneration. By then, the moderate, ethical, and activist Sufi tradition that evolved in Palestine had long been entrenched in the fabric of social and communal life, and many mainstream Sufis had been recognized both as arbiters of *al-ʿilm* and *al-ʿamal* (alongside other men of profound religious learning) and as charismatic figures, channels to God.

The religious and social practices, sites, and spaces that grew up around transmission of the knowledge and guidance of the Sufi *walī* and the bestowal of his divine grace led to the expansion of a Sufi-inspired local following of disciples, companions, and devotees. Orbiting around him during his lifetime, these followers continued and expanded around his tomb.

AUTHORITY AND FOLLOWING

The accounts of the lives and teachings of the *awliyā'* do not indicate the existence of any organized community of Sufis around a charismatic shaykh in terms of initiation, confirmation of status by one specific individual, or rules that demand obedience to a definitive superior. Similarly, receiving the Sufi cloak (the *khirqa*) does not seem to signify a unique affiliation to one particular master and even less to a fraternity but is one of many spiritual influences.[49] Nor do the accounts describe the *ṭarīqa* as an institutional social organization. Rather, people are described as aspirants and followers of a certain *walī* who practices his spiritual method *(ṭarīqa)* through the transmission of ritual guidance, knowledge, and blessing and passes on his morals *(akhlāq)* at the same time.

The term *shaykhuna,* which appears repeatedly in the sources, further attests to the highly individual character of affiliation and association. Indeed, as argued persuasively by Denis Gril and others, the emergence of circles of devotees around a shaykh of recognized charismatic authority and his tomb came to be the prime manifestation of the consolidation of Sufism as a social phenomenon during the middle periods.[50] With many gathering around those whom they believed to have possessed divine grace, connection with Sufism as a frame for devotional and communal life was often through the "cult of saints," which from the twelfth century became central to the religious experience and life of individuals and the community throughout the Muslim world.

The available sources use the expression *ahl al-ṭarīqa* or *ahl al-ṭarīq* to designate the set of people who centered around a certain Sufi *walī* of well-established spiritual authority. Their accounts suggest the existence of at least two circles around him. A small inner group consisted of his committed disciples (the *aṣḥāb* or *murīdūn* or *talāmīdh*) surrounded by companions, who are the "lovers"-supporters of the shaykh and his congregation. A wider circle consisted of occasional visitors who visited the shaykh's lodge or tomb to seek his blessing or simply to be close to him. For all its diffusive affiliations and informal, fluid social networks, the *ahl al-ṭarīqa,* during the later middle period, developed into the prime religiously based and led association in the public sphere of Islamic societies. Moreover, this lack of formal observances and binding links or commitments is precisely what enabled Sufism to expand its horizons.

The accounts about the two famous Qādirī shaykhs, Ibn Arslān and his disciple and successor al-Jaljūlī, provide a glimpse of the diverse circles that gathered around a charismatic Sufi shaykh. Believers from various Muslim countries set out on journeys to visit Ibn Arslān, and the number of *talāmīdh* (disciples) and followers *(atabāʾ)* around him wherever he turned grew constantly. He educated a group *(jamāʿa)* of disciples, advancing each aspirant on the path in accordance with his state of spiritual advancement regardless of his rank *(wa-shaghala kullān fīmā yarā ḥālahu yalīqu bihi fī l-najāba wa-ʿadamihā)* and bestowed his *baraka* on the people *(al-nās)*. He then dressed a group of disciples from al-Shām and Egypt in his *khirqa* and bestowed his *baraka* on them.[51] When a certain *faqih* paid a visit to al-Jaljūlī in his *zāwiya* (in Ramla), he found among his group *(jamāʿa)* "the poor and the affluent, the righteous and the corrupt [literally, unruly] alike."[52] The *faqih* consider the presence of the latter inappropriate since, in his view, only the righteous deserve to be included in a shaykh's companionship *(ṣuḥbat al-shaykh)*. Reading the *faqih*'s thought, the shaykh referred to the model of the revered ʿAbd al-Qādir al-Jilānī, whose *jamāʿa* always included both the righteous and evildoers: the first became more zealous, while in the case of the evildoers, "God turned them from their sins through companionship with him *(ṣuḥbatihi).*"[53]

Although no details are supplied about the content of the renowned Palestinian Qādirī shaykhs' teachings and method of instruction, the accounts of their activities, as with other *awliyā'*, clearly demonstrate that their transmission of knowledge and guidance did not center on training in the secrets of Sufism. Nor was it confined to a few select disciples and intimates. Rather, the typical *walī* would teach society the fundamentals of its religion, foster piety that revolved around the Koran and the Sunna, and propagate his moral precepts and practices among his fellow believers. This dissemination of knowledge and guidance took a variety of forms. Most evident was public recital of the prophetic traditions: the many instances of large crowds attending such recitals in al-Aqṣā mosque during the period under consideration come to mind. Even shaykhs who were engaged in a struggle for their own spiritual perfection interacted with the general populace *(al-nās)*, leading them in prayer or relating prophetic traditions to them. Consider, for example, Shaykh Shams al-Dīn Abū ʿAbd Allāh Muḥammad al-Quramī (d. 788/1386), who moved to Jerusalem from Damascus, where he continued to lead a life of constant worship, withdrawal from worldly affairs *(inqiṭā')*, *dhikr,* fasting, prayer, and, above all, Koran recital. It was related that he used to read the entire Koran three times daily and that he surpassed all other pious worshipers in the performance of the Islamic ordinances. As his fame spread due his pietistic and ascetic practices, many sought his transmission of *ḥadīth.* At first, he declined, preferring the practice of spiritual retreat to the leading of public worship. However, toward the end of his life he took the opportunity of his attendance at al-Aqṣā for the Friday congregational prayer to recite the sayings of the Prophet to a large crowd.[54] Opening the *dhikr* ritual sessions to lay believers and the bestowal of *baraka* were also significant modes through which the

Sufi shaykh disseminated his teachings. Nevertheless, social integration and interaction remained the most important means of all.

The following stories illustrate my central proposition that the Sufi shaykh's concurrently diffused Sufism in the form of ethical community-oriented tradition and extended the horizons of his following. The first tale tells of a disciple of Ibn Arslān who appealed for his help against acts of injustice inflicted by the Mamluk district chief *(kāshif)* of Ramla. The governor had refused to deal with the case unless Ibn Arslān's supernatural powers were manifested in the palm trees standing in front of him. At that moment, the trees were uprooted by a sudden storm. Accompanied by his entourage, the governor then turned to Ibn Arslān in repentance. Attributing the miraculous deed to God alone, Ibn Arslān demanded that they should turn to him and renew their religious belief.[55] Our sources do not tell us exactly what the shaykh required from the ruler who now sought his spiritual guidance. Was it a narrow commitment to adherence to the tenets of just rule as laid down in the Shariʿa and the Sunna or a general commitment to Islam? The moral intent of the episode and its concluding requirement is nevertheless evident. Al-Jaljūlī—whose following included several distinguished *ʿulamāʾ* as well as people from the fringes of society, even lawbreakers—took under his protection Qāsim b. Zanlal, a soldier and one of the "valiant and ill-tempered people." To rescue a woman, he had killed a Mamluk officer in the service of the governor of Aleppo who was about to violate her. Fleeing along the coast, Qāsim arrived in Jaljuliyya and sought the shaykh's help. The shaykh invoked God in his favor. He rebuked Qāsim for the killing (about which he knew, due to his special powers) but interceded for him with the authorities and saved him from punishment: "Allāh shielded him from the persecutors through the *baraka* of the shaykh." Qāsim's encounter with the shaykh led to his repentance and transformation. Thereafter, he refrained from the ways of the villainous and ill-tempered. The shaykh assigned to him the job of water carrier, and Qāsim persisted in the work and in pursuing the state *(ṭaur)* of the *fuqarā'* until he became a renowned figure.[56]

These stories afford a further glimpse of the dynamic of growth of the *walī*'s following. The more that his extraordinary virtues were publicly manifested, the more his fellow believers turned to him. The more that he met their spiritual and nonreligious needs by using his divine powers, the greater his following and authority as a charismatic guide became. A select few disciples and colleagues sought his spiritual advice in the hope of achieving an elevated mystical state. Far more people turned to him for instruction in the essentials of their religion, for guidelines in correct Islamic behavior, and for a word of blessing. Shared by all local believers, veneration of the Sufi friend of God cut across social boundaries and blurred the distinctions between the so-called popular and elitist varieties of religion. In view of the shaykh's growing local following, members of the cities' ruling and religious institutions joined in, fitting themselves into the existing practices that were enacted by others. The participation of a Mamluk governor in the spiritual life of the local community did not transform him into a native member of society, but it did provide him with an entry into the public sphere. At the same time, because worship of the Sufi *walī* was open to the active participation of the political authorities, the barriers between the official and public spheres became at least bridgeable if not obliterated.[57]

Disciples and intimates expressed their admiration and gratitude to the charismatic shaykh by clinging to him wherever he settled or traveled, by relating and recording stories about his life and extraordinary traits, or by commemorating his memory and tending his grave.[58] Commoners supplied the ascetic *walī* with the food that was necessary for his subsistence (for example, Ibrāhīm al-Hudma), while rulers established charitable endowments for the construction of the *walī* lodge and for guaranteeing a permanent supply of food to his *zāwiya*.[59] They even set up revenues of a village as *waqf* for his benefit. Such tokens of gratitude and affection on the part of the rulers became especially apparent when the *awliyāʾ* stood by them, stirring the jihad fervor among their troops. Abū Thawr participated in the conquest of Jerusalem by the Ayyubids. Some time later, Saladin's son instituted as *waqf* for him a village near Bāb al-Khalīl. ʿAlī al-Bakkāʾ is one of three indigent Sufi shaykhs who were named as being present at the siege of the fortified city of Arsuf by Baybars (in 1265). He was among a large crowd of religious figures, many of them Sufis of various types, who backed the Sultan during the fight against the Franks.[60] Baybars's provincial military governor constructed a *zāwiya* for the shaykh, which was later enlarged by other members of the ruling elite until it grew into a whole complex (the second citation in the epigraph to this chapter). Commonplace throughout Bilād al-Shām during the Mamluk period, this assistance in the form of patronage intensified the integration of the ruling authorities into the public sphere and tightened the bond of shared beliefs and practices between the official sphere and the community. While experiencing their encounters with the Sufi *walī* in a variety of ways, believers of all social classes shared the belief in his ability to manipulate divine forces for their cause, which shaped his image as a charismatic figure. Whether seeking spiritual guidance or blessing or taking part in the growing practices surrounding local holy men, they all flocked around whomever they believed to be their "channel to God," recognizing his charismatic spiritual authority.[61]

Muḥammad al-Quramī, mentioned above as venerated by the people due to his pietistic and ascetic practices, was one of the *awliyāʾ* designated as the spiritual poles *(aqṭāb)* of their generation. It is related that the *awliyāʾ* turned to him and that kings flocked to his doorstep.[62] Another, more concrete example of the *walī*'s prominence in society is contained in the biography of Shaykh Muḥammad b. ʿAbd Allāh (d. 844/1440–1441), who arrived in Jerusalem and devoted himself to worship in al-Aqṣā. He made many pilgrimages to Mecca on foot, and many *karāmāt* and *mukāshafāt* were attributed to him. So highly regarded was he by the *'ulamā'* of Jerusalem that they entrusted to him the keys of the Dome of the Rock. At the same, he is cited as an example of a *walī* who had complete authority *(ṣatwa)* over the Sufis in the Ṣalāḥiyya *khānqāh*.[63] Abū l-'Awn al-Jaljūlī's prerogatives and influence in the public sphere were no less impressive. He supervised the annual pilgrimages in the district of Ramla and the religious endowments of at least one tomb *(mashhad)* standing there. This was the tomb of 'Ali b. 'Alīm (Mashhad Sīdnā 'Alī) south of Arsuf.[64] On some occasions, his authority might have transformed into temporal power. We are told that al-Jaljūlī moved freely, acting without restriction in the presence of the kings of Syria and Egypt, who would obey his directions. Moreover, he meddled in the affairs of the authorities, making persecutors obey his words through the mere power of his mind and spirit *(khāṭir)*. It was out of fear of this supernatural power that the governor of Damascus warned his counterpart in Aleppo, advising him to accept the intercession of the shaykh for Qāsim, the soldier he was shielding.[65]

With the passage of time, renowned Sufi *awliyā'* established roots in Palestinian cities and their environs. Consequently, during the Mamluk period, Sufi-inspired communities, while still augmented by newcomers, came to be dominated by a number of local shaykhs, who passed on their positions as spiritual authorities to their closest disciples or to their sons and other relatives. One of the most famous was al-Sayyid Badr al-Dīn Muḥammad (d. 650/1253), a member of one of the families of Sufis, scholars, and *ashrāf* by the name of Abū l-Wafā' (or the Wafā'iyya). The origins of his family are to be found in twelfth-century Iraq, where the famous *walī* Abū l-Wafā' Tāj al-'Ārifīn (d. 561/1166) had been a teacher of 'Abd al-Qādir al-Jilānī.[66] Badr al-Dīn left Iraq for Palestine, probably during the short time of renewed Crusader dominance over Jerusalem (1229–1244), and settled in a place called Dayr al-Shaykh, according to Mujīr al-Dīn, a small village in Wādī al-Nusūr, west of al-Quds al-Sharīf.

Mujīr al-Dīn, whose *al-Uns* is the sole textual source on the Abū l-Wafā' family in Jerusalem and its hinterland, depicts Badr al-Dīn as a *quṭb* of great renown: "All the *awliyā'* of his generation obeyed him, and the high and low *(al-khāṣṣ wa-l-'āmm)* never ceased congregating around him."[67] His reputation for virtue and closeness to God attracted many disciples who came to live near him and his family in the village of Dayr al-Shaykh. He was buried in his *zāwiya,* and his burial place became a site for *ziyāra. Awliyā'* and common people, as well as animals, we are told, used to pay him tribute.[68] Badr al-Dīn had eight sons. The eldest, al-Sayyid Muḥammad (d. 663/1264–1265), is described as one of those who attained elevated mystical states *(aḥwāl)* and spiritual perfection through constant struggle against the passions and the drives of the lower soul *(mujāhadāt)* and firm intention *('azm)* in worship. He guided a great number of people, and miraculous states were revealed in him.[69] Later, his son 'Abd al-Ḥāfiẓ (d. 696/1296–1297) is said to have guided a group and eventually to have become the leader of the people of this spiritual path in his lifetime *(intahat ilāyhi ri'āsat ahl hadhihi al-ṭarīqa fī zamānihi).*[70] However, as the village in Wādī al-Nusūr became too small to accommodate all al-Sayyid Badr al-Dīn's descendants, he gave up his revenues from his land for their benefit and moved to a village named Shafarāt on the outskirts of Jerusalem, later named by him Sharafāt, after the *ashrāf,* members of his family who settled and established roots there.[71] It was in this village that Dāwūd, the son of 'Abd al-Ḥāfiẓ (d. 701/1301), erected a *zāwiya* and a tomb where his descendants, all described as virtuous and charismatic figures, were buried. The most famous of them were al-Sayyid 'Alī and al-Sayyid Muḥammad al-Bahā', who were considered the "pillars" of the Holy Land and its surroundings *(wa-kānā a'mida al-arḍ al-muqaddasa wa-mā ḥawlahā).* It is related that notables and commoners frequented their residence and that a huge crowd sought their *baraka.* In their times, Manjak al-Sayfī—who, according to Mujīr al-Dīn, was then the governor of al-

Shām[72]—intended to institute the entire village of Sharafāt as *waqf* for them. Refusing at first to accept this pious endowment, ʿAlī eventually changed his mind so that the land might be available to the shepherds and cultivators.[73]

The activities and social ascent of members of the Abū l-Wafāʾ family continued with Tāj al-Dīn Muḥammad (the son of ʿAlī; d. 801/1401). Having made the final move to Jerusalem, he brought what was to become known as the "*zāwiya* of the Wafāʾiyya," across from the western edge of the Ḥaram enclosure.[74] His descendents are designated "the shaykhs of the Wafāʾiyya *ṭarīqa* in Jerusalem." His son Taqī al-Dīn Abū Bakr (d. 859/1454) was venerated by the people as the "healer of hearts" and assumed the leadership of the Sufis *(fuqarāʾ)* in Jerusalem. He was the first member of the family to pass on his authority to his son by dressing him in the *khirqa* of the Wafāʾiyya—which was an external sign of the permission that was granted to him to train his own disciples in the spiritual path—and was the first to whom Mujīr Dīn gives the *nisba* al-Ḥusaynī (after Ḥusayn b. ʿAlī).[75] Thereafter, the Ḥusaynīs came to be one of the leading families of the city in the Mamluk and Ottoman periods, and they continue to be such to the present day.

The stories about Badr al-Dīn, his descendants, and followers, notwithstanding their obvious fictional elements and the missing parts of the puzzle, contain major characteristics of other Sufi shaykhs of recognized virtue who lived in Palestine during the Mamluk period. These men—sometimes settled but more frequently migrants—struck roots in their places of residence, turned their *zāwiya* homes into a focal point of devotional life, and along the way won over both the hearts of the local population and the patronage of the Mamluk authorities. It was through their activities and efforts that self-perpetuating locally embedded Sufi-inspired communities, tied together by shared veneration and loyalty to "their" shaykh, were formed and that Islam was further imprinted on the human and physical environment.

LODGE AND TOMB

During the Mamluk period, the *zāwiya* became the principal institutionalized expression of Sufism and the cradle of a spiritual family that could survive and thrive after his death.[76] Originating as small cells or spaces in large mosques, many of the *zāwiya*s in Mamluk Jerusalem and Hebron that were listed in *al-Uns* developed into independent buildings that served as a residence for their shaykh and a focal point of his activities. There the master cultivated his followers—among them *'ulamā'*, members of the ruling elite, and commoners—or simply bestowed his *baraka* on them. The term *shaykh* connoted Sufi master as well as teacher of the Islamic religious and legal sciences, and the shaykhs of the *zāwiya*s sometimes taught *ḥadīth*, jurisprudence, and other subjects in those very institutions or in *madrasa*s.[77]

During the Mamluk period, the *zāwiya* often grew into a whole complex, including a tomb, a dome (or several domes) that signified the sanctity of the complex, a courtyard, an entrance gate, a prayer hall, and a peripheral wall. The complexes that first developed in the Mamluk period incorporated the basic functional and symbolic plan that was characteristic of dozens of other local shrines and sanctuaries in the landscape of Palestine.[78] Consider, for instance, the growth of the *zāwiya* compound of al-Shaykh 'Alī al-Bakkā', whom Mujīr al-Dīn designates as "*ṣāḥib al-zāwiya bi-madīnat sayyidinā al-Khalīl*". In 668/1269, a Mamluk provincial military governor *(amīr)* constructed the *zāwiya* in honor of this ascetic *walī*, and several years later, another *amīr* erected a dome over his grave. Finally (in 720/1320), the *nā'ib* of al-Malik al-Nāṣir b. Qalāwūn added an entrance gate and a minaret to the building (see the second citation in the epigraph to this chapter).

The *zāwiya*-tomb compound of the Abū l-Wafā' family is perhaps the most illustrative example of the compound development (figure 3.3). The first *zāwiya* attributed to the family was probably built in Dayr al-Shaykh while Badr al-Dīn, head of the local branch of the family, was still alive. A detailed survey of

Figure 3.3. The *zāwiya* in Dayr al-Shaykh

the site by Andrew Petersen (in 1994) applies the source material and methodology of historical geography to reconstruct a picture of the site. The complex, which developed over several hundred years and belongs to the category of large shrines with regional significance, has four main parts—a courtyard, a prayer hall, a shrine or *maqām* (the grave itself), and a crypt. The exact sequence of construction is problematic. Still, the earliest building seems to have included the domed *maqām* (with a vaulted extension or *iwān* to the rear), the entrance to the crypt, and a hall roofed with a pointed barrel unit that may have been a doorway to the vault at the back of the *maqām* (leading nowadays to the prayer hall through an arched opening).[79] The next complex that is attributed to the family is in the village of Sharafāt. Surrounded by a wall, it contains a prayer hall, a tomb, and a number of rooms that might have served as cells for the people of the *zāwiya*. Over the years, the site has undergone construction. What remains of the original complex consists of the domed cell that is believed to be the tomb of ʿAbd al-Ḥāfiẓ and the prayer hall, which today is a mosque.[80] On the south side of Ṭarīq Bāb al-Nāẓir, adjacent to the gate itself and bounded by the wall of the Ḥaram al-Sharīf, stands to this day the Wafāʾiyya *zāwiya*, including a hall, a courtyard, and three floors, with a set of rooms on both the first and second floors. Mujīr al-Dīn provides us with a description of the building that provides an idea of the various building periods:

> *Al-zāwiya* al-Wafāʾiyya—next to Bāb al-Nāẓir, and above it is a house, which forms part of the complex and was known as the house of the shaykh Shihāb al-Dīn b. al-Hāʾim, and later as the house of the Abū l-Wafāʾ family because they took up residence their. Formerly, it was known as the house of Muʿāwiyya.[81]

A thorough survey of Mamluk architecture in Jerusalem by Michael Hamilton Burgoyne shows that the early stages of the Wafāʾiyya *zāwiya*'s construction predate the Mamluk period, being presumably Ayyubid. During the Mamluk period, the *zāwiya* consisted of two floors with a house above; in Ottoman times, a third floor was added. Bordering the Ḥaram, the *zāwiya* compound was located in one of the most prestigious areas of Jerusalem. Its close proximity to the Manjakiyya *madrasa* that was founded by al-Amīr Manjak and to other Mamluk cultural foundations may be interpreted as another sign of the close relations forged between members of the Abū l-Wafā' family and the ruling authorities, their high standing in society, and their favored positions as candidates for patronage through *waqf*.[82]

It was the close association of the *zāwiya* with the first *walī* of great renown buried in its complex that turned it into a sanctuary. Stories about miraculous events relating to the foundation of the complex reinforced its sacredness. This last point is nowhere more clearly illustrated than in the story about the *zāwiya* in the village of Sharafāt preserved in *al-Uns:*

> Dāwūd (the son of ʿAbd al-Ḥāfiẓ) was one of the *awliyā'* of extraordinary traits *(aṣḥāb al-karāmāt)*. He lived in the village of Sharafāt (where his father settled), which was inhabited by a few Christians but not by any Muslims apart from him, his family and his followers. He was totally absorbed in worship, and God eventually revealed him as a miracle worker. The reason for this was that the Christian villagers used to squeeze the grapes and sell their wine to Muslim sinners. Profoundly disturbed by this deed, Dāwūd turned to almighty God. And from that time onward, whenever the grapes were squeezed, the wine was turned into vinegar or—as some other people relate—to water. The Christians called him a "magician" *(sāḥir)* and abandoned [the lands]. Having heard about the district tax collector's concern (caused by the loss of revenues), Dāwūd leased the village's lands from him. He then erected a *zāwiya* and a domed shrine there, where he and all of his descendants were buried. One day, a bird was seen flying at great speed toward the *zāwiya*, thereby causing the collapse of the building. On hearing from the builder about the occurrence, Dāwūd ordered the rebuilding of the *zāwiya*. . . . When the task had been completed and the bird again approached the building, Dāwūd pointed to it, and at that moment, the bird dropped dead behind the *zāwiya*. When brought before him by his disciples at

> the lodge, it turned out to be a man of perfect creation. . . . Dāwūd covered him in shrouds, prayed for him, and buried him in the shrine. . . . He said, "This is my cousin, Aḥmad b. al-Ṭayr, a man of the noblest intentions of all. God wished him to be the first to be buried in this shrine."[83]

Apart from the Wafā'iyya, two other dominant local branches of spiritual paths in Mamluk Jerusalem—the Bisṭāmiyya and the Qalandariyya—had *zāwiya*s that were said to have been erected by their shaykhs or directly attributed to them. That of the Bisṭāmiyya (located in the northeastern part of the city) figures prominently in our sources. As noted above, the first shaykh or *ṣāḥib* of the Bisṭāmiyya *zāwiya* in Jerusalem was 'Abd Allāh al-Asadābādī al-Bisṭāmī, successor of al-Shaykh 'Alī al-Ṣafī al-Bisṭāmī, who was one of the most famous Sufi guides and miracle workers of his time. With successive generations of adherents to his *ṭarīqa* buried by al-Ṣafī's side, his tomb became the nucleus of the Bistāmiyya plot *(ḥawsh)* located in the great al-Māmilā cemetery west of the city. The dervish Qalandars, who had their origins in Central Asia and spread to Egypt and Syria-Palestine during the first half of the thirteenth century, converted an old church known as Dayr al-Ahmar in the middle of al-Māmilā cemetery into their *zāwiya.* By dwelling in a cemetery area, the Jerusalem Qalandars manifested the dervish who strove for poverty *(faqr).* Thereafter, a tomb complex grew up around the *zāwiya,* as an extension of it. In 794/1391–1392, the first mausoleum in this complex was built for the founder of the *zāwiya,* Shaykh Ibrāhīm al-Qalandarī, by a woman admirer named Tonsuq. However, unsupported by *waqf,* the Qalandarī *zāwiya* did not survive long.[84]

At the close of the Mamluk period, the Palestinian cities (notably Jerusalem and Hebron) and their hinterland were dotted with Sufi lodges and saintly tombs, as evidenced in pilgrimage guides and travelers' accounts. Successive generations of families and individual tombs were built side by side in *zāwiya*s or in the cemetery areas outside the gates of Jerusalem, clustering around a *walī* whose tomb had become an important focus of pilgrimage. Of the tombs of Ibn Arslān and ʿAbd Allāh al-Qurashī, for instance, lying side by side in al-Māmilā cemetery, Mujīr al-Dīn declared: "Whoever invokes God's name while standing between the graves of Ibn Arslān and al-Qurashī, God will grant all his wishes."[85]

Tombs were also constructed in stages, parallel to the spread of the belief in the *baraka* of the holy men buried there and their appropriation by a prominent shaykh and his community of followers, "the people of his path." Consider al-Jaljūlī's burial place in Ramla. Sometime during the Ottoman period, it developed into a compound as a great building was erected on the top of and around his grave that became a pilgrimage site where his blessings might be received.[86] The same al-Jaljūlī was the first to renovate and enlarge the tomb of ʿAlī b. ʿUlaym (widely known as Sīdnā ʿAlī) that was under his supervision. Mujīr al-Dīn tells: "He reconstructed the *mashhad,* restored it, organized the pilgrimages, and turned the place into a beautiful site. He covered the holy tomb with marble in the year AH 886; previously there had been a wooden tomb. He dug a well in the courtyard of the mosque until he reached the spring water. Thereafter, he built, atop the *iwān* (sitting room), a tower for the purpose of the holy war, for the sake of Allāh, may he be glorified. . . . [The tower] was completed after the year AH 890."[87] During the Ottoman period, the rooms on the second floor and the inscription now located opposite the *miḥrāb* were added.[88]

Sharing the belief that the invocation of God's name at a *walī*'s tomb is answered and his *baraka* granted, simply by touching the stones placed on the grave, different segments of society played a role in the proliferation of saintly tombs. They would initiate the construction and renovation of tombs or would attribute existing tombs to a renowned *walī* whose place of burial was unknown. An illustrative story relates to a shrine in Māmilā cemetery that the people *(al-nās)* imagined was the grave of al-Wāsiṭī, a revered *walī* to whom they ascribed many

Figure 3.4. Mashhad Sīdnā ʿAlī south of Arsuf-Apollonia

miraculous deeds. Though a well-known tomb, the object of *ziyāra,* and one on which great stones were placed, no one knew who was buried there, since no name was inscribed on the tombstone. On one occasion, Mujīr al-Dīn relates, several people, probably desiring that the shaykh's *baraka* be transferred to them through the stones, removed the stones from the grave and placed them somewhere else. Yet early the next morning, they found that the stones had returned to their former place, "and this is one of al-Wāsiṭī's numerous *karamat.*"[89]

As complexes of Sufi lodges and saintly tombs proliferated, they turned into public space and the focus of rituals that were common to the whole of the entire local community. Like other buildings that were founded by endowments, the contribution of these compounds to the shaping of an Islamic space and to al-

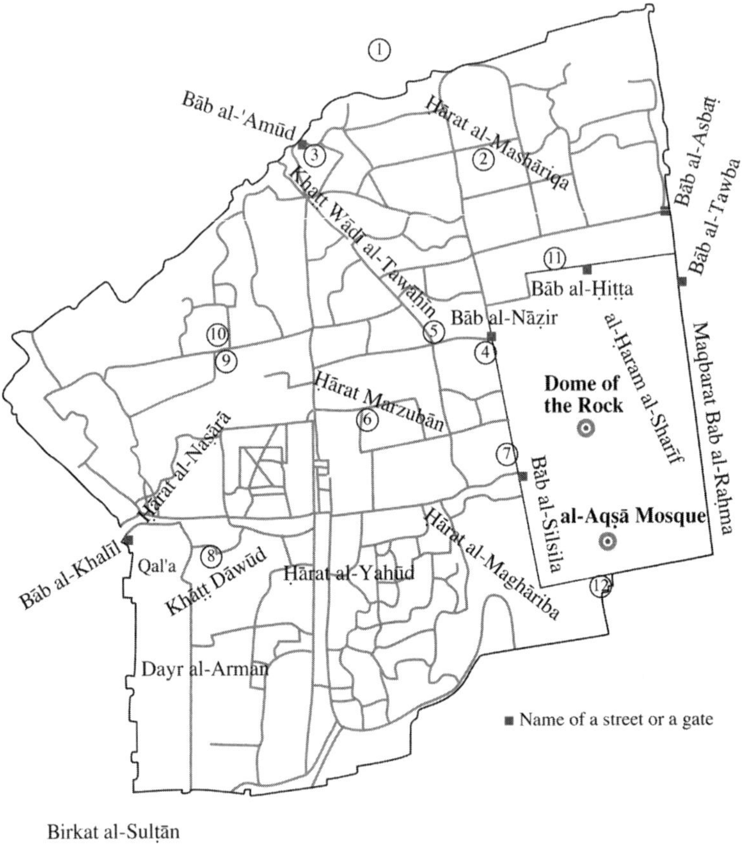

1. al-Zāwiya al-Aduhamiyya
2. al-Zāwiya al-Bisṭāmiyya
3. al-Zāwiya al-Lu'lu'iyya
4. al-Zāwiya al-Wafā'iyya
5. al-Zāwiya al-Muḥamadiyya
6. Zāwiyat al-Shaykh Muḥammad al-Quramī
7. al-Madrasa al-Ashrafiyya (designed for both Sufis and lawyers)
8. Zāwiyat al-Shaykh Ya'qūb al-Ajamī
9. al-Khānqāh al-Ṣalāhiyya
10. al-Zāwiya al-Ḥamārā'
11. al-Khānqāh al-Dawādāriyya
12. al-Zāwiya al-Ḥanthaniyya

Figure 3.5. Map of Sufi establishments in Mamluk Jerusalem

tering the layout of cities can hardly be overestimated (figure 3.5). The construction of mosques, *madrasas*, and *zāwiyas* in cities and towns did not occur in isolation but often served as a stimulus for further building.[90] But it was in the countryside of medieval Palestine that the spread of *zāwiya* had a profound effect. Entire villages sprang up from and around the *zāwiya* compound, and a new and transformed cultural landscape was created. Changes in the names of sites or villages and the frequent occurrence of the word *dayr* (monastery) indicate the conversion of a formerly Christian site or area into a Muslim one.[91] The most visible changes of this kind were initiated by members of the Abū l-Wafā'. Their role as agents of the Islamization of the cultural landscape around Jerusalem is nowhere more clearly revealed than in the development of the villages of Dayr al-Shaykh and Sharafāt.[92] This development was not peculiar to rural areas in medieval Palestine. The modes of operation of the Abū l-Wafā' shaykhs in the Jerusalem area were in many ways similar to the activities of Sufis saints who played a crucial role in the Islamization of Anatolia.[93] Like the "bearers" of Islam in Anatolia, Badr al-Badr al-Dīn and his descendants arrived at an area that was under Islamic rule, settled in the heart of Christian villages, built lodges, enjoyed the patronage of the rulers, and played a crucial role in the Islamization of the area (figure 3.6).

Another important example of Islamization of space in the hinterland of medieval Jerusalem is the development of the village that came to be known as Dayr Abū Thawr (today Abū Tūr). A mid-sixteenth-century guide for Muslim pilgrims to Jerusalem and its environs that was written by Nāsir al-Dīn Muḥammad b. Khiḍr al-Rūmī has further information on the burial-place *(turba)* of Abū Thawr (Shaykh Abū l-'Abbās Aḥmad, whom we have already encountered).[94] By the time of the author, the compound that grew up around Abū Thawr's tomb had become an integral part of the pilgrim circuit, was listed as one of the stations along the route, and was the site of various rituals that had developed around veneration of the

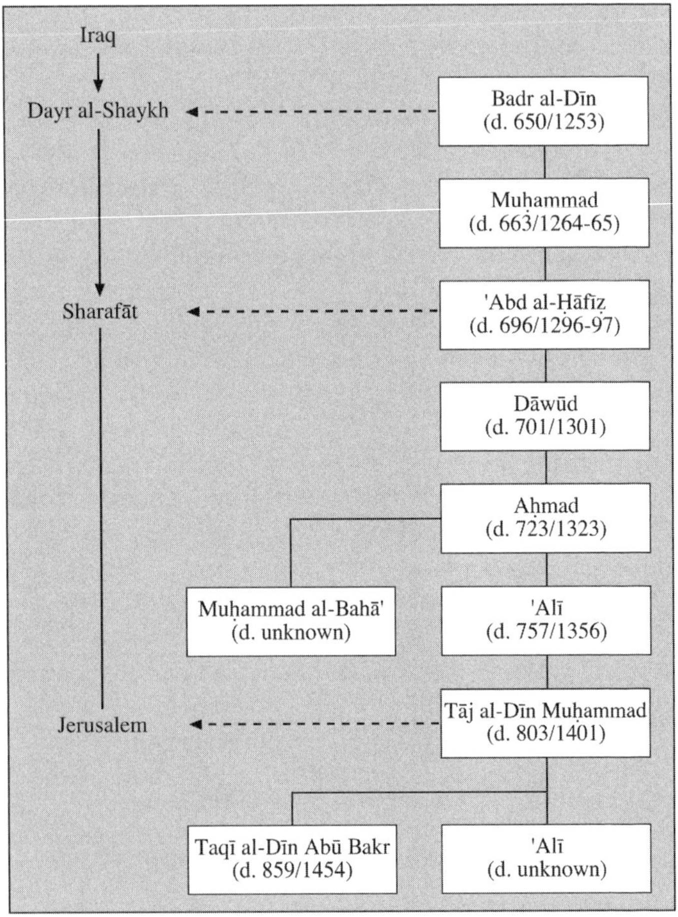

Figure 3.6. The Abū l-Wafā' Palestinian branch (early generations)

shaykh. According to the guide, it was situated on a mountain near Mount Zion. The author also quotes a *ḥadīth* from a book called *Kitāb al-wasiṭ* that describes Mount Abū Thawr, its *wādī,* and its waters. They are all from heaven, and he who comes to the grave of its *walī* will be granted plentiful bounty. When entering the place, the visitor must pray at the gate of the grave's building. When nearing the grave, he will find the Koran *(muṣḥaf)* of ʿAlī b. Abū Ṭālib and should kiss it, stand beside it, and pray.[95]

While intensifying the integration of Palestinian spiritual centers into the cosmopolitan world of Islamic piety that surrounded Sufi shaykhs of recognized virtue, the veneration of the Sufi-*walī* led to the evolution of devotional Sufism as a focus of local communal life. As an ever-more diverse following clustered around local Sufi *awliyāʾ* and their tombs, the expansion of Sufism in Mamluk Palestine must have significantly tightened the bonds between different segments of society and the affinity between local communities and the general religious landscape. Biographers portrayed the life and activities of the Sufi-*walī* within his community, which reasserted and nourished his local ties. The reservoir of local charismatic figures has been enlarged ever since. The articulation and circulation of living traditions about Palestinian Qādirī *awliyāʾ* and their centrality to the religious and social life of contemporary local communities of followers are examined in the epilogue to this book.

Table 3.1 *Khānqāhs* and *zāwiyas* in Ayyubid and Mamluk Jerusalem and Hebron*

Khānqāhs and Zāwiyas	*Foundation and Restoration*	*Beneficiaries and Associates*	*Founder*	*Location*
Al-Zāwiya al-Naṣriyya (or al-Ghazzāliyya)	Late eleventh century, restored by the Ayyubid prince al-Malik Muʿaẓẓam	Followers of Naṣr al-Maqdisī	Naṣr al-Maqdisī (developed out of his lodge)	Jerusalem: near Bāb al-Raḥma (the Gate of Mercy)
Al-Khānqāh Ṣalāḥiyya	Instituted as *waqf* in 585/1189	The "virtuous Sufis," local as well as visitors	Saladin	Jerusalem: the Patriarch's House near the Church of Resurrection
Al-Zāwiya al-Ḥanthaniyya	Late twelfth century	Jalāl al-Dīn Muḥammad al-Shāshī (d. 587/1191) and followers	A prayer chamber in al-Aqṣā bequeathed as *waqf* by Saladin	Jerusalem: in al-Aqṣā mosque, behind the prayer niche
Zāwiyat al-Shaykh Muḥammad al-Qurashī	Late twelfth century	Shaykh Muhammad al-Qurashī (d. 590/1193)	Home of the shaykh	Jerusalem: Ḥārat Marzubān
Zāwiyat al-Jarāḥiyya	Late twelfth century		Al-Amīr Ḥusām al-Dīn al-Jarāḥī	Jerusalem: northern part of the city

* The table outlines the description in Mujīr al-Dīn, *al-Uns al-jalīl*. The term *zāwiya* refers both to a lodge and to a prayer chamber or corner in a mosque.

Al-Zāwiya al-Naḥwiyya	Instituted as *waqf* in 604/1207	Sufis & Ḥanafīs	Al-Malik Muʿaẓẓam	Jerusalem: adjacent to al-Aqṣā mosque
Zāwiyat al-Darakā	Instituted as *waqf* in 613/1216 (originally a Byzantine governmental center)		Shihāb al-Dīn Ghāzī (son of Saladin)	Jerusalem: in the vicinity of the Bīmāristān
Zāwiyat al-Shaykh al-Bakkāʾ	668/1269; restored in 681/1289, 720/1320	Shaykh ʿAlī al-Bakkāʾ (d. 670/1271)	Instituted as *waqf* by al-Amīr ʿIzz al-Dīn Aydamar	Hebron: in a village north to the city
Al-Khānqāh al-Dawādāriyya	695/1295	Members of the local Sufi community and foreign Sufis	Sanjar al-Dawādārī	Jerusalem: north to the Ḥaram
The *zāwiya* in Dayr al-Shaykh	Early thirteenth century	The Wafāʾiyya	Badr al-Dīn Abū l-Wafāʾ (d. 650/1252)	Jerusalem hinterland: Dayr al-Shaykh (originally a Christian area)
Al-Zāwiya al-Kabkiyya	Late thirteenth century		Al-Amīr ʿAlāʾ al-Dīn al-Kabkī (d. 688/1289)	Jerusalem: Māmilā cemetery (west to the city wall of our day)
The *zāwiya* in Sharafāt	Late thirteenth century	The Wafāʾiyya	Dāwūd Abū l-Wafāʾ (d. 701/1301)	Jerusalem hinterland: Sharafāt (originally a Christian village)

Table 3.1 (continued)

Khānqāhs and Zāwiyas	*Foundation and Restoration*	*Beneficiaries and Associates*	*Founder*	*Location*
Zāwiyat al-Maghāriba	703/1303	Shaykh Masʿūd al-Maghrabī (d. unknown)		Hebron: Ḥārat al-Maghāriba
Al-Zāwiya al-Mihmāziyya		Shaykh Kamāl al-Dīn al-Mihmāzī (d. unknown), followers, and descendants	Instituted as *waqf* by al-Malik Ismāʿīl b. al-Naṣr Muḥammad b. Qalāwūn	Jerusalem: north to Bāb al-Ḥiṭṭa (the Gate of Remission)
Al-Zāwiya al-Bisṭāmiyya	Before 770/1368	The Bisṭāmiyya	Instituted as *waqf* by Shihāb al-Dīn al-Asdābādī al-Bisṭāmī (d. 794/1391)	Jerusalem: Ḥārat al-Mashāriqa
Al-Zāwiya al-Aduhamiyya	Mid-fourteenth century	Dāwūd Badr al-Aduhamī (d. 777/1375), and the Aduhamiyya	Al-Amīr Manjak (governor of al-Shām)	Jerusalem: in a cave, north to the city wall of our day
Al-Zāwiya al-Muḥammadiyya	Mid-fourteenth century		Instituted as *waqf* by Muḥammad al-Nāṣrī (?)	Jerusalem: northwest to the Ḥaram

Al-Zāwiya al-Qalandariyya	Mid-fourteenth century; in 794/1391, Tonsuq built a mausoleum for the founder of the *zāwiya*	The Qalandariyya	Shaykh Ibrāhīm al-Qalandarī	Jerusalem: Dayr al-Aḥmar in the middle of al-Māmilā cemetery
Zāwiyat al-Shaykh Muḥammad al-Quramī	Late fourteenth century	Muḥammad al-Quramī (d. 778/1374)	Home of the shaykh; endowed by al-Amīr Naṣr al-Dīn Muḥammad	Jerusalem: Ḥārat Marzubān
Al-Zāwiya al-Shaykhūniyya	Instituted as *waqf* in A.H. 761/1359		Al-Amīr Sayf al-Dīn Qaṭīsha' b. 'Alī; nominated his son Shaykhūn as supervisor of the *waqf*	Jerusalem: near al-Ṣalāḥiyya Madrasa, north to the Ḥaram
Zāwiyat 'Umar al-Mujarad	Late fourteenth century	Shaykh 'Umar al-Mujarad (d. 795/1391)		Hebron: Ḥārat al-Akrād
Al-Zāwiya al-Wafā'iyya, known as Dār Abū l-Wafā'	Early fifteenth century	The Wafā'iyya	Tāj al-Dīn Abū l-Wafā' (d. 803/1400)	Jerusalem: on the southern side of Ṭarīq Bāb al-Nāẓir, adjacent to the gate itself and bounded by the wall of the Ḥaram al-Sharīf

Table 3.1 (continued)

Khānqāhs and Zāwiyas	*Foundation and Restoration*	*Beneficiaries and Associates*	*Founder*	*Location*
Zāwiyat al-Shaykh Shams al-Dīn b. al-Shaykh ʿAbd Allāh al-Baghdādī; or Zāwiyat al-Yaʿqūb al-ʿAjamī or al-Zāwiya al-Bakkāʾiyya	Late fifteenth century Enlarged by Shaykh Shams al-Dīn	Shaykh Shams al-Dīn b. al-Shaykh ʿAbd Allāh al-Baghdādī (d. 885/1490)	Home of the shaykh	Jerusalem: adjacent to the Citadel (originally a Byzantine church)
Zāwiyat al-Hunūd		Indian shaykhs		Jerusalem: Bāb al-Asbāṭ
Zawiyat al-Ḥaḍir				Hebron
Zāwiyat al-Rāmī				Hebron
Zāwiyat al-Samāniyya				Hebron; adjacent to the *zāwiya* of al-Shaykh al-Mujarad
Zāwiyat al-Shaykh al-Ḥanafī				Jerusalem
Zāwiyat al-Shaykh Ibrāhīm al-Mizī		Shaykh Ibrāhīm al-Mizī (d. unknown)		Hebron
Zāwiyat al-Shaykh Raḍwān		Shaykh Raḍwān (d. unknown)		Hebron

Zāwiyat al-Shaykh ʿAbd al-Raḥmān al-Arzrūmī	Shaykh ʿAbd al-Raḥmān al-Arzrūmī (d. unknown)	Hebron
Zāwiyat al-Kanʿūsh al-Adhamī		Hebron
Zāwiyat al-Shaykh Muḥammad al-Baiḍa		Hebron
Al-Zāwiya al-Ṣālaṭiqa		Hebron: by the pool as an extension of al-Zāwiya al-Adhamiyya
Al-Zāwiya al-Ṣamādiyya		Jerusalem: adjacent to al-Zāwiyya al-Bisṭāmiyya
Al-Zāwiya al-Bisṭāmiyya	The Bisṭāmiyya	Hebron: northern part of the city, near al-Jāwilī mosque
Al-Zāwiya al-Ḥamrāʾ (the "Red" *zāwiya*)	The Wafāʾiyya	Jerusalem: near al-Ṣalāḥiyya Khānqāh
Zāwiyat al-Āʿnaṣ		Hebron
Zāwiyat Abū Kamāl	Shaykh Abū Kamāl (d. unknown)	Hebron
Zāwiyat al-Azraq	Shaykh Ibrāhīm al-Azraq (d. unknown)	Jerusalem: southern part of the city; surrounded by a graveyard

Table 3.1 (continued)

Khānqāhs and Zāwiyas	*Foundation and Restoration*	*Beneficiaries and Associates*	*Founder*	*Location*
Al-Zāwiya al-Amīniyya				Jerusalem: on a road leading to the Ḥaram
Al-Zāwiya al-Qādiriyya		The Qādiriyya		Hebron
Al-Zāwiya al-Ẓāhiriyya				Jerusalem: west of the Ḥaram, on Khaṭṭ Wādī al-Ṭawāḥīn (the Street of the Valley of the Mills)
Zāwiyat al-Qawāsima			Al-Amīr Aḥmad al-Qāsamī al-Junaydī (d. unknown)	Hebron: near Zāwiyat ʿAlī al-Bakkāʾ
Al-Zāwiya al-Luʾluʾiyya			Badr al-Dīn Luʾluʾ al-Ghāzī (d .unknown)	Jerusalem: near Bāb al-ʿAmūd
Zāwiyat al-Mawqaʿ				Hebron

NOTES

1. See especially Hodgson, *The Venture of Islam,* 2:210–22; Hourani, *A History of the Arab Peoples,* 153–57.
2. The most recent and extensive work on the growth of the cult of Muslim saints in the Islamic medieval world is Meri, *The Cult of Saints.* See also Joseph Meri, "The Etiquette of Devotion in the Islamic Cult of Saints," in James Howard-Johnston and Paul A. Hayward, eds., *The Cult of Saints in Late Antiquity and the Middle Ages: Essays on the Contribution of Peter Brown* (Oxford: Oxford University Press, 1999), 263–86, for the development of visits to the graves of venerated holy persons into a fundamental aspect of Muslim spirituality. A full-length recent study of visitations of the tombs of the dead during the Mamluk period is Christopher S. Taylor, *In the Vicinity of the Righteous: Ziyāra and the Veneration of Muslim Saints in Late Medieval Egypt,* Islamic History and Civilization, Studies and Texts, vol. 32 (Leiden: Brill, 1999). Taylor focuses on Egypt (1200 to 1500) but provides insightful observations on the evolution of the phenomenon of *ziyārāt* and saint worship as a whole. See also Taylor's extensive bibliography on this field.
3. Mujīr al-Dīn, *al-Uns al-Jalīl,* 2:72.
4. Jonathan Berkey makes this point in *The Formation of Islam,* 239.
5. See Hodgson, *The Venture of Islam,* 2:210–20; Berkey, *The Formation,* 236–40.
6. Trimingham, who in his *The Sufi Orders* coined the common translation of *ṭarīqa* as "order," was also the first to describe a historical pattern that applies to all Sufi orders. For recent interpretations of the character and operation of the early *ṭarīqa*s, see Geoffroy, "Ṭarīka," *EI2.* On the understanding of the *ṭarīqa* in the context under study, see further below.
7. For al-Ṣafī, see Mujīr al-Dīn, *al-Uns al-jalīl,* 2:157.
8. On al-Asadābādī, see ibid., 162; Murtaḍā al-Zabīdī, *Itḥāf al-aṣfiyya bi-raf' salāsil al-awliyā',* ms. fol. 10; Muḥammad b. al-Ḥanbali Raḍī al-Dīn, *Durr al-Ḥabab fi ta'rīkh a'yān ḥalab,* ed. M. al-Fakhūrī and Y. 'Abbāra, 2 vols. (Damascus, 1973), 1:543 (on his origins and training). See also Geoffroy, *Le Soufisme,* 233.
9. Geoffroy, *Le Soufisme,* 233.
10. Ibid., 225–26, 228. See the discussion below on the great Palestin-

ian Qādiri shaykhs. See also Trimingham, *The Sufi Orders,* 43, for the spread of the Qādiriyya in Iraq and Syria.

11. On this matter, see Geoffroy, *Le Soufisme,* 216–17.
12. For examples, see ibid., 237, 359–60 (especially with regard to the Qādiriyya).
13. For major Sufi establishments in Mamluk Jerusalem, see Figure 3.5 below.
14. On the Sufi population of Mamluk Jerusalem generally, see Joseph Drory, "Jerusalem during the Mamluk Period," in Benjamin Z. Kedar, ed., *Jerusalem in the Middle Ages: Selected Papers* (Jerusalem: Yad Ben-Zvi, 1979), 159–61 (in Hebrew). For their lodgings and institutions, see Michael Hamilton Burgoyne, "Tariq Bab al-Hadid: A Mamluk Street in the Old City of Jerusalem," *Levant* 5 (1973): 12–20.
15. Ibn Khaldūn, *The Muqaddimah: An Introduction to History,* 2nd ed., trans. Franz Rosenthal, 3 vols. (Princeton, NJ: Princeton University Press, 1967), 2:435–36. For a full citation of the passage on the Turkish benefactors, see F. E. Peters, *Jerusalem: The Holy City in the Eyes of Chroniclers, Visitors, Pilgrims, and Prophets from the Days of Abraham to the Beginning of Modern Times* (Princeton, NJ: Princeton University Press, 1985), 381–82.
16. Mujīr al-Dīn, *al-Uns al-jalīl,* 2:43. For the dedication inscription that was affixed to the front wall, see Van Brechem, *Matériaux,* 197 n. 64.
17. Mujīr al-Dīn, *al-Uns al-jalīl,* 2:43. For the dedication inscription, see Van Brechem, *Matériaux,* 200 n. 65.
18. For these observations, especially with regard to Mamluk Cairo, see Berkey, *The Transmission of Knowledge,* 47–50, 56–60. On this subject generally, see also Fernandes, *The Evolution of a Sufi Institution,* 33 ff., 97–108.
19. Mujīr al-Dīn, *al-Uns al-jalīl,* 2:35–36. See there for a detailed history of the construction of the *madrasa* and an architectural description. For an English translation, see Peters, *Jerusalem,* 413–15.
20. Ibid. See also S. Tamari, "Al-Ashrafiyya: An Imperial Madrasa in Jerusalem," in Y. Manṣūr, ed., *Studies in Arabic and Islam* (Ramat Gan, 1974), 9–40 (in Hebrew).
21. Cited by Van Brechem, *Matériaux,* 214 n. 70. For a brief account

of the *khānqāh*'s construction and founder, see Mujīr al-Dīn, *al-Uns al-jalīl,* 2:39.

22. Apart from the extensive list provided by Mujīr al-Dīn, the evidence of Sufi establishments that were constructed in Mamluk Jerusalem may be derived from the Jerusalem *sharʿī* court documents and the large cache of documents discovered in the Islamic Museum atop the Ḥaram (in 1974 and 1976) and dating from the Mamluk era in Jerusalem. For an account of this discovery and a survey of the contents, see D. Little, "The Significance of the Haram Documents for the Study of Medieval Islamic History," *Der Islam* 57 (1980): 189–219. ʿAsalī, in his *Maʿāhid al-ʿilm fi bayt al-maqdis* and *Wathāʾiq maqdisiyya taʾrīkhiyya,* employed these documents extensively and effectively.
23. See Kamal S. Salibi, "The Banū Jamāʿa: A Dynasty of Shāfiʿite Jurists in the Mamluk Period," *Studia Islamica* 9 (1958): 97–109.
24. Mujīr al-Dīn, *al-Uns al-jalīl,* 2:150–51. For a fuller biography, see Salibi, "The Banū Jamāʿa," 98–99, based on Mujīr al-Dīn and al-Subkī, *Ṭabaqāt al-shāfiʿiyya al-kubrā,* 5:46–47.
25. Mujīr al-Dīn, *al-Uns al-jalīl,* 2:169.
26. Gril, *La Risāla,* 232–33, and the references to the Arabic text and the full bibliography there. On his days in Jerusalem, see Mujīr al-Dīn, *al-Uns al-jalīl,* 2:145.
27. For the many precedents of this conjunction, see, most famously, al-Iṣfahānī's *Ḥilyat al-awliyāʾ* and al-Hujwīrī's *Kashf al-mahjūb.* See also Mojaddedi, *The Biographical Tradition,* chaps. 2 and 5.
28. Ernest Gellner, "Doctor and Saint," in Nikki R. Keddie, ed., *Scholars, Saints, and Sufis: Muslim Religious Institutions in the Middle East since 1500* (Berkeley: University of California Press, 1972), 307–26. For a criticism of this approach in the context of premodern Morocco, see Vincent J. Cornell, *Realm of the Saint: Power and Authority in Moroccan Sufism* (Austin: University of Texas Press, 1998), xxvii. In an attempt to avoid the popular versus elitist model, Cornell suggests two levels of Moroccan Sufism: local and universal (or extralocal and pan-Islamic).
29. For recent studies on premodern Islamic societies that show that the popular and elitist levels of religion were not separate realms but rather constituted a whole, see Talmon-Heller, "The Shaykh and the Community"; Marín, "The Zuhhād of al-Andalus"; Maribel Fierro, "Opposition to Sufism in al-Andalus," in F. de

Jong and R. Radtke, eds., *Islamic Mysticism Contested: Thirteen Centuries of Controversies and Polemics* (Leiden: Brill, 1999), 174–97.

30. Mujīr al-Dīn, *al-Uns al-jalīl,* 2:164. See also Ibn Qādi al-Shuhba, *Ṭabaqāt al-shāfiʿiyya* (Beirut, 1987), 4:300–01.
31. Geoffroy makes this observation in *Le Soufisme,* 164.
32. Y. Frenkel makes this observation based on ample examples in "*Mutasawwifa* versus *Fuqarāʾ*: Notes Concerning Sufi Discourse in Mamluk Syria," in Alfonso Carmona, ed., *El Sufismo y las normas del Islam,* Trabajos del IV Congreso Internacional de Estudios Jurídicos Islámicos: Derecho y Sufismo (Murcia: Consejería de Educatión y Cultura, 2006), 291–307 (English text). See also Geoffroy, *Le Soufisme,* 37–38, on the belief in the existence of *karāmāt* as expressed in the hagiographic literature by religious scholars, commencing with the treatises on the Qādiriyya.
33. For a richly documented exposition of this literature, see Frenkel, "*Mutaṣawwifa* versus *Fuqarāʾ*."
34. Mujīr al-Dīn, *al-Uns al-jalīl,* 2:197–98.
35. Ibid., 2:209.
36. See Shams al-Dīn Muḥammad al-Sakhāwī, *al-Ḍauʾ al-lāmiʿ li-ahl al-qarn al-tāsiʿ,* 6 vols. (Cairo, AH 1353), 1:282–83. See also Mujīr al-Dīn, *al-Uns al-jalīl,* 2:174–76; al-Nabhānī, *Jamīʿ karāmāt al-awliyāʾ,* 1:533.
37. Al-Sakhāwī, *al-Ḍauʾ al-lāmiʿ,* 1:283.
38. Mujīr al-Dīn, *al-Uns al-jalīl,* 2:177.
39. For early manifestations of the recurring theme of purity in dietary matters, see Bonner, *Aristocratic Violence,* 125–27 (in relation to the famous ascetic Ibrāhīm Adham (d. 161/777–778).
40. Mujīr al-Dīn, *al-Uns al-jalīl,* 2:169.
41. Ibid., 2:144–45.
42. Ibid., 2:153.
43. Peter Brown makes this observation in his own 1998 revision of his "The Rise and Function of the Holy Man in Late Antiquity," *Journal of Roman Studies* 61 (1971): 80–101. As he himself admits, the sociological and psychological models that he used converged to attribute to the holy man a greater degree of separateness from his followers than he may, in fact, have possessed. Peter Brown, "The Rise and the Function of the Holy Man in Late An-

tiquity 1971–1997," *Journal of Early Christian Studies* 6:3 (1998): 368.

44. For *ṣalāḥ* as a social virtue, see Cornell, *Realm of the Saint,* 6.
45. Cf. Peter Brown's observation that the holy man's activities, though usually presented in retrospect as dramatic and utterly exceptional, were in reality no more than a highly visible peak in a "spiritual landscape" that rose gently from the expectations and activities of ordinary Christians in towns and villages. Peter Brown, *Authority and the Sacred: Aspects of the Christianisation of the Roman World* (Cambridge: Cambridge University Press, 1995), 60.
46. For general remarks on the roles that were assumed by the Sufi *walī* beginning in the twelfth century, see Lapidus, *A History of Islamic Societies,* 171. For a vivid picture of his various roles in the particular context of a Palestinian-Syrian rural community, see Talmon-Heller, "The Shaykh and the Community," 103–20. See also Ephrat, *A Learned Society,* 144–47, for the activities of pious and charismatic leaders in the society of eleventh- and early twelfth-century Baghdad.
47. See Geoffroy's discussion in *Le Soufisme,* 23–24, of various sources for the study of Sufism in the Mamluk period.
48. Najm al-Dīn al-Ghazzī, *al-Kawākib al-sā'ira bi-a'yān al-mi'a al-'ashira,* ed. J. Jabbūr, 3 vols. (Beirut: al-Maṭba'at al-Amīr Kāniyya, 1945), 1:74–76.
49. Denis Gril makes this point in light of the treatises of *khirqa* that were composed during the Mamluk period. Denis Gril, "Sources manuscrites de l'histoire du Soufisme à Dār al-Kutub: Un premier Bilan," *Annales Islamologiques* 28 (1994): 102.
50. Gril, *La Risala,* 72. See also Ira Lapidus's observation that from the tenth to the fourteenth centuries, individual Sufis and their disciples and lay believers were the basic unit of Sufism. Lapidus, *A History,* 171. Several recent studies have shown that this observation is applicable to later periods as well. Thus, Nehemia Levtzion argues that up to the eighteenth century, most Sufi fraternities were diffuse affiliations without a central organization or strong links between their members. Nehemia Levtzion, "Eighteenth-Century Sufi Brotherhoods: Structural, Organizational and Ritual Changes," in P. R. Riddell and T. Street, eds., *Islam: Essays on Scripture, Thought and Society* (Leiden: Brill, 1997), 147–66. In

somewhat similar vein, Albrecht Hofheinz observes that in the Sudan people saw themselves as belonging to a particular brotherhood simply because they regarded a particular person as their shaykh. Hofheinz, *Internalizing Islam,* 1:18. For adherence to the shaykh rather than the *ṭarīqa* as a social organization with regard to the Naqshbandiyya, see Buehler, *Sufi Heirs,* chaps. 5–6.

51. Al-Sakhāwī, *al-Ḍau',* 1:282–84.
52. Al-Ghazzī, *al-Kawākib,* 1:75
53. Ibid.
54. Mujīr al-Dīn, *al-Uns al-jalīl,* 2:161. See also Ibn Ḥajar, *al-Durar al-kāmina fî a'yān al-mi'a al-thāmina,* 5 vols. (Cairo: Dār al-Kutub al-Ḥadītha, 1966–1967), 3:425–26.
55. Mujīr al-Dīn, *al-Uns al-jalīl,* 2:146.
56. Al-Ghazzī, *al-Kawākib,* 1:75–76, 2:240–42. Geoffroy relates to this story in *Le Soufisme,* 115–16.
57. This conclusion is in line with recent studies that focus on the world of religious learning but suggest a much greater degree of integration and acculturation of the Mamluks into Muslim society than is described by religious scholars and historians. The pioneering work on this subject is that of Ulrich Haarmann, especially his "Arabic in Speech, Turkish in Lineage: Mamluks and Their Sons in the Intellectual Life of Fourteenth-Century Egypt and Syria," *Journal of Semitic Studies* 33 (1988): 81–114.
58. For example, see the story about Alā' al-Dīn al-'Ajamī above.
59. An example is a decree issued by Sultan Qalāwūn requiring two sacks of wheat to be delivered every month to the *zāwiya* of the shaykh Abū 'Abd Allāh Muḥammad al-Maqdisī in Nablus. See Mujīr al-Dīn, *al-Uns al-jalīl,* 2:151.
60. See Reuven Amitai, "The Conquest of Arsūf by Baybars: Political and Military Aspects," *Mamlūk Studies Review* 9:1 (2005): 73–74. Amitai notes that it was also during the campaign that Baybars took some time off to visit the nearby tomb of Shaykh 'Alī b. 'Alīm (Sīdnā 'Alī) as "it was particularly convenient to have a Muslim saint 'just down the block'" (ibid., 74).
61. See N. Z. Davis's important suggestion about the need to examine the range of people's relations with the sacred and the supernatural to avoid fragmenting practices, beliefs, and institutions that for different segments of the community of believers constitute a whole. N. Z. Davis, "Some Tasks and Themes in the Study of Pop-

ular Religion," in C. Trinkhaus, ed., *The Pursuit of Holiness* (Leiden: Brill, 1974), 312–13.

62. Mujīr al-Dīn, *al-Uns al-jalīl,* 2:161; Ibn Ḥajar, *al-Durar,* 3:426.
63. Mujīr al-Dīn, *al-Uns al-jalīl,* 2:173–74.
64. Ibid., 2:73.
65. Al-Ghazzī, *al-Kawākib,* 2:242. For this and other examples, see Geoffroy, *Le Soufisme,* 140–43.
66. See Eliyahu Ashtor, "Jerusalem in the Late Middle Ages," *Yerushalayim: Review for Eretz-Israel Research* 2 (1955): 109 (in Hebrew), which is a discussion of the family's origins and important role in the scholarly life of Mamluk Jerusalem. This family is not related to the Abū l-Wafā' of Egypt, nor does their Wafā'iyya *ṭarīqa* appear to have any connection to the Wafā'iyya of Cairo. On the various Wafā'iyya families and their origins, see McGregor, *Sanctity and Mysticism,* 52.
67. Mujīr al-Dīn, *al-Uns al-jalīl,* 2:146.
68. Ibid., 2:147. Mujīr adds that his father was the brother of the aforementioned Tāj al-ʿĀrifīn. For a detailed study of the Abū l-Wafā' family's activities and influence in the Jerusalem hinterland, see Nimrod Luz, "Aspects of Islamization of Space and Society in Mamluk Jerusalem and Its Hinterland," *Mamlūk Studies Review* 6 (2002): 133–53. Applying the methodology and source material of geographical studies, Luz focuses on the role played by members of the family in creating a new, Islamic landscape through their settlements and work. For information on the location of Dayr al-Shaykh, see Luz at 137 n. 18 and the map on 153. For local folktales about Badr al-Dīn that are based on the collective memory of people from the Jerusalem area in the early twentieth century, see Andrew Petersen, "A Preliminary Report on Three Muslim Shrines in Palestine," *Levant* 28 (1996): 99–103.
69. Mujīr al-Dīn, *al-Uns,* 2:147.
70. Ibid.
71. Ibid.
72. See Luz, "Aspects of Islamization," 140–41, for his comments on the uncertainty about the exact date of the endowment and the position of the Mamluk official at the time.
73. Mujīr al-Dīn, *al-Uns al-jalīl,* 2:148–49.
74. Ibid., 2:149.
75. Ibid., 2:185–86.

76. On this phenomenon in Syria and Egypt in general, see Geoffroy, *Le Soufisme,* 165–67.
77. As in the Naḥwiyya *zāwiya,* where shaykhs instructed grammar to disciples affiliated with the Ḥanafī school of law. See above, chapter 2, note 125. Several shaykhs of the Bisṭāmiyya *zāwiya,* including Shihāb al-Dīn al-Ḥalabī al-Bisṭāmī, taught in the Ṣalāḥiyya *madrasa.* See Mujīr al-Dīn, *al-Uns al-jalīl,* 2:197.
78. On this matter, see the comprehensive survey of Taufik Canaan, "Mohammeden Saints and Sanctuaries in Palestine," *Journal of the Palestine Oriental Society* 4 (1924): 1–84, in which he presents textual and pictorial descriptions of such sites.
79. Petersen, "A Preliminary Report," 99. See also ibid., 99–103, for a detailed history and description of the *zāwiya,* the village of Dayr al-Shaykh, and its immediate surroundings.
80. See Luz, "Aspects of Islamization," 144, based on his survey of the site.
81. Mujīr al-Dīn, *al-Uns al-jalīl,* 2:37.
82. Michael Hamilton Burgoyne, *Mamluk Jerusalem: An Architectural Study* (London: British School of Archaeology in Jerusalem, 1987), 456–59.
83. Mujīr al-Dīn, *al-Uns al-jalīl,* 2:147–48.
84. Ibid., *al-Uns al-jalīl,* 2:64–65. See also Geoffroy, *Le Soufisme,* 235–36; Karamustafa, *God's Unruly Friends,* 54.
85. Mujīr al-Dīn, *al-Uns al-jalīl,* 2:175.
86. Al-Ghazzī, *al-Kawākib,* 1:77.
87. Mujīr al-Dīn, *al-Uns al-jalīl,* 2:73.
88. On the architectural development of the site, see Hana Taragan, "The Tomb of Sayyidnā 'Alī in Arsuf: The Story of a Holy Place," *Journal of the Royal Asiatic Society* 14:2 (July 2004): 83–102.
89. Mujīr al-Dīn, *al-Uns al-jalīl,* 2:152.
90. See the comments by Hoexter on the contribution of *waqf* to the forming and shaping of Islamic urban space. Hoexter, "The Waqf and the Public Sphere," 128. Ethel Sarah Wolper focuses on medieval Anatolia and the role of the dervish lodge in transforming the urban space. Ethel Sarah Wolper, *Cities and Saints: Sufism and the Transformation of Urban Space in Medieval Anatolia* (University Park: Pennsylvania State University Press, 2003).
91. On changes to the toponymic map as one of the most common indications of demographic, ethnic, and religious changes in an area,

see the extensive discussion by Roni Ellenblum, *Frankish Rural Settlement in the Latin Kingdom of Palestine* (Cambridge: Cambridge University Press, 1998), 179–256. See also Dominique Chevallier, ed., *L'Espace social de la ville arabe* (Paris: Maisonneuve et Larose, 1979), on the theme of cultural landscape.

92. On the direct bearing of the role of the family on the process of Islamization, see Luz "Aspects of Islamization," 146–50. On the population and agricultural production of Dayr al-Shaykh up to the mid-1940s, see W. Hütteroth and K. Abdulfattah, *Historical Geography of Palestine: Transjordan and Southern Syria in the Late Sixteenth Century* (Erlangen: Selbstverlag, 1977), 113; C. R. Conder and H. H. Kitchener, *A Survey of Western Palestine: Memoirs of the Topography, Orography, Hydrography and Archaeology* (London: Committee of the Palestine Exploration Fund, 1881), 3:23–25; W. Khalidi, ed., *All That Remains: The Palestinian Villages Occupied and Depopulated by Israel in 1948* (Washington, DC: Institute for Palestinian Studies, 1992), 288.
93. See Vryonis, *The Decline of Hellenism,* esp. 351–402.
94. Elad, *Medieval Jerusalem,* appendix, 165–73. About the archeological excavations and the Byzantine church on Jabal Abū Thawr, see A. Ovadiah, *Corpus of the Byzantine Churches of the Holy Land* (Bonn: Hantein, 1970), 30–81 and bibliography.
95. Cited by Elad, *Medieval Jerusalem,* 171.

Conclusion

In the period between the rise of Islam and the spread of Ottoman rule, Sufism thrived in Palestine. Its social and regional contributions to shaping an Islamic society and space allow it to be seen as a social history of Sufism as viewed from a particular geographic vantage point.

This transition from a cosmopolitan elite of mystical wayfarers to locally embedded Sufi-inspired communities—called in the sources studied for this book "the people of the way" *(ahl al-ṭarīqa)*—began as early as the late tenth century. The general thrust of this study proposes that the heart of the birth and growth of the local *ahl al-ṭarīqa* resides in the dissemination of Sufism as an ethical community-oriented tradition that built bridges between Sufis and jurists and between Sufis and the society as a whole. Furthermore, the message spread by representatives of the tradition and their modes and frameworks of operation within the society eventually rendered Sufism accessible to Muslim believers who could never reach the heights of mystical experience.

The social evolution of Sufism begins with the early Islamic period in Palestine and the classical period in the history of Sufism and Islam as a whole. During the first four centuries of Islamic rule, the stage was set for the diffusion of the tradition that came to be known as Sufism—in Palestinian cities (notably,

Jerusalem and Hebron), in the garrison towns on the Mediterranean shores, and in the rural areas surrounding cities and towns. Transients and immigrants disseminated the teachings of ascetic and mystical movements that had their origins in the eastern and western Muslim world and thereby incorporated the places they frequented or in which they lived into the universal world of Sufism. At the same time, a diverse Sufi tradition was beginning to put down roots in this geographical and historical setting.

The diffusion of ascetic and Sufi piety in Palestine must have been influenced by the sanctity of its cities and their long-established position as centers of pilgrimage as well as by the examples set by and the direct encounters with Christian monks and holy men. The names of *zuhhād* who lived in Palestine during the early centuries of Islamic rule are to be found in the pages of standard biographical dictionaries devoted to celebrated *ḥadīth* experts—men and women known for their pious practices and righteous conduct. The ascetic piety that these early role models practiced was perceived to be an essential stage for any seeker of mystical ascent and came to be the prime virtue of a true Sufi. My examination of the classical period of Sufism in Palestine has emphasized both the affinity between mystical and ascetic discourse as well as the close association between guidance along the stages and stations of the path and the inducement to emulate ascetic practices and spiritual etiquette. At the end of classical Sufism in the late tenth century, small circles of wayfarers occasionally orbited around several mystic mentors who combined teaching with directing. They eventually constituted the core of "the people of the way."

Also in the late tenth century, a mainstream Sufi tradition emerged that embraced the ethical postures and religious outlook of the early inner-worldly *zuhhād* and the "*ḥadīth* folk" in general and shifted the emphasis from the mystical and ecstatic to the sober and ethical aspects of Sufi piety. The science of the tradition matured, and by the twelfth century, its path had become accepted as a legitimate version of the prophetic Sunna. Representatives of the main Sufi tradition in Palestine during this period engaged in the study and transmission of the traditional and legal sciences and gained recognition and fame as *ḥadīth* and legal experts. The reconciliation between Sufis and jurists and the integration of Sufism within the scholarly world of the jurists of the *madhhab*s allowed learned Sufi shaykhs to assume teaching positions in the great *madrasa*s founded in Jerusalem for members of the Shāfiʿī rite of jurisprudence, the dominant Sunni rite in the Ayyubid and Mamluk periods.

Within the inner world of the Sufis, the emphasis placed on the ethical dimensions of Sufism resulted in a changed concept of the essence of guidance for advancement along the path, leading in turn to a change in the relationship between master and disciple. The accomplished Sufi master embodied the ethical positions of the Prophet. Replicating the prophetic personal model of discipleship, he closely supervised the moral behavior of his disciples, thereby establishing his spiritual position as a moral guide and gathering around him a circle of committed disciples. As early as the latter part of the tenth century, the mobile grouping of early wayfarers gave way to the particular Sufi congregation, which centered on a single authoritative spiritual and moral guide. Around the Sufi guide, who settled in a Palestinian spiritual center and its environs, a coherent, locally embedded congregation of committed followers of his spiritual method *(ṭarīqa)* crystallized, gradually growing and extending its horizons in the course of the Islamic middle periods.

Through the embodiment of the virtues associated with Sufism (above all, mild asceticism, humility, generosity, and altruism), the scope of the Sufi shaykh's sway expanded and the horizons of Sufism came to extend beyond the core of small circles of seekers of the spiritual path. Prominent Sufi spiritual and moral guides in Palestine during the so-called Sunni revival and the middle periods acted as arbiters of religious knowledge and practice alongside the scholars of the established legal schools within which they integrated. Moreover, parallel with their integration within the scholarly and institutional world dominated by jurists of the *madhhab*s, they developed their own modes and frameworks of operation and devised their own ways of integrating into the fabric of social and communal life. Their transmission of knowledge and guidance did not center on training in the secrets of Sufism. Nor was it confined to a few select disciples and intimates. Rather, the typical Sufi guide fostered piety that centered directly on the Koran and the Sunna. He disseminated his norms and values throughout the local community and practiced his virtues within the society by interacting with its members. The road was thus paved for the transformation of Sufism into a highly significant religiously based and led association.

During the Mamluk period (1250 to 1517), the Sufi-inspired community (the *ahl at-ṭarīqa*) became the focus of social identity and affiliation in the urban and rural public sphere of Palestine. An in-depth study of this period brings to light the particular local and individual context of Sufi associations and the heterogeneous character of early Sufi institutionalization—a development that departs from the typical historical pattern of the birth and early extension of all Sufi orders or groups.

In Palestine, the structuring of the Sufi experience and the expansion of its social horizons normally took place outside the framework of an established and widespread *ṭarīqa*. Some of the venerated shaykhs around whom the "people of the way" gathered were affiliated with major mystical schools that originated in other parts of the Muslim world—primarily the Bisṭāmiya and Qādiriyya. However, many others do not appear to belong fully and exclusively to one or another particular spiritual path. Moreover, the term *ṭarīqa* often denotes a method of spiritual guidance that was practiced by a particular Sufi guide rather than a method practiced by an institutional Sufi order or even a well-established route in terms of doctrine, rules, and rituals. Accordingly, the set of people collectively known as *ahl al-ṭarīqa* are described as disciples and followers of a certain charismatic shaykh rather than as members of a *ṭarīqa* as a social organization. It was precisely the informal and unstructured character of the early *ṭarīqa*, I have argued, that ensured its flexibility and inclusiveness.

The personal, master-centered model of the Sufi association also explains the importance of the Sufi lodge known as *zāwiya* in the expansion of Sufism in Mamluk Palestine. Regardless of its type and function, the *zāwiya* was the home, realm, and burial place of the charismatic shaykh. This is why the *zāwiya*, rather than the much more formal Sufi institution of the *khānqāh*, transformed into an Islamic public space. It became a focus of religious and communal life for Muslims of all social segments who sought to receive the shaykh's guidance and blessing and partake in his community, each individual and group in its own way.

The proliferation of the *zāwiya*-tomb complex under the Mamluks helped structure the Sufi experience and extend its horizons. Because Sufi lodges and saintly tombs were built in cities and villages where a charismatic shaykh settled and were supplied with endowments granted to the shaykh by the local governors, they also made a significant contribution to the Islamization of the landscape. The growth of sites and spaces around the charismatic shaykh is one of the main topics that this book has sought to address. The role of Sufis in Islamizing places by creating of a new cultural landscape in medieval Palestine and in other parts of the medieval Muslim world is an issue that needs to be studied further.[1]

Another aim of this book has been to offer ways to embed the history of Sufism within a local context and to investigate the nexus of Sufism and society in a particular setting. Throughout, I have fleshed out the norms that were embodied and spread by the charismatic shaykh and the mechanisms that he employed to assert his influence and enlarge his following.

In reconstructing the life stories of the subjects of this book, I have read the texts on their own terms and in their entirety, rather than confining my examination to literary formulas that impose a normative homogeneity on the Sufi holy man or separating out those portions considered historically reliable and interpreting them apart from the rest. This holistic approach helps to expose the various elements of the Sufi *walī* persona and the various dimensions in which he acted. Here I have followed the line of recent research that argues for moving away from the old classifications into categories of *fuqahā'* versus *fuqarā'* and from the tendency to assume neat divisions between the high Sufism of the great Sufi masters and popular spiritual Sufism with its holy figures and the worship of saints at their tombs.[2]

In examining the growth of sites and spaces around the Sufi shaykh and the impact of Sufis and their institutions on the landscape, I have pointed out the importance of source material other than biographical and hagiographical texts. Bureaucratic documents such as endowment deeds (*waqfiyya*s), inscriptions, and architectural remnants can complement the classical written texts by providing a fuller picture of the local context of Sufism's physical expansion.

Finally, my hope is to advance the usage of biographical and hagiographical material as valuable sources for the study of the social and historical dimensions of Sufism and to offer ways of employing the historical material contained in them. The working hypothesis of this study has been that biographies were not written outside of history but within a particular milieu that lent them their meaning. Regarding the universal model of the righteous Sufi and holy man, it was only by depicting him within a community of believers that the norms that he embodied and the message that he spread could be effective. Similarly, only by localizing or appropriating the ideal of the Sufi "friend of God" could his life be commemorated for later generations of local believers. This is probably why his figure was portrayed in concrete terms and explicit examples illustrated his outstanding virtues and miraculous deeds. Beyond the legendary layer and idealizing terms and expressions, there thus exist details about the life of the charismatic shaykh and accounts about his relationships with the world around him. In-depth inquiry into the tales that are contained in the biographies or are transmitted orally to this day affords insights into the concerns and practices of the society surrounding the Sufi *walī* and of later generations of Muslim believers as they worked to create a reservoir of role models and interpret their own heritage.

NOTES

1. Nehemia Levtzion was the first to offer models for understanding the importance of the Sufis, among other agents of Islamization, in pushing forward the conversion of non-Muslims both within and beyond the lands ruled by Muslims. See Nehemia Levtzion, "Toward a Comparative Study of Islamization," in Nehemia Levtzion, ed., *Conversion to Islam* (New York: Holmes and Meier, 1979), 16–18. A number of studies have been published since then that offer additional theoretical and historical perspectives.
2. For examples of that kind of approach, see especially Cornell, *Realm of the Saint,* and Dina Le Gall, *A Culture of Sufism: Naqshbandis in the Ottoman World* (Albany: SUNY Press, 2004).

Epilogue

During the twentieth century, some aspects of Sufism were strongly criticized by reformist and fundamentalist Muslim thinkers, and Sufism in general found itself under increasing attack. Sufis had to face challenges from the West and even more from the increasing interventions by authoritarian secularized states and hostile Islamic fundamentalists. Under these conditions, many Sufi fraternities have declined, lost the dominance in the public sphere of Islamic societies they enjoyed for many centuries, or disappeared altogether. Nevertheless, other *ṭarīqa*s have survived by adapting themselves to the changing circumstances.[1]

In recent decades, the opposition of both Muslim and non-Muslim governments to radical fundamentalism and the growing demand for Islamic forms of personal and collective piety have resulted in a marked revival in Sufi activities. Several Sufi fraternities have managed to preserve their traditions, develop new forms of disseminating their teachings and legacies, and even expand into new enterprises in the various realms of religious, social, and political life. Moreover, Sufi-framed performances and discourse still maintain their significance as a source of social identity and solidarity and offer channels for Sufis to participate in the public sphere.[2] Several major features of this general trend are noticeable in contemporary Israel as well.

During the latter part of the Ottoman period, the major widespread Sufi fraternities in Palestine (such as the Naqshbandiyya) were of limited scope and social significance (or declined and disappeared altogether, as in the case of the Mawlawiyya and Rifāʿiyya). However, three *ṭarīqa*s—the Qādiriyya, Yashuriyya, and Khalwatiyyah-Raḥmaniyya, in ascending order of success—were able to adapt themselves to the challenges of modernity and the Israeli reality. The latter two were urban in origin and considered to be Shariʿa-oriented in doctrine and practice, and they penetrated into the villages of the Galilee and the rural areas of Hebron and Nablus in the nineteenth century.

Since Mamluk times, the more deeply rooted but less dominant Qādiriyya had various local groups of the *ṭarīqa* that had been active in Palestine in both rural and urban areas. Although those groups disintegrated after the war of 1948, new, fragmented groups have appeared in recent decades, partly due to the renewal of contacts with the Palestinians of the West Bank and Gaza in the wake of the Six-Day War.[3] Their pattern of appearance and growth is similar to that of the earliest *ṭarīqa*s in Palestine. Small local congregations are united by a collective devotion to a particular charismatic shaykh, either a descendant of a local leading family or a successor in a genealogical chain of spiritual ancestors. This noninstitutional form of the *ṭarīqa* still explains the evolution of Sufism into a generalized religious pattern that is accessible to every believer and that leads beyond the confines of exclusive affiliations and enforced loyalties.

ʿAbd al-Salām Manāsra, a former communist from Nazareth, is one the leading Qādirī shaykhs in contemporary Israel.[4] He makes his claim for religious authority and leadership status on a direct nomination by his own shaykh, who had induced him into the *ṭarīqa*. His disciples and followers are dispersed in several cities, towns, and villages around the country and the West Bank, but their main concentration is in the Jezreel Valley and the Lower Galilee, with its stronghold in Nazareth.

The center of operations for the shaykh is a modest apartment on the main street of the city, which Shaykh Manāsra calls "our *zāwiya.*" It provides a hall for prayer and *dhikr* rituals, a library-in-the-making, and a space for other personal and collective activities—all within the dual frame of the Lights of Peace Association *(jamʿīya anwār al-salām),* which has a strong universal message, and the Association for Diffusion of the Prophet's Tradition *(jamʿīya nashr āthār al-nabī).* Shaykh Manāsra entertains the hope that "with the help of God," the library will form the nucleus of an educational center containing books about Sufism and the Islamic creed and history in general. Moreover, the *zāwiya* is designed to turn into a center for the distribution of charity and assistance in school studies.

No less important are ʿAbd al-Salām's newly established paper—*al-Burhān* (The Proof)—and an Internet site. The shaykh uses them to strengthen a sense of community among his followers and to spread the message of his *ṭarīqa* to diverse audiences far beyond his group. In this teaching, he follows the traditional way of the Qādiriyya—sober Sufism with a strong emphasis on the primacy of the Sunna and the Shariʿa and, above all, on moral conduct. One of the shaykh's most intimate disciples repeats the motto of the centrality of moral conduct in the definition of Sufism that has its origins in the *adab* literature of the great medieval Sufi masters. In his words: "Sufism is not only a theory but a way of life and mode of ethical behavior *(ṭarīq al-akhlāq).* To be a Sufi is to habitually exercise the purity of one's heart *(ṣafāʾ al-qalb)*—to cater for others, be generous, and honest." Spreading the moral message of the path is explicitly identified with the dissemination of the true religion of Islam. This message is designed not only for a small circle of devoted wayfarers but also for all Muslims—in fact, for all human beings. Although he stresses the orthodox position of the supremacy of Islam over other monotheistic religions, Shaykh Manāsra insists that all components are but different traditions of the one universal religion.

The modern devices that are used for the propagation of the religion do not substitute for traditional modes. Emphasis on the personal and devotional bonds between the shayk and his closest disciples continues to be the main structuring code. In Shaykh Manāsra's perception, nothing can replace the highly personal relationships that he has forged with his followers ever since his nomination as their shaykh—"for knowledge and guidance pass from heart to heart by direct and prolonged tie *(rābiṭa)* between master and disciple." The shaykh's closest disciples frequent the *zāwiya* in Nazareth as a matter of course, and everyone seeking his spiritual and moral guidance or practical advice in daily matters of personal and public piety and morality may approach him. Every Thursday, the shaykh and his group come to the *zāwiya* for the collective performance of the *dhikr,* which, as they stress, is open to any Muslim who wishes to participate in their spiritual life. Non-Muslims are also invited to visit and observe.

In common with earliest followers of the Sufi path, the Qādirī flock present themselves as faithful adherents of their shaykhs and their lines of spiritual leaders rather than as members of the *ṭarīqa* as a social organization. When ʿAbd al-Hādī of the village of Sulaim was asked about the meaning of being a Qādirī, he answered, "It is paying visits to my shaykh whenever I can, faithfully practicing the religion of Islam, frequenting the local mosque, and reading the litanies *(wird)* of our greatest master, ʿAbd al-Qādir, every day. To be recognized as our shaykh, one has to prove the purity of his heart and his moral virtues through deeds."

Shaykh Manāsra's lineage *(silsila)* of illustrious Palestinian Qādirī leaders begins with Shaykh Ṣāliḥ al-Sarnīnī, who settled in Jerusalem about 120 years ago. A well-known tradition tells how this branch of the *ṭarīqa* first appeared and established roots in Palestine around the figure of Shaykh Ṣāliḥ. At the age of forty, Shaykh Ṣāliḥ, a pious and ascetic worshiper, left his homeland of Tunisia for Baghdad to live near the *zāwiya* compound of ʿAbd al-Qādir ("the great founding father and the source of the path") and join his community of followers there. But his physical and spiritual journeys had not yet ended. About twenty years later, in a dream, he saw a loaf of bread and heard a voice ordering him to direct his steps to Jerusalem, where the loaf—symbolizing the Qādirī legacy, which he was to carry on—was to be found. Shaykh Ṣāliḥ tried to ignore the divine message (preferring to travel to Tunisia for a family visit instead) and, as a result, lost consciousness for almost two years. But when the same dream and mental condition recurred, he finally left Baghdad for the holy city of Jerusalem, where he engaged in constant preaching and gained fame due to his spiritual perfection, wisdom, and Sufi virtues. Many flocked around him. Of his disciples, the native-born Shaykh Hāshim al-Baghdādī came to be seen as the most promising. He shadowed his master wherever the shaykh turned, attended to all his needs, and washed, fed, and cared for him when he was old. On his deathbed, Shaykh Ṣāliḥ nominated Shaykh Hāshim to succeed him as leader of the local branch of the *ṭarīqa* by handing over to him his head cover. About sixteen years ago, this same Shaykh Hāshim passed on his position to Shaykh Manāsra after his "conversion" *(tawba)* to Sufism.

Shaykh Manāsra's own close disciple, Khālid, is currently completing master's studies (in the field of Arabic language) at the Hebrew University, acting as the leader of prayer *(imām)* of the congregational mosque in his village of al-Jawamis (near Nazareth), and performing service to his shaykh. Khālid sits before the shaykh to listen to the *tawba* story, which he has probably heard many times before. Shaykh Manāsra's first encounter with his shaykh took place on a stormy night in the latter's *zāwiya*-home in Jerusalem. The purpose of the visit was to ask Shaykh Hāshim questions about matters of true faith and religious practice to which no one had as yet succeeded in providing satisfactory answers. In Shaykh Hāshim's words, the Koranic verses he recited, and finally the touch of his hand on ʿAbd al-Salām's chest (astonishingly, as this is the habit of the monks of Nazareth) left him temporarily paralyzed, as if the shaykh had used magic on him. Ever since that long night of learning and intimacy, he has loved the shaykh more than his own self and has sworn unstinting allegiance and docility to his every command. This, in brief, is how the tradition of the leading shaykhs of the *ṭarīqa* local branch is carried on—through oral transmission, with each successor relating his illustrious shaykh's teachings and deeds, repeating the motif of dramatic initiation and "conversion" leading to daily performances of spiritual purity and moral qualities, and locating the stories in the specific environment.

Two local domed shrines are the object of occasional *ziyāra* for the shaykh, his disciples, and others who identify themselves as Qādirīs or as Sufis in general. They direct their steps to those sites to receive the *awliyā*'s blessings and perform the *dhikr* rituals there. One is the tomb of the Qādirī *imām* al-Nasāwī in Ramla, traditional center of the *ṭarīqa* and home of the Abū Labāb, the leading Qādirī family of the Ottoman period. The other is the alleged tomb of Daḥiyya in the Lower Galilee, around which sprang the village of Daḥī in the late Ottoman period.

Located on the top of Mount Moria, overlooking the entire Jezreel Valley, and surrounded by a graveyard, the tomb in Daḥī is said to be that of one of the Prophet's companions, a devout warrior who was Syrian in origin and who was killed there in one of the battles with the Byzantines over Palestine in the seventh century. Over the years, the building was restored, the first restoration being in Saladin time. The village itself began to grow up around the tomb about 120 years ago, and its first inhabitants came from a number of surrounding small villages, including Sulaim, home of the famous Zūʿabī local family. Most members of the family in both Syria and Palestine had already relinquished their Sufi identity. But to this day, they share with their Sufi neighbors admiration of the *walī*, which was appropriated long ago by the local community to meet its quest for spirituality and sanctity and for a focus of individual and communal devotion. According to local tales, Daḥiyya was an extremely pious warrior and as handsome as the angel Gabriel. As a companion of the Prophet, he is considered to be a Sufi and, as such, a model of virtue, a charismatic figure, and a channel to God. He is venerated by the local Qādirīs, who consider him their shaykh as well.

Various local traditions continue to circulate that interweave stories about Daḥiyya with tales about other venerated models of virtue who are labeled Sufis and who came to live in the cities and towns of Palestine or were born there. Tales are told about their teachings, moral conduct, and extraordinary deeds and about the communities, sites, and spaces that have grown up around them from the early Islamic period to our day.

NOTES

1. For a general discussion of the debate on Sufism in the twentieth century, see Carl F. Ernst, *Sufism: An Essential Introduction to the Philosophy and Practice of the Mystical Tradition of Islam* (Boston: Shambhala, 1977), 199–228; Elizabeth Sirriyeh, *Sufis and Anti-Sufis: The Defense, Rethinking and Rejection of Sufism in the Modern World* (Richmond, Surrey: Curzon, 1999), chaps. 4–6.
2. For a recent study that analyzes the various ways in which different Sufi brotherhoods in Syria and Palestine have responded to the challenge of modernity and the peculiar political circumstances in which they live, see Itzchak Weismann, "Sufi Brotherhoods in Syria and Israel: A Contemporary Overview," *History of Religions* 43 (2004): 303–18.
3. Frederick de Jong, "The Sufi Orders in Nineteenth- and Twentieth-Century Palestine," *Studia Islamica* 58 (1983): 149–80; Weismann, "Sufi Brotherhoods," 315–16.
4. This section is based on an interview with Shaykh Manāsra and several of his disciples at his *zāwiya* in Nazareth, as well as visits to the villages of Daḥī and Sulaim in the Lower Galilee (September and October 2005).

Bibliography

PRIMARY SOURCES

Al-Anṣārī, ʿAbd Allāh-i Harawī. *Ṭabaqāt al-ṣūfiyya*. Ed. ʿAbd al-Hayy-I. Kabul, AH 1341.

Al-Dhahabī, Shams al-Dīn Muḥammad. *al-ʿIbār fī khabar man ghabar*. Ed. Ṣ. al-Dīn Munājid and F. Sayyid. 4 vols. Kuwait, 1961–1966.

———. *Kitāb tadhkirat al-ḥuffāẓ*. 4 vols. Hyderabad: Dā'irat al-Maʿārif al-ʿUthmāniyya, 1968–70.

———. *Siyar aʿlām al-nubalā'*. Ed. S. al-Arna'ūṭ et al. 25 vols. Beirut: Mu'assasat al-Risāla, 1981–1985.

Al-Ghazzālī. *Ayyuha al-walad*. Beirut, 1959.

Al-Ghazzī. Najm al-Dīn. *al-Kawākib al-sāʾira bi-aʿyān al-miʾa al-ʿashira*. Ed. J. Jabbūr. 3 vols. Beirut: al-Maṭbaʿat al-Amīr Kāniyya, 1945.

Al-Hujwīrī. *Kashf al-maḥjūb*. Trans. R. A. Nicholson. London: Luzac, 1976.

Ibn ʿAsākir. *Ta'rīkh madinat dimashq*. Ed. M. Abū Saʿīd and ʿU. al-ʿAmrawī. 40 vols. Beirut, 1995.

Ibn al-Athīr. *al-Kāmil fī l-ta'rīkh*. 12 vols. Beirut, 1966.

Ibn Ḥajar al-ʿAsqalānī. *Tahdhīb al-tahdhīb*. Ed. M. Hārūn. Hyderabad, AH 1327.

———. *al-Durar al-kāmina fī aʿyān al-miʾa al-thāmina*. 5 vols. Cairo: Dār al-Kutub al-Ḥadītha, 1966–1967.

Ibn al-ʿImād al-Ḥanbalī. *Shadharāt al-dhahab fī akhbār man dhahab*. 8 vols. Beirut, n.d.

Ibn al-Jawzī, Abū l-Faraj. *Ṣifat al-ṣafwa*. 4 vols. Hyderabad: Da'irat al-Maʿārif al-ʿUthmāniyya, AH 1355–1357.

———. *al-Muntaẓam fī ta'rīkh al-muluk wa-l-umam*. 6 vols. Vols. 5–10. Hyderabad: Da'irat al-Maʿārif al-ʿUthmāniyya, AH 1358–1359.

Ibn Kahīr, Abū l-Fidā'. *al-Bidāya wa-l-nihāya*. 14 vols. Cairo: Maṭbaʿat al-Ṣalāfiyya, AH 1351.

Ibn Khaldūn. *The Muqaddimah: An Introduction to History*. 2nd ed. Trans. Franz Rosenthal. 3 vols. Princeton, NJ: Princeton University Press, 1967.

Ibn Khallikan. *Wafayāt al-aʿyān wa-abnā' al-zamān*. Ed. I. ʿAbbās. 8 vols. Beirut: Dār Beirut: Dār Ṣādir, 1971.

Ibn Mulaqqin, Abū Ḥafṣ ʿUmar. *Ṭabaqāt al-awliyā'*. Ed. N. Sharība. Cairo: Maṭbaʿat Dār al-Ta'līf, 1973.

Ibn Qādi al-Shuhba. *Ṭabaqāt al-shāfiʿiyya*. Beirut, 1987.

Ibn Saʿd, Muḥammad. *Kitāb al-ṭabaqāt*. Leiden: Brill, 1905.

Al-Iṣfahānī, Abū Nuʿaym. *Ḥilyat al-awilyā' wa-ṭabaqāt al-aṣfiyā'*. 10 vols. Beirut: Dār al-Kitāb al-ʿArabī, n.d.

Al-Jāmī, ʿAbd al-Raḥmān. *Nafaḥāt al-uns min ḥaḍarāt al-quds*. 2nd ed. Ed. M. A. al-Jādur. 2 vols. Beirut: Dār al-Kutub al-ʿIlmiyya, 2003.

Al-Jazarī, ḅ. al-Athīr. *al-Lubāb fī tahdhīb al-ansāb*. 3 vols. Beirut: Dār Ṣādir, n.d.

Al-Kalābādhī, Abū Bakr. *The Doctrines of the Ṣūfīs*. Trans. A. J. Arberry. Cambridge: Cambridge University Press, 1989.

Al-Khaṭīb al-Baghdādī, Abū Bakr. *Ta'rīkh baghdād*. 14 vols. Cairo: Maṭbaʿat al-Saʿada, AH 1349.

Khusraw, Nāṣir-ī. *Diary of a Journey through Syria and Palestine*. Trans. from the Persian and annotated by G. Le Strange. *Palestine Pilgrims Text Society* 4 (1893). Reprint, New York: AMS Press, 1971.

Al-Maqdisī, Aḥmad b. Muḥammad. *Muthīr al-gharām bi-faḍā'il al-Quds wa-l-Shām*. Ed. Aḥmad Ṣāliḥ al-Khālidī. Jaffa, 1946. (A printed edition of the last part of the manuscript)

Mujīr al-Dīn, ʿAbd al-Raḥman b. Muḥmmad, al-Ḥanbalī, al-ʿUlaymī.

al-Uns al-jalīl bi-ta'rīkh al-Quds wa-l-Khalīl. 2nd ed. 2 parts. Baghdad, 1995.

Al-Munāwī, ʿAbd al-Ra'ūf. *al-Kawākib al-durriyya fī tarājim al-sāda al-ṣūfiyya*. Ed. M. H. Rabīʿ. 2 vols. Cairo, n.d.

Al-Muqaddasī, Shams al-Dīn. *Aḥsan al-taqāsīm fī maʿrifat al-aqālīm*. 2nd ed. Ed. M. J. de Goeje. Leiden: Brill, 1906.

Al-Nabhānī, Yūsuf Ismā'īl *Jamī' karāmāt al-awliyā'*. 2nd ed. 2 vols. Beirut, 1988.

Al-Ṣafadī, Khalīl b. Aybak. *al-Wāfī bi-l-wafayāt*. Ed. H. Ritter, S. Dedering, et al. 22 vols. Istanbul: Deutsche Morgenländische Gesellschaft, 1931–.

Al-Qushayrī, Abū l-Qāsim. *al-Risāla al-qushayriyya fī ʿilm al-taṣawwuf*. Ed. M. Zuriq and ʿA. al-Balṭajī. Damascus, 1988. Partial translation by B. R. Von Schlegell. *Principles of Sufism by al-Qushayri*. Berkeley: Nizam Press, 1990.

Raḍī al-Dīn, Muḥammad b. al-Ḥanbalī. *Durr al-ḥabab fī-ta'rīkh aʿyān Ḥalab*. Ed. M. al-Fakhūrī and Y. ʿAbbāra. 2 vols. Damascus, 1973.

Al-Sakhāwī, Shams al-Dīn Muḥammad. *al-Ḍau' al-lāmiʿ li-ahl al-qarn al-tāsiʿ*. 6 vols. Cairo, AH 1353.

Al-Samʿānī, Abū Saʿd. *al-Ansāb*. 5 vols. Beirut, 1988.

Al-Sarrāj, Abū Naṣr. *Kitāb al-lumaʿ fī l-taṣawwuf*. Ed. M. ʿAbd al-Ḥalīm and S. al-Bāqī. Cairo: Dār al-Kutub al-Ḥadītha, 1960.

Al-Shaʿrānī, ʿAbd al-Wahhāb. *al-Ṭabaqāt al-kubrā*. 2 vols. Cairo, 1954.

Al-Subkī, Tāj al-Dīn. *Ṭabaqāt al-shafiʿiyya al-kubrā*. Ed. ʿA. F. M. al-Ḥilw and M. M. al-Tanāḥī. 10 vols. Cairo: Maṭbaʿat ʿIsā al-Bābī al-Ḥalbī, 1964–1976.

Al-Suhrawardī. *A Sufi Rule for Novices*. Trans. and abridged by Menahem Milson. Cambridge, MA: Harvard University Press, 1975.

Al-Suhrawardī, Abū al-Najīb. *Kitāb ādāb al-murīdīn*. Ed. with an introduction by M. Milson. Jerusalem: Jerusalem Studies in Arabic and Islam, 1978.

Al-Suhrawardī, Shihāb al-Dīn ʿUmar. *The ʿAwārifu-l-Maʿārif*. Trans. H. Wilberforce Clarke. New York: Weiser, 1970.

Al-Sulamī, Abū ʿAbd Allāh al-Raḥmān. *Kitāb ādāb aṣ-ṣuḥba.* Ed. M. J. Kister, Jerusalem: Israel Oriental Society, 1954.

———. *Jawāmiʿ ādāb al-Ṣūfiyya* and *ʿUyūb al-Nafs wa-Mudāwāthuhā.* Ed. with an introduction by E. Kohlberg. Jerusalem: Institute of Asian and African Studies, Hebrew University, 1976.

———. *Manāhij al-ʿārifīn.* Ed. E. Kohlberg, Jerusalem: Jerusalem Studies in Arabic and Islam, 1979.

———. *Ṭabaqāt al-ṣūfiyya.* 2nd ed. Ed. N. Shurība. Aleppo, 1986.

Al-Yafiʿī, ʿAbd Allāh. *Mirʾāt al-jinān wa-ʿibrat al-yaqẓān fī maʿrifat ḥawādith al-zamān.* 2nd ed. 4 vols. Beirut, 1970.

Al-Zabīdī, Murtaḍā. *Itḥāf al-aṣfiyya bi-rafʿ salāsil al-awliyāʾ.* Ms. fol. 10. n.d.

SECONDARY WORKS

Alman, Charles. "Two Types of Opposition and the Structure of Latin Saints' Lives." *Mediaevalia et Humanistica* n.s. 6 (1975): 1–11.

Amitai, Reuven. "The Conquest of Arsūf by Baybars: Political and Military Aspects." *Mamlūk Studies Review* 9:1 (2005): 62–83.

Andrae, Tor. *Islamische Mystiker.* Stuttgart: Kohlhammer, 1960 (trans. from the Swedish).

———. "Zuhd and Mönchtum." *Le Monde Oriental* 25 (1931): 296–327.

Arberry, A. *Sufism: An Account of the Mystics of Islam.* 5th ed. New York: Harper and Row, 1970.

Al-ʿAsalī, Kamāl al-Dīn. *Maʿāhid al-ʿilm fī bayt al-maqdis.* Amman, 1981.

———. *Wathāʾiq maqdisiyya taʾrīkhiyya.* Amman, 1983–1989.

Ashtor, Eliyahu. "Jerusalem in the Late Middle Ages." *Yerushalayim: Review for Eretz-Israel Research* 2 (1955): 71–116 (in Hebrew).

Baldick, J. *Mystical Islam: Introduction to Sufism.* London: Tauris, 1989.

Bausani, A. "Religion in the Seljuk Period." In J. A. Boyle ed. *The Cambridge History of Iran: The Saljuk and Mongol Periods.* Cambridge: Cambridge University Press, 1968. 5:283–303.

Berger, P. L., and T. Luckmann. *The Social Construction of Reality: A*

Treatise in the Sociology of Knowledge. London: Lane, Penguin Press, 1969.

Berkey, Jonathan P. *The Formation of Islam: Religion and Society in the Near East, 600–1800.* Cambridge: Cambridge University Press, 2003.

———. *Popular Preaching and Religious Authority in the Medieval Islamic Near East.* Seattle: University of Washington Press, 2001.

———. *The Transmission of Knowledge in Medieval Cairo: A Social History of Islamic Education.* Princeton, NJ: Princeton University Press, 1992.

Binns, John. *Ascetics and Ambassadors of Christ: The Monasteries of Palestine, 314–631.* New York: Oxford University Press, 1994.

Bonner, Michael. *Aristocratic Violence and Holy War: Studies in the Jihad and the Arab Byzantine Frontier.* New Haven, CT: American Oriental Society, 1996.

Bosworth, C. E. "The Rise of the Karrāmiyya [sic] in Khurāsān." *Muslim World* (1960): 6–14.

Brenner, Louis. "Separate Realities: A Review of Literature on Sufism." *International Journal of African Historical Studies* 5 (1972): 637–58.

Brock, Sebastian P. *Syriac Perspectives of Late Antiquity.* London: Variorum Reprints, 1984.

Broom, Leonard, Philip Selznick, Dorothy H. Broom. *Essentials in Sociology.* 3rd ed. Itasca, ILL: Peacock Press, 1985.

Brown, Peter. "The Rise and the Function of the Holy Man in Late Antiquity." *Journal of Roman Studies* 61 (1971): 80–101.

———. *The Body and Society: Men, Women, and Sexual Renunciation in Early Christianity.* New York: Faber and Faber, 1988.

———. *Authority and the Sacred: Aspects of the Christianisation of the Roman World.* Cambridge: Cambridge University Press, 1995.

———. "The Rise and the Function of the Holy Man in Late Antiquity 1971–1997." *Journal of Early Christian Studies* 6:3 (1998): 353–76.

Buehler, Arthur F. *Sufi Heirs of the Prophet: The Indian Naqshbandiyya and the Rise of the Mediating Sufi Shaykhs.* Columbia: University of South Carolina Press, 1998.

Bulliet, Richard W. *The Patricians of Nishapur: A Study in Medieval*

Islamic Social History. Cambridge, MA: Harvard University Press, 1972.

———. *Islam: The View from the Edge*. New York: Columbia University Press, 1994.

Burgoyne, Michael Hamilton. "Tariq Bab al-Hadid. A Mamluk Street in the Old City of Jerusalem." *Levant* 5 (1973): 12–20.

———. *Mamluk Jerusalem: An Architectural Study*. London: British School of Archaeology in Jerusalem, 1987.

Cahen, Claude. "The Turkish Invasion: The Selchūkids." In K. Setton, ed. *A History of the Crusades*. 2nd ed. Madison: University of Wisconsin Press, 1969. Vol. 1.

Canaan, Taufik. "Mohammeden Saints and Sanctuaries in Palestine." *Journal of the Palestine Oriental Society* 5 (1924): 1–84.

Chabbi, Jacqueline. "Khānkāh," and "Ribāt," *Encyclopedia of Islam*, 2d ed. Leiden: Brill, 1960–.

———. "La fonction du ribāṭ à Baghdad du Ve siècle au début du VIIe siècle." *Revue des études islamiques* 42 (1974): 101–21.

———. "Réflexions sur le soufisme iranien primitif." *Journal Asiatique* 266/1–2 (1978): 37–55.

———. "Remarques sur le développement historique des mouvements ascétiques et mystiques au Khurasan." *Studia Islamica* 46 (1977): 5–72.

———. "Fudayl b. ʿIyad: Un precurseur du Hanbalisme (d. 187/803)." *Bulletin d'études orientales* 30 (1978): 331–45.

Chevallier, Dominique, ed. *L'Espace social de la ville arabe*. Paris: Maisonneuve et Larose, 1979.

Chih, R., and D. Gril, eds. *Le saint et son milieu: ou comment lire les sources hagiographiques?* Cairo: Institut Français d' Archéologie Orientale, 2000.

Chittick, William C. *Sufism: A Short History*. Oxford: Oneworld, 2000.

Chitty, D. J. *The Desert a City*. Oxford: Oxford University Press, 1966.

Chodkiewicz, Michel. Review of Julian Baldick, *Mystical Islam*. *Studia Islamica* 73 (1991): 167.

Conder, C. R., and H. H. Kitchener. *A Survey of Western Palestine:*

Memoirs of the Topography, Orography, Hydrography and Archaeology. London: Committee of the Palestine Exploration Fund, 1881.

Constable, Giles. "Moderation and Restraint in Ascetic Practices in the Middle Ages." In Haijo J. Westra, ed., *From Athens to Chartres: Neoplatonism and Medieval Thought. Studies in the Honour of Edouard Jeauneau.* Leiden: Brill, 1992. 315–27.

Cooperson, Michael. *Classical Arabic Biography: The Heirs of the Prophet in the Age of al-Ma'amūn.* Cambridge: Cambridge University Press, 2000.

Cornell, Rkia E. *Early Sufi Women.* Louisville, KY: Fons Vitae, 1999.

Cornell, Vincent, J. *Realm of the Saint: Power and Authority in Moroccan Sufism.* Austin: University of Texas Press, 1998.

Davis, N. Z. "Some Tasks and Themes in the Study of Popular Religion." In C. Trinkhaus, ed., *The Pursuit of Holiness.* Leiden: Brill, 1974. 307–38.

De Jong, Frederick. "Review of *The Sufi Orders in Islam.*" *Journal of Semitic Studies* 17:2 (Autumn 1972):279.

———. "The Sufi Orders in Nineteenth- and Twentieth-Century Palestine." *Studia Islamica* 58 (1983): 149–80.

De Jong, Frederick and H. Algar. "Malāmatiyya," *Encyclopedia of Islam,* 2d. ed. Leiden: Brill, 1960–.

Deweese, Devin. *Islamization and Native Religion in the Golden Horde: Baba Tūkles and Conversion to Islam in Historical and Epic Traditions.* Pennsylvania: the Pennsylvania State University Press, 1994.

Drory, Joseph. "Jerusalem during the Mamluk Period." In Benjamin Z. Kedar, ed., *Jerusalem in the Middle Ages: Selected Papers.* Jerusalem: Yad Ben-Zvi, 1979. 148–84 (in Hebrew).

———. *Ibn al-'Arabī of Seville: Journey to Eretz Israel (1092–1095).* Ramat Gan: Bar Ilan University Press, 1993 (in Hebrew).

Ellenblum, Roni. *Frankish Rural Settlement in the Latin Kingdom of Palestine.* Cambridge: Cambridge University Press, 1998.

Elad, Amikam. "The Coastal Cities of Palestine during the Early Middle Ages." *Jerusalem Cathedra* 2 (1982): 146–67 (in Hebrew).

———. *Medieval Jerusalem and Islamic Worship: Holy Places, Ceremonies, Pilgrimage.* Leiden: Brill, 1995.

Ephrat, Daphna. *A Learned Society in a Period of Transition: The Sunni 'Ulama' of Eleventh-Century Baghdad.* Albany: SUNY Press, 2000.

———. "In Quest of an Ideal Type of Saint: Some Observations on the First Generation of Moroccan *Awliyā Allāh* in *Kitāb al-tashawwuf.*" *Studia Islamica* 94 (2002): 67–84.

———. "Religious Leadership and Associations in the Public Sphere of Seljuk Baghdad." In M. Hoexter, S. N. Eisenstadt, and N. Levtzion, eds., *The Public Sphere in Muslim Societies.* Albany: SUNY Press and Van Leer Jerusalem Institute, 2003. 31–48.

Ernst, Carl W. *Sufism: An Essential Introduction to the Philosophy and Practice of the Mystical Tradition of Islam.* Boston: Shambhala, 1977.

———. *Teachings of Sufism.* Boston: Shambhala, 1999.

Ernst, W. Carl and Lawrence, B. Bruce. *Sufi Martyrs of Love: The Chishti Order in South Asia and Beyond.* New York: Palgrave, 2002.

Fernandes, Leonor E. *The Evolution of the Sufi Institution in Mamluk Egypt: The Khanqah.* Berlin: Klaus Schwarz Verlag, 1988.

Fierro, Maribel. "Opposition to Sufism in al-Andalus." In F. de Jong and R. Radtke, eds., *Islamic Mysticism Contested: Thirteen Centuries of Controversies and Polemics.* Leiden: Brill, 1999. 174–97.

Frenkel, Y. "The Endowment of al-Madrasa al-Ṣalāḥiyya in Jerusalem by Saladin." In J. Drory, ed., *Palestine during the Mamluk Period.* Jerusalem: Yad Ben-Zvi, 1993. 64–85 (in Hebrew).

———. "*Mutasawwifa* versus *Fuqara'*: Notes Concerning Sufi Discourse in Mamluk Syria." In Alfonso Carmona, ed., *El Sufismo y las normas del Islam.* Trabajos del IV Congreso Internacional de Estudios Jurídicos Islámicos: Derecho y Sufismo. Murcia: Consejería de Educatión y Cultura, 2006. 291–307 (English text).

Frye, Richard N., ed. *The Histories of Nishapur.* Cambridge, MA: Harvard University Press, 1965.

Gabrielli, Francesco. *Arab Historians of the Crusades: Selected and Translated from the Arabic Sources.* 3rd ed. London: Melbourne and Henleym, 1984.

Gellens, Sam I. "The Search for Knowledge in Medieval Muslim Societies: A Comparative Approach." In Dale F. Eickelman and James

Piscatori, eds., *Muslim Travellers: Pilgrimage, Migration, and the Religious Imagination.* Berkeley: University of California Press, 1990. 50–65.

Gellner, Ernest. "Doctor and Saint." In Nikki R. Keddie, ed., *Scholars, Saints, and Sufis: Muslim Religious Institutions in the Middle East since 1500.* Berkeley: University of California Press, 1972. 307–26.

Geoffroy, Éric. *Le Soufisme en Égypte et en Syrie sous les Derniers Mamelouks et les Premiers Ottomans: Orientations Spirituelles et Enjeux Culturels.* Damascus: Institut Français. 1995.

———. "Ṭarīka," *Encyclopedia of Islam* 2d ed. Leiden: Brill, 1960–.

Gil, Moshe. *A History of Palestine, 634–1099.* Trans. Ethel Broido. Cambridge: Cambridge University Press, 1992.

Gilbert, Joan E. "Institutionalization of Muslim Scholarship and Professionalization of the 'Ulamā' in Medieval Damascus." *Studia Islamica* 32 (1980): 105–34.

Goffman, E. *The Presentation of Self in Everyday Life.* New York: Doubleday Anchor Press, 1959.

Goitein, S. D. "The Sanctity of Jerusalem and Palestine in Early Islam." In S. D. Goitein, ed., *Studies in Islamic History and Institutions.* Leiden: Brill, 1966. 135–48.

———. *A Mediterranean Society: The Jewish Communities in the Arab World as Portrayed in the Documents of the Cairo Geniza.* 5 vols. Berkeley: University of California Press, 1967–1988.

Goldziher, I. "Arabische Synonymik der Askese." *Der Islam* 8 (1918): 204–13.

———. *Introduction to Islamic Theology and Law.* Trans. A. Hamori and R. Hamori. Princeton, NJ: Princeton University Press, 1981.

Graham, Terry. Review of Mojaddedi, *The Biographical Tradition. Journal of Islamic Studies* 13:3 (2002): 339–42.

Gramlich, R. *Alte Vorbilder des Sufitums.* Wiesbaden: Steiner Verlag, 1995.

Gril, Denis. *La Risāla de Ṣafī al-Dīn ibn al-Manṣūr ibn Ẓāfir: Biographies de maîtres spirituels connus par un cheikh égyptien du VIIe/XIIIe siècle.* Cairo: Institut Français d'Archéologie Orientale, 1986.

———. "Sources Manuscrites de l'Histoire du Soufisme à Dār al-

Kutub: Un Premier Bilan." *Annales Islamologiques* 28 (1994): 97–105.

Haarmann, Ulrich. "Arabic in Speech, Turkish in Lineage: Mamluks and Their Sons in the Intellectual Life of Fourteenth-Century Egypt and Syria." *Journal of Semitic Studies* 33 (1988): 81–114.

Hall, C. "Asceticism." In *Encyclopedia of Religion and Ethics*. Ed. James Hastings, New York: Clark, 1964.

Hodgson, Marshall G. S. *The Venture of Islam: Conscience and History in a World Civilization*. Vol. 2, *The Expansion of Islam in the Middle Periods*. Chicago: Chicago University Press, 1974.

Hoexter, Miriam. "The Waqf and the Public Sphere." In M. Hoexter, S. N. Eisenstadt, and N. Levtzion, eds., *The Public Sphere in Muslim Societies*. Albany: SUNY Press and Van Leer Jerusalem Institute, 2003. 119–38.

Hofheinz, Albrecht. *Internalizing Islam: Shaykh Muhammad Majdhūb, Scriptural Islam and Local Context in the Early Nineteenth-Century Sudan*. Ph.D. thesis, University of Bergen, 1996.

Holt, P. M. *The Age of the Crusades: The Near East from the Eleventh Century to 1517*. London: Longman, 1986.

Hourani, Albert. *A History of the Arab Peoples*. Cambridge, MA: Harvard University Press, 1991.

Hurvitz, Nimrod. "Biographies and Mild Asceticism: A Study of Islamic Moral Imagination." *Studia Islamica* 85 (1997): 41–65.

———. *The Formation of Hanbalism: Piety into Power*. London: Curzon, 2002.

———. "From Scholarly Circles to Mass Movements." *American Historical Review* 108:4 (October 2003): 985–1008.

Hütteroth, W., and K. Abdulfattah. *Historical Geography of Palestine: Transjordan and Southern Syria in the Late Sixteenth Century*. Erlangen: Selbstverlag, 1977.

Johansen, B. "The All-Embracing Town and Its Mosques: Al-Miṣr al-Ǧāmī." *Revue de l'Occident musulman et de la Mediteranée* 32 (1981–1982): 139–61.

Kaḥḥāla, ʿUmar Riḍā. *Muʿjam al-muʾallifīn*. Damascus: Maṭbaʿat al-Taraqī, 1960.

Karamustafa, Ahmet. *God's Unruly Friends: Dervish Groups in the Is-*

lamic Later Middle Period, 1200–1500. Salt Lake City: University of Utah Press, 1994.

Khalidi, W. ed. *All That Remains: The Palestinian Villages Occupied and Depopulated by Israel in 1948*. Washington, DC: Institute for Palestinian Studies, 1992.

Kihnberg, Leah. "What Is Meant by *Zuhd?*" *Studia Islamica* 61 (1985): 27–44.

Kissling, Hans J. "Abdāl," *Encyclopedia of Islam*, 2d. ed. Leiden: Brill, 1960–.

Kister, J. "You Shall Only Set out for Three Mosques: A Study of an Early Islamic Tradition." *Le Moséon* 82 (1969), 173–196.

———. "A Comment on the Antiquity of Traditions Praising Jerusalem." *Jerusalem Cathedra* 1 (1981): 185–86.

Kiyānī, Muḥsin. *Tārīkh-i-khānaqāh dar Irān*. Teheran: Kitābkhānayi Ṭahūrī, 1990.

Knysh, Alexander. *Islamic Mysticism: A Short History*. Leiden: Brill, 2000.

Kōprūlu, Mehmed Fuad. *Islam in Anatolia after the Turkish Invasion*, trans. and ed. G. Leiser. Salt Lake City: University of Utah Press, 1993.

Lapidus, Ira M. *A History of Islamic Societies*. New York: Cambridge University Press, 1988.

Lecomte, Gerard. "Sufyān al-Thawrī: Quelques remarques sur les personnage et son oeuvre." *Bulletin d'études orientales* 30 (1978): 51–60.

Leder, S. "Charismatic Scripturalism: The Ḥanbali Maqdisis of Damascus." *Der Islam* 74 (1997): 279–304.

Le Gall, Dina. *A Culture of Sufism: Naqshbandis in the Ottoman World*. Albany: SUNY Press, 2004.

Le Strange, G. *Palestine under the Muslims: A Description of Syria and the Holy Land from a.d. 650 to 1500*. Boston: Riverside Press, 1890.

Levtzion, Nehemia. "Eighteenth-Century Sufi Brotherhoods: Structural, Organizational and Ritual Changes." In P. R. Riddell and T. Street, eds., *Islam: Essays on Scripture, Thought and Society*. Leiden: Brill, 1997. 147–60.

———. "Toward a Comparative Study of Islamization." In Nehemia Levtzion, ed. *Conversion to Islam.* New York: Holmes and Meier, 1979, 1–23.

Lewisohn, Leonard, ed. *Classical Persian Sufism: From Its Origins to Rumi.* London: Khaniqahi-Nimatullahi Publications, 1993.

Little, Donald P. "The Significance of the Haram Documents for the Study of Medieval Islamic History." *Der Islam* 57 (1980): 189–219.

———. "Mujīr al-Dīn al-ʿUlaymī's Vision of Jerusalem in the Ninth/Fifteenth Century." *Journal of American Oriental Society* 115:2 (April–June 1995): 237–47.

Livne-Kafri, O. *The Sanctity of Jerusalem in Islam.* Ph.D. thesis, Hebrew University, Jerusalem, 1985 (in Hebrew).

———. "Early Muslim Ascetics and the World of Christian Monasticism." *Jerusalem Studies in Arabic and Islam* 20 (1996): 105–29.

———. "Khitām al-Qur'ān." *Maʿof ve-Maʿase* 3 (1997): 107–09 (in Hebrew).

Luz, Nimrod. "Aspects of Islamization of Space and Society in Mamluk Jerusalem and Its Hinterland." *MamlÙk Studies Review* 6 (2002): 133–53.

Makdisi, George. "Muslim Institutions of Learning in Eleventh-Century Baghdad." *Bulletin of the School of Oriental and African Studies* 24 (1961): 1–58.

———. *Ibn ʿAqīl et la resurgence de l'Islam traditionaliste au xi*[e] *siècle* (v[e] *siècle de l'Hégire*). Damascus: Institut Français, 1963.

———. "The Sunni Revival." In D. S. Richards, ed., *Islamic Civilization, 950–1150.* Oxford: Cassier, 1973. 155–68.

———. "The Hanbalite School and Sufism." *Humaniora Islamica* 2 (1974): 61–72.

———. "Ṣuḥba et riyāsa dans l'enseignement médiéval." In *Recherches d'islamalogie: Recueil d'articles offerts à Georges Answati et Louis Gardet par leurs collègues et amis.* Louvain: Editions Peeters, 1978, 207–21.

———. The *Rise of Colleges: Institutions of Learning in Islam and the West.* Edinburgh: Edinburgh University Press, 1981.

———. "Hanbalite Islam." In M. L. Swartz ed. *Studies on Islam.* New York: Oxford University Press, 1981, 216–74.

Malamud, Margaret. "Sufi Organizations and Structures of Authority in Medieval Nishapur." *International Journal of Middle East Studies* 26 (1994): 428–42.

Marín, Manuela. "Zuhhād of al-Andalus (300/912–429/1029)." In M. Fierro and J. Samsó, eds., *The Formation of al-Andalus*. Part 2, *Language, Religion, Culture and the Sciences*. Aldershot: Ashgate, 1998. 103–31.

Massignon, L. *Essai sur les origines du lexique technique de la mystique musulmane*. Paris: Geuthner, 1922. Trans. Benjamin Clark as *Essay on the Origins of the Technical Language of Islamic Mysticism*. Notre Dame: University of Notre Dame Press, 1997.

———. *Recueil de textes inédits concernant l'histoire de la mystique en pays de l'Islam*. Paris: Geuthner, 1929.

Masud Muhammad, Khalid. "Sufi Understanding of *Hajj* Rituals." In Alfonso Carmona, ed., *El Sufismo y las mormas del Islam*, Trabajos del IV Congreso Internacional de Estudios Jurídicos Islámicos: Derecho y Sufismos. Murcia: Consejeríade Educatión y Cultura, 2006). 271–90 (English text).

Mauss, M. "La Notion de Personne, Celle de Moi." In *Sociologie et Entropologie*. 6th ed. Paris: PUF, 1995.

McGregor, Richard J. Review of Josef W. Meri, *The Cult of Saints among Muslims and Jews in Medieval Syria*. Oxford: Oxford University Press, 2002. *H-Mideast-Medieval@H-net*, June 2004.

———. *Sanctity and Mysticism in Medieval Egypt: The Wafā' Sufi Order and the Legacy of Ibn 'Arabi*. Albany, NY: SUNY Press, 2004.

Meier, Fritz. "Hurasan und das Ende der klassischen Sufik." In *Atti del Convengo internationale sul Tema: La Persia nel Medioevo*. Rome, 1970. 131–56.

———. *Abū Saʿīd-i Abū al-Ḥayr (357–490/967–1049): Wirklichkeit und Legende*. Leiden: Brill, 1976.

———. "The Mystic Path." In Bernard Lewis, ed., *The World of Islam: Faith, People, Culture*. London: Thames and Hudson, 1992. 117–28.

———. "Khurāsān and the End of Classical Sufism." In *Essays on Islamic Piety and Mysticism*. Trans. John O'Kane with editorial assistance of Bernd Radtke. Leiden: Brill, 1999. 189–219.

Melchert, Christopher. "The Transition from Asceticism to Mysticism at the Middle of the Ninth Century C.E." *Studia Islamica* 83:1 (1996): 51–70.

———. "The Piety of the Hadith Folk." *International Journal of Middle East Studies* 34:3 (2002): 425–39.

Meri, Joseph. "The Etiquette of Devotion in the Islamic Cult of Saints." In James Howard-Johnston and Paul A. Hayward, eds., *The Cult of Saints in Late Antiquity and the Middle Ages: Essays on the Contribution of Peter Brown.* Oxford: Oxford University Press, 1999. 263–86.

———. *The Cult of Saints among Muslims and Jews in Medieval Syria.* Oxford: Oxford University Press, 2002.

Mojaddedi, Jawid A. "Legitimizing Sufism in al-Qushayrī's Risāla." *Studia Islamica* 90 (2000): 37–70.

———. *The Biographical Tradition in Sufism: The Ṭabaqāt Genre from al-Sulamī to Jāmī.* Richmond, Surrey: Curzon, 2001.

Monawwar, Muhammad b. E. *Les étapes mystiques du shaykh Abu Saʿid.* Trans. and annotated by M. Achena. Paris: Sindbad, 1974.

Mottahedeh, Roy, P. *Loyalty and Leadership in an Early Islamic Society.* Princeton, NJ: Princeton University Press, 1980.

Netton, I. "The Breath of Felicity: *Adab, Aḥwāl, Maqāmāmt* and Abū Najīb al-Suhrawardī." In Leonard Lewisohn, ed., *Classical Persian Sufism: From Its Origin to Rumi.* London: Khaniqahi-Nimatullahi Publications, 1993. 457–82.

Nicholson, Reynold, A. *The Mystics of Islam.* 4th ed. London: Arkana, 1989.

Nwyia, P.·*Exégèse coranique et language mystique.* Beirut, 1970.

Ovadiah, A. *Corpus of the Byzantine Churches of the Holy Land.* Bonn: Hantein, 1970.

Patlagean, Evelyne. "Ancienne hagiographie byzantine et histoire sociale." *Annales esc.* 23 (1968): 106–26.

Patrich, J. *The Judean Desert Monasticism in the Byzantine Period: The Institutions of Sabas and His Disciples.* Jerusalem: Yad Ben-Zvi, 1995 (in Hebrew).

Paul, J. "Au début du genre hagiographique dans le Khorasana." In D. Aigle, ed., *Saints orientaux.* Paris: DeBoccard, 1995. 27–34.

Peters, F. E. *Jerusalem: The Holy City in the Eyes of Chroniclers, Visitors, Pilgrims, and Prophets from the Days of Abraham to the Beginning of Modern Times.* Princeton, NJ: Princeton University Press, 1985.

Petersen, Andrew. "A Preliminary Report on Three Muslim Shrines in Palestine." *Levant* 28 (1996): 97–113.

Pinto, Paulo G. "Performing *Baraka:* Sainthood and Local Spirituality in Syrian Sufism." In G. Stauth, ed. *On Archaeology of Sainthood and Local Spirituality in Islam: Past and Present Crossroads of Events and Ideas. Yearbook of the Sociology of Islam 5.* Bielefeld: Transcript Verlag, 2004. 195–211.

Radtke, Bernd. "Theologen und Mystiker in Hurāsān und Transoxanien." *Zeitschrift der Deutschen Morgenlandischen Gesellschaft* 136:1 (1986): 536–69.

Radtke, Bernd, and John O'Kane. *The Concept of Sainthood in Early Islamic Mysticism: Two Works by al-Ḥakīm al-Tirmidhī.* Richmond, Surrey: Curzon, 1996.

Reinert, B. *Die Lehre vom tawakkul in der klassischen Sufik.* Berlin: de Gruyter, 1968.

Renard, John. *Historical Dictionary of Sufism.* Oxford: Scarecrow Press, 2005.

Richards, D. S. ed. *Islamic Civilization 950–1150.* Oxford: Cassirer, 1973.

Rousselle, Aline. *Pomeia: de la maîtrise du corps à la privation sensorielle.* Paris: Presses Universitaires de France, 1983. Trans. Felicia Pheasart as *Pomeia: On Desire and Body in Antiquity.* Cambridge: Blackwell, 1993.

Salibi, Kamal S. "The Banū Jamāʿa: A Dynasty of Shāfiʿite Jurists in the Mamluk Period." *Studia Islamica* 9 (1958): 97–109.

Schacht, Joseph. "Ibn al-Qaysarānī," *Encyclopedia of Islam,* 2d. ed. Leiden: Brill, 1960–.

Schimmel, Annemarie. *Mystical Dimensions of Islam.* Chapel Hill: University of North Carolina Press, 1975.

Selznick, Philip. *Leadership in Administration.* New York: Row, Peterson, 1957.

Sezgin, P. *Geschichte des arabischen Schrifttums*. 9 vols. Leiden: Brill, 1967–.

Shoshan, Boaz. *Popular Culture in Medieval Cairo*. Cambridge: Cambridge University Press, 1993.

Silvers-Alario, Laury. "The Teaching Relationship in Early Sufism: A Reassessment of Fritz Meier's Definition of the *shaykh al-tarbiyya* and the *shaykh al-taʿlīm*." *Muslim World* 93 (January 2003): 69–97.

Sirriyeh, Elizabeth. *Sufis and Anti-Sufis: The Defense, Rethinking and Rejection of Sufism in the Modern World*. Richmond, Surrey: Curzon, 1999.

Smith, Margaret. *Studies in Early Mysticism in the Near and Middle East*. London: Sheldon Press, 1931.

Sviri, Sara. "wa-rahbāniyatan ibtadaʿūhā." *Jerusalem Studies in Arabic and Islam* 13 (1990): 195–208.

———. "Ḥakīm Tirmidhī and the Malāmatī Movement in Early Islam." In Leonard Lewisohn, ed., *Classical Persian Sufism: From Its Origins to Rumi*. London: Khaniqahi-Nimatullahi Publications, 1993. 583–602.

———. "Self and Its Transformation in Ṣūfīsm, with Special Reference to Early Literature." In David Shulman and Guy G. Stroumsa, eds., *Self and Self-Transformation in the History of Religions*. Oxford: Oxford University Press, 2002. 195–215.

Talmon-Heller, Daniella. "The Shaykh and the Community: Popular Hanbalite Islam in 12th–13th Century Jabal Nablus and Jabal Qāsyūn." *Studia* Islamica 79 (1994): 103–20.

———. "Religion in the Public Sphere: Rulers, Scholars, and Commoners in Syria under Zangid and Ayyubid Rule (1150–1260)." In M. Hoexter, S. N. Eisenstadt, and N. Levtzion, *The Public Sphere in Muslim Societies*. Albany: SUNY Press and Van Leer Jerusalem Institute, 2003. 49–63.

———. *Islamic Piety in Medieval Syria: Mosques, Cemeteries, Shrines*. Leiden: Brill, 2007.

Tamari, S. "Al-Ashrafiyya: An Imperial Madrasa in Jerusalem." In Y. Manṣūr, ed., *Studies in Arabic and Islam*. Ramat Gan, 1974. 9–40 (in Hebrew).

Taragan, Hana. "The Tomb of Sayyidnā ʿAlī in Arsuf: The Story of a

Holy Place." *Journal of the Royal Asiatic Society* 14:2 (July 2004): 83–102.

Taylor, Christopher S. *In the Vicinity of the Righteous: Ziyāra and the Veneration of Muslim Saints in Late Medieval Egypt.* Islamic History and Civilization, Studies and Texts, Vol. 32. Leiden: Brill, 1999.

Touati, Houari. *Islam et Voyage au Moyen Âge.* Paris: Éditions du Seuil, 2000.

Trimingham, J. Spencer. *The Sufi Orders in Islam.* Oxford: Oxford University Press, 1998. (1st. ed. Oxford: Clarendon, 1971.)

Van Brechem, M. *Matériaux pour un Corpus Inscriptionum 'Arabicarum, deuxième partie. Syrie du sud, Jérusalem, Ville.* Cairo, 1922.

Van Ess, J. *Theologie und Gesellschaft im 2. und 3. Jahrhundert Hidschra.* Berlin, 1992–1996.

Vööbus, Arthur. *A History of Asceticism in the Syrian Orient.* Louvain: Secretariat du Corpus SCO, 1958–.

Vryonis, Speros. *The Decline of Hellenism in Asia Minor and the Process of Islamization from the eleventh through the fifteenth Centuries.* Berkeley: University of California Press, 1971; rpt. 1986.

Weber, Max. *The Sociology of Religion.* Trans. Ephraim Fischoff. Introduction by Tolcott Parsons. Boston: Beacon, Press, 1963.

———. *The Theory of Social and Economic Organization.* Trans. A. M. Henderson and Talcott Parsons. Ed. with an introduction by P. Talcott. New York: Free Press, 1947.

Weismann, Itzchak. "Sufi Brotherhoods in Syria and Israel: A Contemporary Overview." *History of Religions* 43: 303–18.

Wilson, Stephen, ed. *Introduction to Saints and Their Cults: Studies in Religious Sociology, Folklore and History.* Cambridge: Cambridge University Press, 1983.

Wolper, Ethel Sarah. *Cities and Saints: Sufism and the Transformation of Urban Space in Medieval Anatolia.* University Park: Pennsylvania State University Press, 2003.

Index

HARVARD MIDDLE EASTERN MONOGRAPHS

1. *Syria: Development and Monetary Policy,* by Edmund Y. Asfour. 1959.
2. *The History of Modern Iran: An Interpretation,* by Joseph M. Upton. 1960.
3. *Contributions to Arabic Linguistics,* Charles A. Ferguson, Editor. 1960.
4. *Pan-Arabism and Labor,* by Willard A. Beling. 1960.
5. *The Industrialization of Iraq,* by Kathleen M. Langley. 1961.
6. *Buarij: Portrait of a Lebanese Muslim Village,* by Anne H. Fuller. 1961.
7. *Ottoman Egypt in the Eighteenth Century,* Stanford J. Shaw, Editor and Translator. 1962.
8. *Child Rearing in Lebanon,* by Edwin Terry Prothro. 1961.
9. *North Africa's French Legacy: 1954-1962,* by David C. Gordon. 1962.
10. *Communal Dialects in Baghdad,* by Haim Blanc. 1964.
11. *Ottoman Egypt in the Age of the French Revolution,* Translated with Introduction and Notes by Stanford J. Shaw. 1964.
12. *The Economy of Morocco: 1912-1962,* by Charles F. Stewart. 1964.
13. *The Economy of the Israeli Kibbutz,* by Eliyahu Kanovsky. 1966.
14. *The Syrian Social Nationalist Party: An Ideological Analysis,* by Labib Zuwiyya Yamak. 1966.
15. *The Practical Visions of Ya'qub Sanu',* by Irene L. Gendizier. 1966.
16. *The Surest Path: The Political Treatise of a Nineteenth-Century Muslim Statesman,* by Leon Carl Brown. 1967.
17. *High-Level Manpower in Economic Development: The Turkish Case,* by Richard D. Robinson. 1967.
18. *Rebirth of a Nation: The Origins and Rise of Moroccan Nationalism, 1912-1944,* by John P. Halsted. 1967.
19. *Women of Algeria: An Essay on Change,* by David C. Gordon. 1968.
20. *The Youth of Haouch El Harimi, A Lebanese Village,* by Judith R. Williams. 1968.

21. *The Problem of Diglossia in Arabic: A Comparative Study of Classical and Iraqi Arabic,* by Salih J. Al-Toma. 1969.
22. *The Seljuk Vezirate: A Study of Civil Administration,* by Carla L. Klausner. 1973.
23. and 24. *City in the Desert,* by Oleg Grabar, Renata Holod, James Knustad, and William Trousdale. 1978.
25. *Women's Autobiographies in Contemporary Iran,* Afsaneh Najmabadi, Editor. 1990.
26. *The Science of Mystic Lights,* by John Walbridge. 1992.
27. *Political Aspects of Islamic Philosophy: Essays in Honor of Muhsin S. Mahdi,* by Charles E. Butterworth. 1992.
28. *The Muslims of Bosnia-Herzegovina: Their Historic Development from the Middle Ages to the Dissolution of Yugoslavia,* Mark Pinson, Editor. 1994.
29. *Book of Gifts and Rarities: Kitāb al-Hadāyā wa al-Tuḥaf.* Ghāda al Hijjāwī al-Qaddūmī, Translator and Annotator. 1997.
30. *The Armenians of Iran: The Paradoxical Role of a Minority in a Dominant Culture: Articles and Documents,* Cosroe Chaqueri, Editor. 1998.
31. *In the Shadow of the Sultan: Culture, Power, and Politics in Morocco,* Rahma Bourqia and Susan Gilson Miller, editors. 1999.
32. *Hermeneutics and Honor: Negotiating Female "Public" Space in Islamic/ate Societies,* Asma Afsaruddin, editor. 1999.
33. *The Second Umayyad Caliphate: The Articulation of Caliphal Legitimacy in al-Andalus,* by Janina M. Safran. 2000.
34. *New Perspectives on Property and Land in the Middle East,* Roger Owen, editor. 2001.
35. *Mystics, Monarchs, and Messiahs: Cultural Landscapes of Early Modern Iran,* by Kathryn Babayan. 2003.
36. *Byzantium Viewed by the Arabs*, by Nadia Maria El Cheikh. 2004.
37. *The Palestinian Peasant Economy under the Mandate: A Story of Colonial Bungling*, by Amos Nadan. 2006.
38. *The Moral Resonance of Arab Media: Audiocassette Poetry and Culture in Yemen*, by W. Flagg Miller. 2007.
39. *Islamicate Sexualities: Translations across Temporal Geographies of Desire,* Kathryn Babayan and Afsaneh Najmabadi, editors. 2008.
40. *Spiritual Wayfarers, Leaders in Piety: Sufis and the Dissemination of Islam in Medieval Palestine,* by Daphna Ephrat. 2008.